BEFORE GENTRIFICATION

BEFORE GENTRIFICATION

The Creation of DC's Racial Wealth Gap

TANYA MARIA GOLASH-BOZA

UNIVERSITY OF CALIFORNIA PRESS

University of California Press
Oakland, California

© 2023 by Tanya Golash-Boza

Library of Congress Cataloging-in-Publication Data

Names: Golash-Boza, Tanya Maria, author.
Title: Before gentrification : the creation of DC's racial wealth gap / Tanya
    Maria Golash-Boza.
Description: Oakland, California: University of California Press, [2023] |
    Includes bibliographical references and index.
Identifiers: LCCN 2023001544 (print) | LCCN 2023001545 (ebook) | ISBN 9780520391161
    (hardback) | ISBN 9780520391178 (paperback) | ISBN 9780520391185 (ebook)
Subjects: LCSH: Gentrification—Washington (D.C.) | Middle class African
    Americans—Housing—Washington (D.C.) | Discrimination in housing—
    Washington (D.C.) | African American neighborhoods—Washington (D.C.)—
    Social conditions.
Classification: LCC HT177.W3 G648 2023 (print) | LCC HT177.W3 (ebook) |
    DDC 307.3/41609753—dc23/eng/20230407
LC record available at https://lccn.loc.gov/2023001544
LC ebook record available at https://lccn.loc.gov/2023001545

32   31   30   29   28   27   26   25   24   23
10   9   8   7   6   5   4   3   2   1

The cover art, *Law and Order*, juxtaposes the label "Superpredator" politicians assigned to Black boys like Halim Flowers with the empathy jurors have had for White boys like Kyle Rittenhouse. The work also highlights how not only Black neighborhoods but also Black dreams have been redlined. As Halim explains on his website:

I am a "Superpredator." After being sentenced to life in prison at the age of 16, this is the title that I was given and fought hard to denounce. Held in a cage for 22 years, I began crafting my method of artistic expression to find some sense of peace in a hopeless place before I resurrected back into the "real" world. I use photography, painting, poetry, and spoken word to further my love revolution.

Contents

Illustrations and Tables

TABLES

Acknowledgments

ACKNOWLEDGMENTS ARE STATEMENTS OF INDEBTEDNESS to others for their time and generosity. Any acknowledgments I write will not suffice as I am indebted to so many generous people who helped me research and write this book. I simply could not have written this book on my own. The research, the writing, and the analysis were done in community.

I must first acknowledge my extraordinary family. My mother's unfaltering moral code and my father's unwavering commitment to building a better world set examples no mere mortal such as myself could attain. My parents moved to Washington, DC, in 1970 to build a revolutionary movement. At eighty years old, my father continues this struggle. In 1976, when I was two years old, my parents bought a home on Fourth and Kennedy Streets, NW, in a neighborhood that was at the tail end of White flight. Growing up White in a Black community means my four siblings and I share a unique bond. No one understands us like we understand one another. I thank my siblings—Ian, Sean, Katrina, and Justin—for helping me understand my experiences in this racialized world.

I also thank my first best friend, Monique Dillard, who took me into her family like a sister. I extend my gratitude to Monique's grandmother, Mrs. Vera Dillard, who taught me, among other things, how to use an iron.

I am grateful to Nmadilaka Ahaghotu, who was my best friend throughout high school and college. Her family became my family, and I am forever grateful for their unconditional love.

I am blessed with a circle of women from DC who are as loyal, fly, and fierce as they come. Thank you, Sabriya Williams, Jamila Frone, Tiffanie Coleman, Amani Allen, Sherrell Jones Whitfield, Traci Hoyle, and Izu Ahaghotu for your friendship and support.

I am also blessed with a circle of academic sisters who help me navigate life in and around the academy. Thank you, Ayu Saraswati, Zulema Valdez, Jemima Pierre, Winddance Twine, Whitney Pirtle, Dalia Magaña, and Christina Lux for being there when I need you.

I am grateful to all the amazing women who have joined us at the Creative Connections Writing Retreat each year. I first shared work from this project at the 2017 retreat in Yosemite and have brought this project every year to our retreats in Bali, Peru, Italy, and Belize, gaining new insights and new friendships with each trip.

This book is based on many interviews and conversations with a wide range of people. I thank all of my interviewees for sharing their stories and helping me understand the effects of the War on Drugs on DC. I also thank Phylicia Fauntelroy Bowman, Sarah Shoenfeld, Mara Cherkasky, Mary Levy, and Delabian Rice-Thurston for sharing their insights about DC history with me.

The book is the result of a great amount of research. I am grateful to the National Science Foundation for funding this project and to a stellar team of researchers and students who made this effort possible. Several capable and dynamic interviewers helped complete the interviews.

Thank you to Tiffanie Coleman, Rodrigo Dominguez-Martinez, Shannell Thomas, Christina Sturdivant, Mark Rivas, and Tyler Hoyle. I am grateful to the undergraduate students in the Racism, Capitalism, and the Law Lab who collected and analyzed data for this project. Special thanks to Ukamaka Ezimora, Louis Perez, Lily Lindros, Alexia Wasson, Ashley Gonzales Oropeza, Jorge Alvarez, Galilea Sanchez, Anais Palomo, Jeni Alvarado, Erika Estrada, Anthony Jansky, Tania Alvarado, Briana Aguilar, and Michael Aquino, all of whom contributed to research for this book. I am fortunate to have an enthusiastic team of graduate students who assisted with background research, creative direction, and managing the undergraduate researchers. Thank you to graduate students Carmen Salazar, Yajaira Ceciliano Navarro, Hyunsu Oh, Patrick Coldivar-Valencia, and Waleed Rajabally.

I have been working on this book since 2016, and a remarkable number of people have given me feedback along the way. I am grateful to Sarah Shoenfeld, Mary Pattillo, and Andrea Leverentz for their detailed and generous comments on the entire manuscript during a book manuscript workshop, funded by the UC Merced Center for the Humanities. Alessandro De Giorgi, Allison Aikon, Andrea Benjamin, Andrea Marston, Anthony Peguero, Carson Byrd, David Farber, Donna Murch, Holly Foster, Irene Yen, Johanna Bochman, Kelly Lytle Hernandez, Lila Sharif, Manuela Picq, Mara Cherkasky, Marjorie Zatz, Natasha Howard, Peter Hudson, Phylicia Bowman, Saida Grundy, Steven Alvarado, Whitney Pirtle, and Zulema Valdez read portions of the manuscript and gave me feedback that has made the book better. A special thanks to Anthony Ocampo for our many conversations about writing. I am also grateful to the readers for UC Press for their insightful comments: Derek Hyra, Treva Lindsay, Alex Vitale, and one anonymous reader. This book also benefited from developmental editing by Audra Wolfe, Kate Epstein, Zoë Ruiz, and Lisa Colleen Moore. Thanks to each of you for helping make the arguments sharper and the prose clearer.

I finished writing this book while I was a visiting professor at l'Unité de Recherche Migrations et Société (URMIS) at the Université Côte d'Azur in Nice, France. I could not have found a better place to be and to write. I am particularly grateful to colleagues who welcomed me to France and gave me excellent feedback on my work. A special thanks to Françoise Lestage, Swanie Potot, Jean-Luc Primon, Patrick Simon, and Milena Doytcheva. I am also grateful to Emmanuelle Peraldo and Nora Galland for their friendship and support during my time in Nice.

I thank the archivists at the DC Public Library, particularly Derek Gray and Ray Barker, for facilitating my access to the Neighbors, Inc., collections.

I am honored that editor extraordinaire Naomi Schneider acquired this book for the University of California Press. Thank you, Naomi, for seeing that my early draft had potential and for stewarding this book through the publishing process. I am also deeply grateful to the wonderful staff at UC Press who made this book what it is. Thank you to the entire editorial, design, and publicity teams.

Last but not least, I am grateful to my wonderful husband, Fernando Boza, and three amazing children, Tatiana, Soraya, and Raymi. I am blessed to have you with me on this journey called life.

INTRODUCTION

IN 1959, MARK'S GRANDPARENTS PURCHASED a two-story, brick, 2,500-square-foot row house with large windows and a finished basement in tree-lined Mount Pleasant. They were among the thousands of African Americans who achieved the American dream of home ownership in the 1950s. Mark's mother grew up in this sunlit and spacious three-bedroom home with ample space for backyard cookouts. She graduated from high school and secured a well-paying job with the federal government. She raised her three children in this home, who in turn raised their children there.[1]

In 1992 Mark was arrested and the federal government seized the house his grandparents had purchased, alleging Mark was using the property in his drug-selling operation, though he had not lived there for years. His mother was able to buy the house back from the federal government, but now she had a mortgage. When she took out a second mortgage to make repairs to the home, the payments ballooned.

She fell behind. Seven years after Mark was incarcerated, his mother lost the house she had inherited from her parents. Today the home is valued at $1.5 million.

The story of Mark's family was the impetus for this book. Or, perhaps more accurately, my reflections on how my life took a different path from Mark's compelled me to write this book.

I went to high school with Mark's younger sister, Traci. My friends and I spent many hours together at Traci's home—as did her extended family of cousins, aunts, and uncles, who came and went as we sat around waiting for Traci to finish getting ready to go out or for one of our boyfriends to give us a ride. Traci and I have remained close friends, and when I spend time with her, our conversation often turns to the family home in Mount Pleasant. The loss of this home was distressing, both financially and emotionally.

When I interviewed Black men from Washington, DC, who had been incarcerated, I heard a version of this story over and over again. Their grandparents had purchased homes in the 1950s, just a few years after schools and lunch counters were desegregated. Their parents struggled to become home owners themselves. Although the homes their grandparents purchased are worth millions today, this has not translated into intergenerational wealth.

White people in the United States have, on average, eight times the wealth of Black people.[2] Wealth is not only the source of social and political power in a capitalist society; it also can be used to create opportunities, maintain financial security, and pass along a legacy to the next generation. Wealth takes on particular importance in a country like the United States where medical expenses and college tuition routinely put people without significant wealth in lifelong debt.

Inequality in home equity accounts for most of the racial wealth gap, which is why scholars who study racial disparities in wealth in the United States focus on home ownership. Less than half of Black people own the home they live in, as compared to three-quarters of White people.[3] White people have more wealth than Black people because they are more likely to own homes and their homes are assessed at a higher value than those of Black owners.[4]

Activists have long fought to narrow the racial home ownership gap because of its relationship to the racial wealth gap. While it seems logical that promoting Black home ownership can narrow the racial wealth gap, my research reveals that simply increasing access to home ownership is unlikely to accomplish this. Anti-Black racism shapes the ways the public and private sectors invest in, and divest from, Black neighborhoods, which in turn leads to devaluing homes in areas where Black people live. In Washington, DC, Black neighborhoods have experienced dispossession, displacement, and disinvestment, followed by *carceral investment*, that is, state investment in policing and prisons, and *racialized reinvestment*, that is, when demographics shape neighborhood reinvestment patterns. These forces have prevented Black people from experiencing upward intergenerational mobility and accumulating wealth. Although there were over fifty thousand Black home owners in DC by 1980—seven times more than in 1940—by 2015 White people in the DC metro area had eighty-one times the wealth of Black people.[5]

Mark was sentenced to life in prison for drug distribution when he was twenty-three years old. During his decades of imprisonment, I often thought about how much of the world I was able to experience while he remained behind bars. I also reflected on how removing thousands of young Black men like Mark from families and communities in DC had lasting consequences. I began this research seeking to understand the experiences of Black men who were incarcerated during the War on Drugs and were released in the twenty-first century to a gentrified city. This investigation led to the unexpected finding that significant numbers of these men had experienced downward intergenerational mobility.

Most research on people who return home from prison focuses on intergenerational poverty. For example, in *Doing Time on the Outside,*

Donald Braman argues that mass incarceration in Washington, DC, has devastated poor Black families and keeps them in poverty. In *Intersecting Lives: How Place Shapes Reentry,* Andrea Leverentz describes how people returning home from prison experience changing neighborhoods and navigate their post-prison experiences. In these works and others, the underlying assumption is that incarcerated people's poverty is intergenerational. In contrast, my conversations with men returning home to Washington, DC, after their incarceration revealed that many of them came from families that had achieved one of the hallmarks of middle-class status: home ownership. I found that incarceration has effects far beyond the people William Julius Wilson calls "truly disadvantaged."[6]

Because my research began with questions about the long-term effects of the War on Drugs, I do not explore in depth the experiences of Black families who were able to avoid the ill effects of mass incarceration. However, most Black families in DC have been affected by the widespread criminalization of Black men in the 1990s: by 1997, half of Black male youth in DC were caught in the carceral web, meaning they were on probation, in prison or jail, out on bail awaiting trial, or had a warrant out for their arrest.[7] To be sure, some of the descendants of African American migrants to Washington, DC, have achieved remarkable success and have far surpassed the social and economic achievements of their parents and grandparents. This book, however, considers the barriers to upward intergenerational mobility (and even to class reproduction) many Black families face and the role that prisons and policing as well as disinvestment in Black communities has played in this.

Before Gentrification explores how Black neighborhoods in Washington, DC, became places that could be gentrified. I argue that disinvestment as well as carceral investment in Black communities in DC displaced and dispossessed Black residents, making gentrification through racialized reinvestment possible. The decision to use prisons and policing to solve the problems in Black communities in DC in the twentieth century, instead of investing in schools, community centers, social services, health care, drug treatment, and violence prevention, facilitated gentrification in the twenty-first century.

These policies also prevented home ownership from leading to intergenerational wealth for Black DC residents. The central argument of this book is that Black neighborhoods in DC have experienced dispossession, displacement, and disinvestment, followed by carceral investment and racialized reinvestment and that this trajectory helps us understand the persistence of the racial wealth gap.

My arguments build on the work of gentrification scholars such as Neil Smith and Ruth Glass, who argue that insofar as gentrification is a process whereby high-income people (the gentry) move into poor, disinvested neighborhoods, disinvestment is a precursor to gentrification.[8] My work also builds on the scholarship of geographers such as David Harvey and Ruth Wilson Gilmore who argue that disinvestment is a form of "organized abandonment" whereby the public and private sectors abandon communities. Gilmore further contends that these abandoned areas become sites of "organized violence," referring to heavy policing and environmental degradation.[9] I considered using the term "organized abandonment" instead of "disinvestment" and the term "organized violence" instead of "carceral investment" but ultimately decided that the language of disinvestment, carceral investment, and racialized reinvestment allows me to highlight the role of *investment* in these phenomena. In the context of racial capitalism, the investments that flow and fail to flow to communities shape their fates. In DC, these investments have created the racial wealth gap.

Lance Freeman explains in *A Haven and a Hell* that the economic prospects of Black people nationwide improved between 1940 and 1970, as average annual wages nearly tripled during this period. These improved economic prospects, along with White flight to the suburbs, allowed some Black people to leave dilapidated inner cities and purchase homes in neighborhoods like Eckington and Petworth that were built for White occupancy. In the Washington, DC, neighborhood of Petworth, where I grew up, there were only 146 home owners who were not White in 1950. By 1960, there were 3,463 Black home owners, accounting for two-thirds of home ownership there.[10]

Most scholarship on the rise in home ownership in the mid-twentieth century focuses on the fact that Black families were locked out of opportunities to own homes and were often confined to public housing projects.[11] In *The Color of Law,* Richard Rothstein explains that prior to the 1968 Fair Housing Act, Black people were not able to access White neighborhoods. Rothstein also discusses neighborhoods like East Palo Alto, where Black people were able to purchase homes, but his account suggests that these neighborhoods overwhelmingly became overcrowded slums. In Washington, DC, many neighborhoods built for White people became majority Black yet did not become slums.

Keeanga-Yamahtta Taylor's book, *Race for Profit,* describes the barriers Black people confronted when trying to obtain traditional home financing. Her work documents a phenomenon she terms "predatory inclusion," which explains how realtors and mortgage brokers convinced low-income Black women to buy substandard homes they couldn't afford to repair. Moreover, they purchased these homes on land installment contracts, which, instead of generating intergenerational wealth, stripped assets. Taylor's account, however, focuses primarily on the 1970s, even though most of the growth in Black home ownership occurred in the decades before that.

I agree with other scholars who argue that Black people have been locked out of opportunities to build wealth.[12] However, whereas many scholars argue that Black people were denied federally subsidized mortgages, I find that thousands of Black people were able to gain access to those mortgages. And whereas other scholars argue that the

TABLE I

US Home Ownership Rates by Race, 1940–2020

Year	% White	% Black
1940	45.7	22.8
1950	57.0	34.4
1960	64.4	38.4
1970	65.2	41.6
1980	67.8	44.4
1990	68.2	43.4
2000	73.8	47.2
2010	74.4	45.2
2020	74.5	44.1

SOURCE: US Census home ownership data.

areas where Black people lived became slums, I argue that many of these areas were not slums, although they did experience disinvestment.[13] A more precise understanding of the mechanisms by which Black people have been denied the opportunity to build wealth is critical as it allows us to create more informed solutions to the racial wealth gap. One thing is clear: simply increasing access to home ownership is unlikely to close the gap. The reason for this is that neighborhoods where Black people live have consistently experienced disinvestment and carceral investment, and this is what needs to change.

Home ownership rates for Black people grew from 22.8 percent in 1940 to 41.6 percent in 1970, according to US Census data.[14] Home ownership among White people grew from 45.7 to 65.2 percent during the same period. (Table I.) Although Black Washingtonians were largely unable to purchase homes in the new all-White suburbs in Maryland and Virginia, they were able to purchase homes in the areas White residents were leaving. In Washington, DC, these formerly all-White areas quickly transformed into segregated all-Black communities, with rows of solid brick homes housing Black working, middle, and upper classes.

Despite the growth of neighborhoods with large numbers of Black home owners in the twentieth century, nearly all scholarship on Black urban communities has focused on the poor. In *The Truly Disadvantaged*, William Julius Wilson describes how the departure of the Black middle class from inner cities in the 1970s led to concentrated poverty and joblessness in many Black urban communities. Similarly, Douglas Massey and Nancy A. Denton focus on the negative consequences of segregation and concentrated poverty in *American Apartheid*. However, as the sociologist Mary Pattillo explains, three-quarters of African Americans are not poor, and many middle-class Black people did not abandon the city.[15]

Although some middle-class African Americans did leave Washington, DC, for the suburbs in the 1970s, many stayed and formed strong communities in this majority-Black city. Washington, DC, however, is unique, and that uniqueness plays a role in the narrative that unfolds in this book. Thus I want to take a moment to explain why DC residents do not enjoy full democratic rights.

The District of Columbia (DC) is a city that is not embedded in a county or a state. Before 1967 Congress had complete control of DC's budget and laws. In 1967 President Lyndon Johnson implemented a plan whereby nine appointed council members were charged with the city's budget and legislation. This decision transferred legislative power from Congress to this newly appointed body, yet Congress retained veto power over its decisions, a power it maintains today. In 1968 the city elected its first school board, its first elected body in decades. Five years later Congress passed the District of Columbia Home Rule Act, which permitted the city to elect a mayor and a city council democratically and set its own budget.[16]

However, the pathway toward DC residents gaining democratic control has been long and beset with setbacks, and it is far from complete. There are four congressional committees that have oversight of DC's laws and budget. None of these four committees is made up of people elected by DC residents. This has budgetary implications for the city but also shapes its relationship to the federal government, as Congress plays some of the roles a state might play. To this day, DC residents do not have a voting representative in Congress.

It is worth pausing to acknowledge that Washington, DC, has implemented anti-Black policies when White people held power and when Black people held power. Before the passage of Home Rule legislation in 1973, a White-dominated Congress controlled the city's budget and laws. It is not surprising that the southern-dominated House Subcommittee on District Appropriations refused to grant the city the funds it needed to serve its majority-Black residents when those same representatives were striving to uphold segregationist policies in their states and communities.

When Home Rule was implemented in 1975, as part of the long, slow, and incomplete march toward civil rights, Congress maintained the right to review all legislation passed by the city council as well as the budget, thereby limiting the power of the city's Black leaders. Congressional mandates limit the city's taxing authority, and the president appoints the city's judges. Thus, although the city had Black leadership, it remained subject to the whims of majority-White federal authorities and thus to a governing body that has long been anti-Black. Nevertheless, as James Forman Jr. explains in his book, *Locking Up Our Own,* the city's Black leadership fully supported the coercive anticrime policies implemented beginning in the 1980s. Middle-class Black DC residents actively voiced their demands for improved schools, expanded city services, drug rehabilitation clinics, and more policing and prisons. The city and the federal government responded most swiftly to this last set of demands—with carceral investment. Despite Black leadership, Black police officers, Black judges, and Black teachers, the city remains embedded in a broader context of White supremacy and anti-Black sentiment that has stymied efforts to support Black people in meaningful ways.[17]

Under Home Rule, Congress retains veto power over legislation and restricts the city government's powers in other ways. Congress has used its veto power to block legislation that would have expanded the rights of same-sex couples, helped avoid the spread of HIV/AIDS, decriminalized medical marijuana, and increased abortion access.[18] A central source of disagreement stems from the fact that about 90 percent of DC voters identify as Democrats, whereas Congress is usually fairly evenly divided between Democrats and Republicans. Congress thus serves as an oversight body that does not share the same values or outlooks of most DC residents. This imbalance is exacerbated when Congress is Republican dominated. This lack of autonomy is unique to the nation's capital and limits the democratic rights of residents.

Home Rule is also tenuous. In 1995, in response to a fiscal crisis, Congress created the Control Board, which took budgetary powers away from elected officials. Then, in 1997, Congress passed the National Capital Revitalization and Self-Government Improvement Act, which allowed it to take control of many of the city's functions. One of the major consequences of this act is that the Federal Bureau of Prisons took over the management of DC residents sentenced to prison. People housed at the city's local prison, Lorton Reformatory, began to be distributed to federal prisons around the country. In 2001 Lorton was closed. To this day, any person sentenced to prison for violating the DC criminal code will be sent to a federal prison, which can be anywhere in the United States. The placement of incarcerated people from DC in prisons hundreds or even thousands of miles away has increased the burden on their loved ones. This is exacerbated by the fact that by 2001 Washington, DC, had become the city with the highest incarceration rate in the world.[19]

In the aftermath of the Great Depression, the federal government implemented a series of policies designed to provide adequate housing to all. Part of this project involved stripping Black people of their land to build public housing. Beginning in the 1930s, public housing projects provided safe and comfortable homes for Black and White residents. These public housing projects included Barry Farm Dwellings, which featured spacious garden apartments and tree-lined walkways, and Langston Terrace Dwellings, which had a terra-cotta frieze in the central courtyard. While Mark's grandparents were moving into their Mount Pleasant home in the 1950s, Black families in other areas of the city were moving into public housing.

By the 1970s public housing in DC was 100 percent Black occupied. As the surrounding neighborhoods became primarily Black, the federal government was reluctant to expand or even maintain public goods in these areas. The city and the federal government as well as the private sector began to disinvest from these communities. DC's housing projects began to decay, and funding for repairs and upkeep was not forthcoming.[20] When Black neighborhoods experienced high rates of joblessness and poverty in the 1970s and 1980s, the city and federal governments could have invested in these communities by improving and expanding public housing, investing in schools, and developing a federal jobs program. But they did not. Instead, they chose to invest in the carceral apparatus—policing and prisons—to deal with the social issues that joblessness and poverty had created. The grandsons of Black people who purchased homes in the 1950s and those who moved into public housing projects in the 1950s faced similarly bleak prospects in the 1990s.

Public schools were failing and murder and incarceration rates were high across Black middle-class, working-class, and poor areas. By the late 1980s, in most public housing in Washington, DC, crime and violence were rampant. In a congressional hearing on February 21, 1989, Rep. Charles Rangel (D-NY) stated, "By now, everyone knows of the damage drugs are doing to America—a murder a day in the District of Columbia, public housing projects made uninhabitable because of violence associated with drug dealing." Six months later, Sen. Daniel

Moynihan (D-NY) stated in a Senate hearing, "Public housing projects have become war zones."[21]

What went wrong? Why didn't home ownership translate into middle-class stability for Black families? Why did public housing projects become overrun with drugs and violence? Why were half of Black men in Washington, DC, under some form of carceral supervision by 1997? And why are some neighborhoods that experienced devastation in the 1980s being gentrified today?

Disinvestment and then carceral investment enabled gentrification through racialized reinvestment. Reinvestment in DC has taken different forms, aligned with the class and racial composition of neighborhoods. Formerly White, then majority-Black neighborhoods like Mount Pleasant and Petworth are experiencing gentrification through White reclamation, whereby White residents move in and renovate the historic housing stock. In contrast, in neighborhoods with large housing projects built for Black residents in the mid-twentieth century large-scale demolition is taking place, accompanied by the construction of new housing. When the new residents of these neighborhoods are White, these neighborhoods undergo a complete transformation. However, when the new residents are Black, there are low levels of public and private investment—continuing the trend of disinvestment in Black neighborhoods.

For White people, government-subsidized home ownership in the 1950s translated into intergenerational wealth as their homes consistently increased in value and their neighborhoods featured well-funded schools as well as employment opportunities. This combination of community assets and intergenerational wealth allowed many of the children of White people who purchased homes in all-White suburbs to become home owners themselves. Public and private investments in White neighborhoods enriched White residents. The logic of racial capitalism, however, did not work the same in Black neighborhoods, where home ownership often has not translated into intergenerational wealth. Public authorities failed to invest in public schools once they became majority Black. When crack swept across the city, further devastating Black communities, the primary government response was carceral instead of supportive. And today neighborhoods experiencing revitalization and private reinvestment are those from which Black residents are being displaced.

Even when public and private investments have flowed to Black communities, they have continued the pattern of dispossession and displacement. When decades of disinvestment led to a rise in violence in the 1980s, the city and the federal government responded with carceral investment. In the twenty-first century, these same communities are experiencing public and private reinvestment through gentrification.

Disinvestment, dispossession, and displacement of Black people are rooted in both racial capitalism—"an economic system that organizes and justifies exploitation by racial classification"[22]—and anti-Black racism—ideologies, policies, and practices that deny Black people opportunities, resources, and power and disproportionately subject them to coercive policies such as incarceration and premature death.[23] Anti-Black ideologies have led decision makers to implement policies that have resulted in the displacement and dispossession of Black people and decades of disinvestment in Black communities. The concept of racial capitalism allows us "to understand the mutually constitutive nature of racialization and capitalist exploitation."[24] In a capitalist system, land is a market commodity that produces wealth and power. Housing prices include not only the value of the bricks and mortar that constitute the house but also the value of the land, which is greatly influenced by the quality of the schools and the level and kinds of neighborhood amenities. The value of homes is also tied directly to anti-Black racism, as homes in neighborhoods with more Black people are valued lower than homes in neighborhoods with more White people.[25]

An analysis based on theories of capital might focus solely on how land value is produced. An analysis based on theories of race might focus solely on racial differences in the price of housing. Racial capitalism, however, offers a useful theoretical lens and a helpful set of tools to understand the relationship between race and land value.

In Washington, DC, majority-Black spaces are devalorized in the real estate market, and this very devalorization creates the possibility for their revalorization. For this revalorization to happen, however, Black people must be displaced. As the urban studies scholar Prentiss Dantzler explained, "Dispossession becomes the antecedent for accumulation, while displacement regenerates this cycle of exploitation."[26] Revalorization happens through gentrification, which the sociologist Zawadi Rucks-Ahidiana has described as a "racialized, profit-accumulating process."[27] The value of the land in the United States is highly dependent on the race of the people who occupy it. This value, then, is not static but is created through the dispossession and displacement of Black people.

My framework of disinvestment, carceral investment, and racialized reinvestment helps us understand how public and private investments have enriched White people and dispossessed Black people. The analysis of changes in Washington, DC, over the past hundred years also makes it clear that both public and private investments in the city are consistently anti-Black. The public and private sectors abandoned not only poor Black neighborhoods like Navy Yard but also working- and middle-class Black neighborhoods like Petworth. High-income neighborhoods on the Platinum Coast such as North Portal Estates and Colonial Village became majority Black in the aftermath of White flight, yet were able to avoid the worst of the waves of disinvestment and surveillance, although they experienced far more public and private disinvestment than comparable White neighborhoods. And when crack swept across the city, further devastating Black communities, the government used its significant resources to target drug-selling crews in Black middle-class neighborhoods. Today neighborhoods that are experiencing revitalization and private reinvestment are those from which Black residents are being displaced.

The ethnographic, historical, and interview data that I collected to write this book show that Washington, DC, has undergone waves of displacement and dispossession that have culminated in gentrification. Several recent books on gentrification in Washington, DC, render the racialized dimensions of this process clear. Derek Hyra's *Cappuccino City,* Brandi Thompson Summers's *Black in Place,* and Sabiyha Prince's *African Americans and Gentrification in Washington, DC* all highlight the physical, cultural, and political displacement of African Americans from DC. These works focus primarily on neighborhoods with relatively high poverty rates such as Shaw and H Streets, NE. In addition to drawing a longer historical arc, I consider gentrification in several other DC neighborhoods, allowing us to consider how gentrification has affected Black neighborhoods across the city, both sites of concentrated poverty and middle-class Black communities. For example, I include Capitol View, which has experienced a form of Black gentrification, as one of the case studies as it provides important insights into how gentrification in Washington, DC, often leads to anti-Black outcomes, even when the newcomers are Black.[28]

The title of this book, *Before Gentrification,* highlights the importance of considering how gentrification was made possible. Gentrification, by definition, does not occur in neighborhoods that already have high levels of public and private investment. So how did so many Black neighborhoods in DC become disinvested? *Before Gentrification* answers this question by employing a comparative analysis that includes case studies of Eckington and Petworth, neighborhoods that were home to the Black middle class in the second half of the twentieth century; Capitol View, formed as a Black middle-class community; and Barry Farm and Navy Yard, where large public housing projects were sited (Map 1). Despite their different historical trajectories, by the 1980s these neighborhoods had become similar in many ways. They all experienced the violence of disinvestment and carceral investment.

This book explains how Black children who grew up in poor, working-class, and middle-class neighborhoods ended up in the grips of the

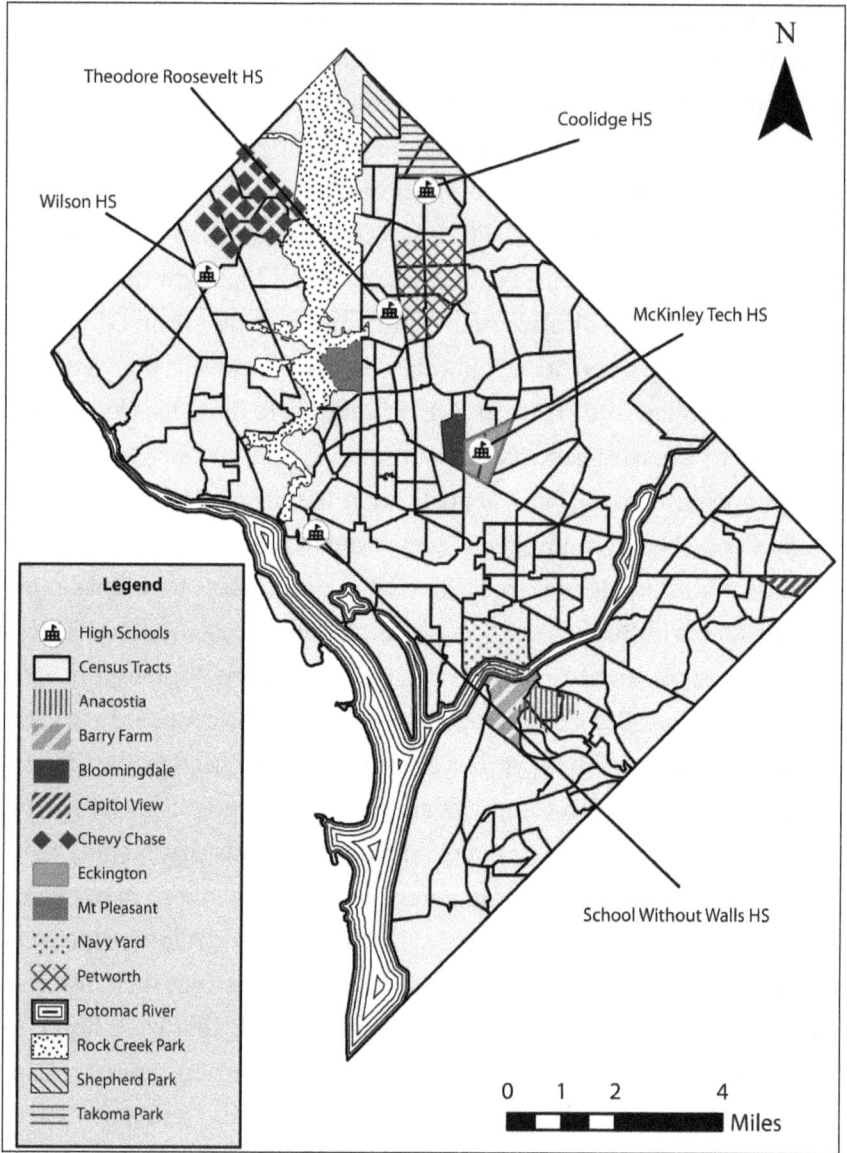

Map 1. DC neighborhoods and high schools of interest.

carceral system, as well as how disinvestment, carceral investment, and racialized reinvestment have made it difficult for these families to pass down wealth to the next generation. Mary Pattillo's *Black Picket Fences* examines how declining labor market opportunities and enhanced criminalization negatively affected middle-class Black youth coming of age in the 1990s in a Chicago neighborhood that is similar in many ways to the DC neighborhoods of Petworth and Eckington.[29] My analysis of Black neighborhoods in Washington, DC, makes it clear how a range of factors, including the changing labor market, the criminalization of Black people, the targeting of Petworth and Eckington during the War on Drugs, and disinvestment in public goods, created obstacles to intergenerational wealth transmission. This in turn helps us understand why White residents of the Washington metropolitan area today have eighty-one times the wealth of Black residents.[30]

Before Gentrification analyzes the role of state-led practices such as segregation and the War on Drugs in creating the devastation that made gentrification possible. Each chapter focuses on a different aspect of carceral and profit-driven investment, disinvestment, and racialized reinvestment. The chapters are arranged chronologically, revisiting several neighborhoods at different points in time.

I draw from a broad range of primary and secondary sources to recount the story of Washington, DC, over the past hundred years. My data include eleven months of ethnographic research conducted between 2016 and 2022, thirty-seven interviews collected between 2016 and 2022, and a comprehensive housing survey of Washington, DC, using Google Street View. The thirty-seven interviews with formerly incarcerated Black men from Washington, DC, were conducted in person before the COVID-19 pandemic and virtually when that was no longer feasible. The interviews were transcribed and coded for major themes. The interviews were with Black men whose first arrest and prison stay were at the height of the War on Drugs—between 1984 and 2000—and who were born between 1965 and 1985. They had served between four and thirty-five years in prison.

In addition, I rely on the oral histories of forty-seven people: thirty-eight of these are held in the DC Oral History Collaborative Collection (including the Barry Farm Oral History Project, the Mapping Segregation Oral History Project, the Fort Totten Storytellers Project, and Women of the WIRE), and nine were collected from long-term residents of Washington, DC, and are on file with the author. Among the oral histories are those of some of the first Black residents to arrive in all-White areas of DC, some of the White residents who left DC for the suburbs, long-term residents of public housing, and people directly affected by the carceral system. I am grateful to the DC Public Library for making these oral histories publicly available and to the research teams for doing the work required to collect and post them. I read the transcripts of each of the oral histories and coded them for themes relevant to my analysis. A list of the interviews and oral histories is presented in the appendixes.

I also draw from the forty boxes of the Neighbors, Inc., papers in the Washingtoniana archive at the DC Public Library, which shed light on processes of neighborhood change in Northwest in the second half of the twentieth century. I use the 1940 US Census rolls to gain insight into neighborhoods prior to slum clearance. I also draw from court cases, newspaper articles, congressional reports and testimonies, and government reports to understand the historical context. Finally, I use several sources of quantitative data, including the US Census, the US Department of Veterans Affairs mortgage information, the National Center for Education Statistics, the Bureau of Labor Statistics, the Bureau of Justice Statistics, and the Metropolitan Police Department arrest and stop and frisk statistics.

Part 1 focuses on disinvestment. Most scholarship on housing for Black people in the mid-twentieth century looks at the barriers to securing housing due to redlining and a racist real estate industry. To the extent that scholars examine Black home ownership during this period, the focus is on how these areas became slums and how Black people were denied traditional mortgages. My research in Washington, DC, reveals a different story. Black home ownership in Washington, DC, increased sevenfold between 1940 and 1980. The areas where Black people purchased homes were thriving neighborhoods with many small businesses and excellent schools. Similarly, public housing initially provided safe and comfortable homes for Black people. However, these areas slowly but surely experienced public and private disinvestment and, eventually, violence.

Chapter 1, "Dispossession and Displacement," uncovers an unrelenting trend in the history of housing in Washington, DC: anti-Black federal and local policies generated wealth for White residents while dispossessing and displacing Black residents. By the mid-twentieth century, there were hundreds of thousands of African Americans in DC, many of them part of the Great Migration. Some of these Black migrants and their descendants purchased homes and formed small communities of landowners, only to have their land taken through eminent domain. Others lived in substandard housing in alley dwellings that were demolished to make way for public housing. The federal government's concentration of public housing east of the Anacostia River and in other remote areas of Southeast and Northeast would shape the future of the surrounding communities for decades. In Eckington and Petworth, real estate agents and the federal government worked together first to keep the neighborhoods White and then to encourage White flight to the suburbs. White flight allowed people like Mark's grandfather to purchase homes in White neighborhoods, yet these same communities would experience public and eventually private disinvestment.

Chapter 2, "The Violence of Disinvestment," describes the ripple effects of disinvestment, when public authorities abandoned public education, public housing, and city services in Black communities. Public schools that had been excellent in the 1950s and 1960s began to experience significant setbacks. Public housing that had been built with much fanfare fell into disrepair as public housing budgets were slashed. As White people fled to the suburbs, so did the jobs. By the early 1980s, half of Black youth were unemployed. The violence of disinvestment did not spare Black middle-class neighborhoods, and many Black families who could afford to leave the city did. Those families that remained lived through a wave of violence: over four thousand Black men were murdered in Washington, DC, between 1988 and 1998.

Part 2 focuses on carceral investment. Whereas most scholarship on policing in Black communities highlights poor areas, the chapters in part 2 discuss both poor and working- to middle-class Black communities to show both the similarities between them and the unique ways in which they were targeted.

Chapter 3, "Cracking Down: The War on Drugs and Downward Mobility," begins in the 1980s and tells the story of how crack came to Washington, DC, via Los Angeles, Colombia, and Central America. The crack trade devastated large swaths of the city, created opportunities for drug-dealing crews, and generated a devastating wave of violence. However, crack did not do this alone. Decades of disinvestment made the spread of crack possible. Crack arrived at a moment when the city had abandoned its most vulnerable residents. The city responded to the rising problems associated with crack by expanding the criminal legal apparatus instead of addressing the root problems of failing schools and widespread economic precarity. This carceral investment in policing and incarceration played a significant role in the dispossession of the Black middle class.

Chapter 4, "Bringing in the Feds: Targeting Black Middle-Class Neighborhoods," focuses on the role of prosecutors and the courts in attacks on middle-class Black communities in DC during the height of the War on Drugs. The criminal legal system in DC is unique as the prosecutor can decide whether to use the DC or the federal code when bringing charges against anyone accused of violating the law. This made Washington, DC, an ideal testing ground for new, harsher penalties for drug possession and selling. This chapter explains how DC and federal prosecutors worked together to bring conspiracy charges against alleged members of drug-dealing crews, leading to life sentences for many. These collaborations produced the highest incarceration rate in the world.[31]

Part 3 focuses on reinvestment. Although the wave of gentrification in DC and other cities came on the heels of the War on Drugs, few scholars have paid attention to the connections between the War on Drugs and subsequent gentrification. Using the War on Drugs as the point of departure, I show how Black middle- and working-class areas were devastated by disinvestment and then carceral investment, making them prime candidates for reinvestment through gentrification.

Chapter 5, "Chocolate City No More: Gentrification through White Reclamation," describes how gentrification has led to Black dispossession and White enrichment in working- to middle-class Black neighborhoods. Petworth and Eckington both experienced White flight, redlining, disinvestment, carceral investment, and reinvestment through gentrification. Redlining led to private disinvestment as these areas became ineligible for loans to improve homes and start or expand businesses. Both public and private disinvestment led to crime, which led to heavy policing. As Black youth were shipped off to prison, many of their families decided to leave the city. These residential areas thus became further disinvested and abandoned, making gentrification through rehabilitation possible and profitable. Low housing prices, record-low interest rates, and tax incentives rendered these neighborhoods attractive to investors. This gentrification has both changed the character of these neighborhoods and made them unaffordable to long-term residents.

Chapter 6, "Racialized Reinvestment: HOPE VI, New Communities, and the End of Public Housing," examines a different trajectory leading to gentrification—one that involves the new urban renewal seen in areas once dominated by public housing. It considers three neighborhoods, Navy Yard, Capitol View, and Barry Farm, to show how racial dynamics shape gentrification. Juxtaposing Navy Yard—the most gentrified neighborhood in the country—to Capitol View—one of the few areas in the city experiencing Black gentrification—makes clear how private investments accompany the arrival of White but not Black gentrifiers. The chapter also compares the experiences of returning citizens—that is, formerly incarcerated people—from these neighborhoods to returning citizens from middle-class neighborhoods.

The concluding chapter considers what it means for the city—and the nation—to reckon with the enduring legacy of the War on Drugs. Locking up a generation of Black boys and men has had far-reaching consequences, for these men, their families, and the nation's capital. One lasting consequence is the number of formerly incarcerated people in the city today: sixty thousand, or 10 percent, of DC's current residents have a criminal conviction. Many of these individuals have returned home to a gentrifying city that is both unaffordable and being policed in new ways.

In this book, I tell Mark's story as well as the stories of dozens of other Black men who experienced incarceration. I also include pieces of my own story. I have rarely discussed my childhood experiences in relation to my scholarship in my published work, as I have not wanted to use my experiences growing up in a Black neighborhood to legitimize my authority as a race scholar. Nevertheless, there is value in providing an example of how White scholars might reflect not only on their White privilege but also on the racialized nature of their networks, relationships, analyses, and backgrounds. Also, explaining where I fit into this narrative feels more honest than pretending as if I don't know some of the people whose stories I recount.

I was in college when Mark was arrested and remember clearly how devastating his arrest, trial, and life sentence were for Traci's whole family. Traci is a gifted artist, but she found it difficult to concentrate on finishing her art degree during her brother's six-month trial and dropped out of college. I moved away from Washington, DC, in the 1990s, and each time I have returned I have thought about how full my life has been while Mark has been behind bars, how it is possible that Traci's family lost a home that rose in value each time I returned, and how much not just Mount Pleasant but also the whole city has changed during Mark's years behind bars.

I am a White person who grew up in the primarily Black neighborhood of Petworth during the 1980s. All my close friends—from childhood through college—were Black. Growing up in a Black community has shaped who I am, how I view the world, and what questions I ask. At the same time, my Whiteness has also shaped who I am and my place in the world.

My family has not experienced the historical traumas of slavery, sharecropping, and Jim Crow that the families of my African American friends have. I grew up reading books in school that featured people who look like me. I grew up conscious of my Whiteness, yet I knew my Whiteness would not be a barrier to achieving my life goals.

My parents' social, cultural, and economic capital made my educational journey relatively easy. When I was in middle school, my teacher suggested I enroll in the basic math class; my father advocated to get me in the more advanced class. When I had trouble with my math homework, my parents paid one of my classmates to tutor me. Both of my parents attended college and were able to help me with my college applications. They also fully funded my undergraduate education so that I have not been burdened with student loans. Not only are my parents financially stable but their siblings are too, so my parents have not had to provide financial support to them.[32]

I worked part-time from the age of fourteen, starting with Mayor Marion Barry's Summer Youth Employment Program. Unlike some of my friends, I didn't have to turn my paycheck over to my parents. Instead, I used that money to buy the designer jeans, bags, and shoes I coveted (and my frugal parents refused to buy for me).

Although my Whiteness and class status protected me in many ways from structural violence, I was not immune to the forces of personal and state violence that shaped my community. By the time I graduated from high school, I had been threatened at gunpoint, had experienced multiple instances of physical and sexual violence, and had witnessed many more. I saw people get shot. I had to lay flat on the sidewalk to avoid flying bullets. My first arrest happened when I was twelve, my first night in jail when I was eighteen. My older brother was hospitalized after getting jumped. My younger brother was arrested and incarcerated and has lived with the stigma of a felony conviction. In the summer of 2019, I had the incredibly painful experience of watching police officers restrain, arrest, and take my mentally ill sister by force to a psychiatric hospital.

My family's ability to guide me into and pay for college meant I was able to leave my neighborhood when I was seventeen and move into the dorms at the University of Maryland. Nevertheless, my experiences make understanding personal and state violence more than just a research endeavor for me. I have a personal investment in understanding how and why my neighborhood became plagued by violence, why so many of my childhood friends were murdered, why a generation of Black boys and men was put behind bars, and why so few of my childhood friends can afford to live in the neighborhood where we were raised.

But violence is only part of the story of my neighborhood. Despite the challenges we faced growing up, I had a very rich life as a teenager. My cup was filled to the brim with friends, fashion, and fandom.

Most weekends when I was a teenager, my friends and I would go to the Ibex, the Black Hole, or the Metro Club to see one of DC's famed go-go bands play live music. Going to the go-go in DC was an immersive experience: we danced most of the night, not caring that we sweated our hair out; and since go-go features callbacks, we would often sing along with the band. Having the opportunity to experience live music on a regular basis was a treat.[33]

Going to the go-go was also practically like going to a fashion show, as DC people take pride in how we look. There was always a photography booth set up near the entrance to the club. For five dollars, the photographer would take a Polaroid shot of the group. Looking back on those photos, I can practically smell the aerosol hairspray, and I am also reminded of how much effort we put into our hair and outfits. Usually when my friends and I went out, I got dressed at Nmadilaka's house because her older sister Ijeoma had the final say on our outfits. If we wanted to go out with Ijeoma, we had to meet her high standards. Nmadilaka and I were pretty goofy when it was just the two of us, but when we were with Ijeoma, we had to be fly.

Once we got our fly selves into a taxi to take us to the club, Ijeoma would lead us in saying the Lord's Prayer. I wasn't raised to be religious, but I took comfort in saying the prayer, as I knew our safety in DC's nightlife was not guaranteed. When we got to the club, we would stick together the whole time. There was no going off to get drinks or to talk to other people on your own. We arrived at the club together, stayed together the whole time, and without exception left together. The fierce loyalty my friends and I had to each other when I was a teenager has profoundly shaped my relationships to this day.

I also grew up with a deep sense of belonging to the city in general and to my neighborhood in particular. We referred to the neighborhood where I lived as "Kennedy Street" or "1–4" (in reference to Fourteenth Street). DC natives rarely refer to neighborhoods by their official name. Instead, we would say "Kennedy Street" or "Montana Avenue" to refer to the street and the area around it. Some neighborhoods are known by a single address, such as "640," which refers to the area and housing project around 640 Morton Street. Other neighborhoods might be referred to by a slightly modified name of a housing project, as in Barry Farms (instead of Barry Farm). Some exceptions, like Mount Pleasant, Chevy Chase, and Anacostia, are known by their official neighborhood names—although even these names generally refer to the broader area, as opposed to the city-defined neighborhood boundaries. Although "Petworth" is not the name most often used by long-term residents, I use it to describe the general area where I grew up because it is recognizable to a broad audience. This is in part because the Petworth Library and Petworth Metro stop make it clear where Petworth is.[34]

This book tells the story of Washington, DC, to explain how anti-Black racism and racial capitalism have shaped the city's trajectory. Where one stands in relation to systems of power and oppression shapes how one understands these systems. As an upper-middle-class White woman, I draw material benefits from living in an anti-Black, racial capitalist system. Nevertheless, my scholarly research, my personal relationships, and my political education as the daughter of anti-racist communists allow me to perceive the negative effects of racial capitalism and anti-Black racism. These structural forces have not only shaped the trajectory of my hometown; they have also shaped the lives of its residents, including my closest friends. Some of the friends I grew up with are no longer with us, including Nmadilaka's younger brother, Alo. Others, like Traci's brother, Mark, have spent decades in the prison system. Others, like my college roommate's boyfriend, Gerald, are still behind bars.

Some of my childhood friends have achieved professional success despite the tremendous barriers erected by anti-Black racism and racial capitalism. Some have even attained professional success despite having spent time in prison. My childhood friends work in a wide range of occupations; they are bus drivers, government workers, legal professionals, and business owners. Some of my former classmates are, like me, college professors. Whereas anti-Black racism and racial capitalism have required my friends to develop unfathomable amounts of strength and resilience to overcome barriers to professional success, these same forces have made my journey relatively easy.

My Whiteness, my class status, my parents' leftist politics, and my experiences growing up in a Black community and attending racially diverse schools have shaped my life experiences, my material conditions, and my perspective on the topics discussed in this book. I am well aware of the politics of being a White woman writing about a Black community, as well as the mistakes many of my White colleagues have made in this endeavor, such as writing sensationalist accounts of violence and poverty and failing to connect this violence and poverty with systemic forms of oppression. I am doing my best to avoid making these mistakes. I will let you, the reader, be the judge of my ability to do that.

PART ONE

DISINVESTMENT

WHEN I ENROLLED IN KINDERGARTEN at our neighborhood school in 1978, I was one of two White children there. The other White child was my brother Ian. When I was in second grade, I transferred to a new school where there were only a handful of students who were not White. My new school had carpeting, a library full of books, and a beautiful playground. My old school had linoleum floors and a sparse library, and we spent recess walking single-file around the block with our teacher.

I spent the rest of my childhood taking the city bus from my primarily Black neighborhood east of Rock Creek Park to primarily White schools west of the park. I would get on the bus across the street from the corner store owned by Mr. Ko where I used to buy Big Mama sausages. We would ride past the liquor store where Monique and I bought cigarettes for her grandmother . . . and later for ourselves. Then we would ride past the funeral home where I attended Erica's funeral after she was gunned down in a drive-by shooting.

1

DISPOSSESSION AND DISPLACEMENT

ELIZABETH PROCTOR THOMAS, A FREE BLACK WOMAN, was one of dozens of Black people who owned property in DC's Brightwood neighborhood before the Civil War. In September 1861, Union troops appropriated her land to build Fort Massachusetts, later renamed Fort Stevens. She fought for years to be compensated for the loss of her property and was finally awarded $1,835 in 1916. She died a year later.[1]

The appropriation of Elizabeth Proctor Thomas's land was not an exception. The city and private developers worked together to eradicate nearly all the Black communities established in DC's Northwest quadrant in the nineteenth century and build subdivisions and public amenities for White residents on land once owned by Black people. Formerly enslaved people and their descendants worked hard to purchase land and homes in DC only to have their property taken from them through eminent domain.

After the Civil War, the Brightwood area remained sparsely populated, with eighty-six White and sixty Black households in 1880. A decade later, real estate developers purchased large tracts of land and built several all-White subdivisions there. By 1950, just one block of Black residents consisting of thirteen households remained in Brightwood. In 1959, developers cleared those houses to build Rockview Apartments.[2]

The process of capitalist accumulation in Washington, DC, began with primitive accumulation when European settlers expelled the Nacotchtank (Anacostan) Indigenous people from the land that the city now occupies. This expulsion was the first step toward transforming the land into private property. Just forty years after the first documented encounter in 1608, when Captain John Smith arrived via the Potomac River, the Nacotchtank population had been reduced by more than three-quarters. By the time the hundred-square-mile area was cut out of the states of Maryland and Virginia to become the nation's capital in 1791, the Indigenous population had been completely displaced.[3]

As a system of exclusive property rights was imposed, commodification and privatization imbued the land with monetary value within a capitalist system.[4] The value of the land was enhanced by the labor of enslaved persons, who were forced to clear trees to make way for boulevards, dig ditches that would become streets, make and lay bricks for houses, and quarry and transport stones to build the White House.[5] In the Americas, there is a long-standing pattern of displacements and dispossessions rooted in settler colonialism wherein Europeans uprooted Indigenous communities to steal their lands and then used enslaved African labor to increase the profit they could extract from them.

Although it was the labor of Black people that increased the value of the land, in the twentieth century, developers, White citizens associations, and government officials worked together to remove Black people and create all-White communities. In Reno City and on Meridian Hill, the city used eminent domain to build parks and schools serving Whites only. In Brightwood, the Federal Housing Administration (FHA) financed new, all-White subdivisions. In the Southeast quadrant, the housing authority used slum clearance and urban renewal policies to level the homes of Black people. In Navy Yard, an integrated working-class neighborhood, the housing authority used these policies to replace homes with segregated public housing for Black residents. In Barry Farm, it used these same powers to remove Black home owners and create public housing. In Capitol View, private developers built homes for middle-class Black residents, and then the housing authority constructed public housing projects in the heart of the community. In each of these cases, anti-Black local and federal policies led to the displacement and dispossession of Black families and the creation of a segregated city.[6]

This chapter introduces five DC neighborhoods that I revisit throughout the book—Navy Yard, Barry Farm, Capitol View, Eckington, and Petworth—and describes the displacement and dispossession of Black families from these and surrounding neighborhoods. Navy Yard, Barry Farm, and Capitol View are in the Southeast quadrant; Eckington is in the Northeast; and Petworth is in the Northwest (Map 2).[7] The displacement and dispossession of Black people from these and other neighborhoods in Washington, DC, was a critical step in the process of enhancing the value of this land. Under capitalism land can be bought and sold, of course, but under racial capitalism, the value imputed to land varies according to the racial composition of the people who live on it. Dispossessions and displacements are not incidental to racial capitalism; they are what make racial capitalism possible.

SLUM CLEARANCE, URBAN RENEWAL, AND PUBLIC HOUSING

The Black population of DC surged during and in the decades after the Civil War (1861–1865). By 1950 there were 280,803 Black residents in Washington, DC.[8] This increase in the Black population, along with segregationist policies, intensified the housing shortage for Black residents. Until

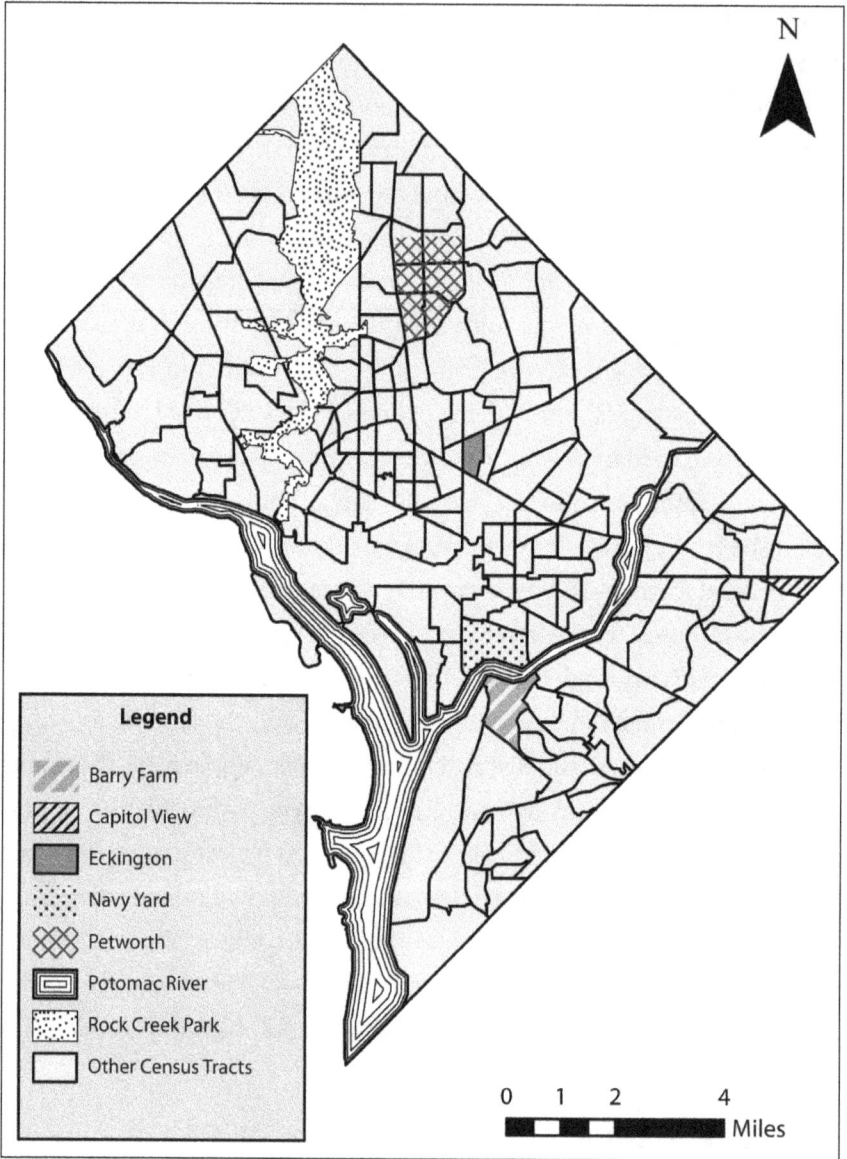

Map 2. DC Neighborhoods: Navy Yard, Barry Farm, Capitol View, Eckington, and Petworth.

the 1950s both public and private housing developments were legally segregated. And despite the great need for housing for Black residents, most new housing was built for Whites only. This made it difficult for Black residents to move out of the central city.[9] In 1947 two-thirds of the Black residents of DC lived within a 2¼-mile radius of downtown.[10]

When formerly enslaved migrants arrived in DC, they often lived in substandard housing called alley dwellings, poorly constructed homes that lined the alleys of the city. In 1866 two hundred people were squeezed into a 200-square-yard space on Rhode Island Avenue. Farther downtown, on the land where the Departments of Commerce and Labor would later be constructed, one hundred families were crowded into dilapidated, makeshift shanties in a 50-square-yard space.[11] The Alley Dwelling Authority (ADA; a precursor to the National Capital Housing Authority [NCHA]) and other government agencies engaged in a prolonged campaign to eliminate so-called slums and alley dwellings, which they viewed as a scourge on the nation's capital.

The construction of public housing helped alleviate the housing shortage, yet there has consistently been more demand than supply. The first public housing project in DC, built in 1937, was Langston Terrace Dwellings, located near the Anacostia River in Northeast. About 2,700 people applied for the opportunity to live in this new complex for Black residents, which could accept only 274 families. In Foggy Bottom, the ADA leveled ninety homes of Black families in 1938 and built St. Mary's Court, a twenty-four-unit public housing complex, in its place.[12] The construction of public housing eliminated and destabilized longstanding Black home owner communities and eradicated integrated neighborhoods. One of these communities was Navy Yard.

Navy Yard: From Integrated to Segregated Housing

The Washington Navy Yard was established in 1799, just eight years after the nation's capital was founded. Many Navy Yard workers built homes nearby and walked to work. The surrounding neighborhood came to be called Navy Yard. Although Navy Yard began as a primarily White neighborhood, during and after the Civil War increasing numbers of African Americans settled there, and it gradually became majority Black. By 1940 Navy Yard's population consisted of about 1,500 White residents and 5,000 Black residents.[13]

The FHA, which had been established in 1934 in response to the financial crisis of the Great Depression, played a significant role in creating segregation in DC. The historians Mara Cherkasky and Sarah Shoenfeld uncovered an FHA map from 1937 that resembles "redlining" maps found in other cities. These maps outlined in red (thus the term "redlining") those areas deemed high risk for investment, that is, those with "'undesirable populations' such as Black, Jewish, Asian, and Mexican households. These areas were more likely to be close to industrial areas and to have older housing." Because the FHA's underwriting policies classified Black and integrated neighborhoods as "risky," they institutionalized racial segregation by primarily underwriting loans in areas that were predominantly White.[14]

The FHA map graded Navy Yard "F," which meant it was "showing effects of negro occupancy; many of the structures are in poor condition and are rapidly tending to become slums if not already in that category."[15] The FHA's labeling of Navy Yard as a slum not only justified the razing of homes in this racially integrated, working-class area; it also made it difficult to secure a loan for buying or upgrading houses there for decades to come. This ensured that the area around the public housing projects would receive minimal private investment. In 1941, the ADA demolished a large swath of homes in Navy Yard and built a 314-unit public housing project for Black residents, Carrollsburg Dwellings.[16] The federal government then refused to adequately fund public housing, leading to deteriorating conditions in the housing projects by the mid-1960s.

The housing authority also built public housing for White residents during World War II, mostly in White working-class neighborhoods in

Southeast, such as Fort Dupont. However, the largest by far, McLean Gardens, which had over 2,000 units, was built west of Rock Creek Park. McLean Gardens only lasted three years as public housing; it was sold in 1946 to a private investor, despite the intense need for more public housing. Two decades later, the housing authority converted an existing building on Connecticut Avenue into public housing. That building, called Regency House, has 160 units and to this day is the only public housing project west of the park.[17]

In Navy Yard, Black and White residents had lived side by side. For example, the 1940 US Census shows that John Williams, a Black man, lived with his wife and their six children and his mother-in-law in a house they rented at 915 Sixth Street, SE. A White man, Kenneth Fugitt, lived with his wife, three children, and father next door in a house they owned. Mr. Williams was a janitor, and Mr. Fugitt was an automobile mechanic.[18] Census block data show that in 1950 the square block where the Williams and Fugitt families lived had eighty-five homes, one-third of which were occupied by home owners. In 1958, the housing authority destroyed this block and the area surrounding it to build the Arthur Capper Dwellings, a 707-unit public housing project. A decade later the Navy Yard area was no longer integrated: it was nearly 100 percent Black. The goals of the public housing program, which were to eliminate slum dwellings and provide decent housing, offered hope to many Black families. Together, Carrollsburg and Arthur Capper Dwellings eventually housed over a thousand low-income residents. However, policies that created segregated public housing combined with FHA guidelines that deterred private investment meant that Navy Yard was transformed from an integrated working-class neighborhood into a site of concentrated poverty and racial isolation.

Navy Yard was not an isolated case. Other residents of integrated neighborhoods in DC's Southwest quadrant were displaced through the use of eminent domain for so-called urban renewal. But this time, instead of building only public housing, the bulldozers primarily made way for upscale, high-rise apartment buildings. Since these buildings were not dilapidated, were not residences, and were going to be sold to for-profit developers, two small business owners challenged the Redevelopment Land Agency's (RLA's) right to clear their land in April 1954. However, in December, the Supreme Court ruled in *Berman v. Parker* that the RLA had the right to destroy 99 percent of the buildings in Southwest, to force 1,500 businesses to move, and to displace nearly all the residents. About half of the displaced residents went to the Southeast quadrant of the city—an area that remains nearly all Black today. Only 12 percent of the displaced families were able to stay in Southwest. In 1970, by the time the massive urban renewal project had been completed, the area had just 9,427 residents, only one-third of whom were Black.[19] Both construction projects displaced nearly all the former residents and transformed integrated neighborhoods into segregated ones.

Barry Farm: From Black Landowners to Public Housing

In 1867, the Freedmen's Bureau made 375 acres in Southeast DC available to formerly enslaved people and their descendants. The land lay between Uniontown, a restricted White residential area, and the Government Hospital for the Insane, later renamed St. Elizabeths. By the end of 1868, most of the one-acre lots had been sold to Black people. Residents built homes for themselves, a school for Black children, and an African Methodist Episcopal church. They named the streets after antislavery lawmakers, including Thaddeus Stevens, Charles Sumner, and Benjamin Wade, as well as Freedmen's Bureau officials, including John Eaton and Oliver Howard. Although the community chose the name Hillsdale, in official records and on maps it remained known as Barry Farm. (James Barry was a white merchant who had previously owned the land.) By 1940, Hillsdale/Barry Farm was a majority-Black community with several small businesses. About half of the residents owned the homes they lived in. Many of these residents had built the homes themselves, and many cultivated gardens around their homes.[20]

In 1941, the government used its power of eminent domain to condemn and destroy a thirty-four-acre section of Barry Farm to build a public housing project for Black families. Twenty-three Black families that owned the land they occupied were uprooted.[21] The FHA's designation of Barry Farm/Hillsdale as a "slum" due to the high percentage of Black residents was used to justify its decision to raze the homes and build the Barry Farm Dwellings housing project in their place. The housing project would provide housing for hundreds of African Americans but also set the stage for a significant shift in the character of this neighborhood—from a community of home owners to an area with relatively few home owners.[22]

Barry Farm Dwellings consisted of large apartments with between two and six bedrooms and featured windows that allowed in natural light. Large trees graced the grounds. The housing project thrived initially. In 1959, the *Washington Post* ran a story on the fifth annual beautification campaign at Barry Farm Dwellings. After seeing the colorful flower gardens created by residents, William R. Simpson, general counsel of the NCHA, "wished out loud that Washington's other fifteen projects were cared for as well" as Barry Farm.[23]

Although the Barry Farm Dwellings provided safe and affordable housing, the government did not fund these housing projects sufficiently to allow them to continue to flourish. In addition, the FHA designated the area as destined for decline, making it difficult for small businesses to secure loans. And the city rezoned the area, allowing for the building of more multifamily homes, which reduced the home ownership rate. Several other public housing facilities were built in the vicinity. The combined effect of these policies and practices was to funnel the poorest Washingtonians into the neighborhood, thereby creating concentrated poverty and racial isolation, which together compound disadvantages for families, especially children.[24]

FEDERALLY FINANCED SUBDIVISIONS

The FHA was established under President Franklin Roosevelt's New Deal. Another component of the New Deal—designed to help the country recover from the Great Depression—was the Home Owners' Loan Corporation (HOLC), which Roosevelt created in June 1933 with an appropriation of $200 million. Within three years, the HOLC had refinanced mortgages for over eight hundred thousand home owners, not only salvaging old mortgages but also creating policies that would help prevent future mortgage crises and promote home ownership. All homes with FHA-insured mortgages had to follow HOLC guidelines, which required that mortgages have both low interest rates (10 percent instead of the standard 30 percent) and repayment periods of twenty-five or thirty years. They also had to meet minimum building standards and be in neighborhoods where HOLC and FHA estimated home values were likely to be stable or increase. Although these New Deal programs provided opportunities to White families to build wealth through home ownership, they were far less likely to benefit Black people. Black people were not, however, entirely excluded. Capitol View is one example.

Capitol View: "America's finest colored community"

In an analysis of the DC housing market in 1940, the FHA warned that, unless offered an alternative, the city's Black residents would eventually move into White areas. The FHA therefore committed to subsidizing a minimal amount of private housing for Black families, in part to save the rest of the city from what it called the "rising tide of color."[25] This may be the reason the FHA subsidized some of the home building in Capitol View, despite the fact that the FHA had graded this area "H," which not only described majority-Black areas but also recommended that structures be razed and new buildings constructed in their place. This grade eventually would give the housing authority license to build public housing in this area, as it had done in Barry Farm.[26]

In the 1920s, a Black developer named John Whitelaw Lewis began developing Capitol View as a residential subdivision for African Americans. In the 1930s he collaborated with the Capital View Realty Company, which was able to secure FHA-insured loans and enable Black families to purchase single-family homes. The Capital View Realty Company convinced the FHA that Capitol View would be a suitable investment by emphasizing its status as an elite Black subdivision. The stone-and-brick homes would feature oak floors and tiled bathrooms with tubs and showers.[27]

In 1936, the *Afro-American* newspaper described Capitol View as "America's finest colored community." Black newspapers frequently ran ads and articles promoting this modern development. In 1939 the Capital View Realty Company built four two-story, brick-and-cinder-block houses between 5333 and 5341 East Capitol Street at a cost of $17,500—or $4,375 each.[28] Harry W. Lucas, a porter for Presidents Harding, Coolidge, Hoover, and Roosevelt, bought the house at 5333 East Capitol Street and lived there until his death in 1950.[29] His wife, Amelia Lucas, was still living there in 1965 when her photo appeared in the *New York Amsterdam News* showing her at the Nassau Golf Club during the Third Annual Pepsi-Cola International Golf Tournament.[30] Mrs. Lucas worked for the Federal Trade Commission for more than thirty-five years and made her mark as an amateur golfer as well as a long-term federal employee. She died at age sixty-nine in 1978.[31]

Capitol View residents worked together to transform their neighborhood from a rural subdivision lacking basic amenities into a thriving urban community. In the early twentieth century, they formed the Capitol View Civic Association to address such issues as unpaved streets and poor access to public transportation.[32] Residents started a church in the home of one of the residents, Mrs. Turner, and eventually secured funding to hire the renowned Black architect R. C. Archer Jr. to build the Capital View Baptist Church in 1947.[33] In July 1938 they succeeded in getting a Metrobus to serve their community. The first elementary school for residents was the George Harris Richardson Elementary School, built in 1948. In 1949 Kelly Miller Junior High opened. It would take nearly another quarter century before Capitol View residents obtained an easily accessible high school, Woodson High.[34] The city's failure to build infrastructure in Capitol View despite persistent pleas by community members is just one of many examples of the ways that Black neighborhoods in DC have seen their tax dollars fund public investments across town while they themselves have not benefited in the same ways.

Insofar as it became a community of Black middle-class home owners living in brand-new subdivisions in the 1930s, Capitol View was exceptional. The character of "America's finest colored community" would change dramatically when the housing authority decided to build one of the city's largest public housing projects in its heart. When the residents of Capitol View learned of these plans, they protested. City officials pointed to the lack of available land in the inner city as well as the need for public housing, particularly for Black residents. And despite residents' protests, in 1952, the National Capital Parks and Planning Commission (NCPPC) approved the construction of the East Capitol Dwellings in this middle-class neighborhood with a high percentage of home owners. This housing project comprised mostly two-story semidetached houses, in addition to a few three-story apartment buildings. It soon became apparent that the housing authority's contractor had not met basic construction standards as the homes quickly fell into disrepair.[35]

Redlining in Capitol View would have enduring consequences. To this day, Capitol View has few amenities and instead shows the signs of decades of public and private disinvestment.

Chevy Chase and Reno City: White Amenities, Black Displacement

Juxtaposing the histories of Barry Farm, Navy Yard, and Capitol View to the history of majority-White Chevy Chase reveals a clear pattern: anti-Black federal and local policies generated wealth for White residents and dispossessed and displaced Black residents. Black home owners were displaced from Barry Farm to make way for public housing. In Chevy Chase Black people were also displaced. But instead of building public housing for Black families to help alleviate the housing shortage, the city built a school for White students and a park. Developers argued that the presence of Black people would devalue the land. They were able to convince legislators to enact policies that would create an all-White community west of the park. One of these decisions involved moving Black people out of a community in Chevy Chase called Reno City.

Local developers and White residents worked together to have this community of 370 families razed. Reno City was founded at the end of the Civil War by George and Ariana Dover, who had been enslaved by White families in Washington, DC. Their settlement grew into a small village, with a school for Black children called the Reno School. The Chevy Chase Land Company, however, worked assiduously over decades to have this community demolished. Eventually, with the help of the all-White Friendship Citizens Association and the buy-in of the NCPPC, Reno City was demolished.[36]

By 1951, when demolition occurred, Reno City was a shadow of its former self. There were only six students left in the Reno School, each in a different grade.[37] In 1951, the NCPPC notified the twelve Black families remaining in Reno City that they must vacate their homes to make room for a recreation center. One of the last Black households to leave was headed by Alexander Lewis, a Treasury Department worker and veteran, who had been given final notice to leave his house by April 30,

1951. Lewis was born in 1890 in Reno City and had graduated from the Reno School in 1910. Despite a search that lasted several weeks, he and his wife were unable to find an affordable house or apartment. Lewis feared they would have to settle for a furnished room.[38] They ultimately found a place in a primarily Black neighborhood just north of Howard University, where Lewis remained until his death in 1979.[39]

I attended the junior high school built on the land once called Reno City. When I attended Alice Deal Junior High, I was on the cross-country team, and our practice involved jogging around Fort Reno Park. I was unaware that the green hills of the park had once been home to generations of African Americans.

By building a school for White students and an expansive park instead of public housing, the city helped ensure that the value of the land in Chevy Chase would remain high and that the area would attract private investment. Today Chevy Chase has several grocery stores, gourmet shops, bookstores, cafés, and restaurants. In contrast, Capitol View has smaller versions of the public amenities available in Chevy Chase and almost none of the private development or investment. Notably, even upper-middle-class Black communities in the 1970s such as Colonial Village and North Portal Estates had few of the public or private amenities found in Chevy Chase.

THE CREATION OF ALL-WHITE SUBDIVISIONS: ECKINGTON AND PETWORTH

The creation of all-White subdivisions in Washington, DC, was made possible by the combined forces of several parties: federal authorities like the FHA and the HOLC, developers, real estate agents, banks, and White property owners. The meticulous research of Prologue DC's Cherkasky and Shoenfeld, which required looking at hundreds of thousands of deeds individually to see if they have language that indicates that the property may not be sold or rented to Black people, revealed that most of the homes in Chevy Chase, Petworth, Mount Pleasant, Bloomingdale, and Eckington had racially restrictive covenants in place, with language such as the following: "the land and premises shall not be rented, leased, sold, transferred, demised or conveyed unto or in trust for any negro or colored person, or person of negro blood or extraction."[40]

The 1937 FHA map for DC consistently graded all-White subdivisions higher than the areas where Black people lived. These higher ratings would likely qualify home buyers for federally subsidized mortgages and home owners for loans to renovate their homes. On the 1937 FHA grading map, Eckington was rated "E," as the homes were built earlier, but this designation meant the area was still green-lighted for investment. It also meant the area qualified for federally subsidized mortgages and loans, making it accessible to White home buyers. Petworth received a "C" because it was all-White and working to middle class. This gave developers, home owners, and small business owners a green light for loans. A "C" rating meant that the FHA predicted the area would "maintain a very high appeal for the middle-class buyer for at least ten years."[41] This designation was prescient, as the neighborhood would begin to change about a decade later. It would continue to be attractive to middle-class buyers in the 1950s, but most of these buyers would be Black.

In addition to the official redlining and the racially restrictive covenants implemented by developers, White home owners played a role in maintaining segregation. In 1924 property owners in Eckington and the adjacent neighborhood of Bloomingdale established a permanent executive committee whose goal was to ensure that the neighborhoods remained White.[42] In 1946, residents of Randolph Street in Petworth banded together to sign an agreement to bar Black residents for fifty years.[43] White home owners formed racially exclusive "citizens associations" across the city, including the North Capitol Citizens Association, the Petworth Citizens Association, the Manor Park Citizens

Association, the Friendship Citizens Association, and the Mount Pleasant Citizens Association, to lobby the city for everything from better streetcar service to new libraries. In addition, they worked to keep their neighborhoods White. One of their strategies was to create multi-property covenants (dubbed "petition covenants" by Cherkasky and Shoenfeld) that forbade selling or renting their homes to Black people. This strategy was important as the petitions covered those homes that did not have racially restrictive covenants.[44] Real estate developers, government policies, citizens associations, and the courts worked in concert to ensure that these new subdivisions, including Eckington and Petworth, would remain all-White until the 1950s, when most of the White residents would leave for the newly built suburbs.

WHITE FLIGHT AND CREATING SUBURBIA

Although developers, the federal government, and White home owners engaged in multiple practices to ensure White subdivisions would remain racially exclusive, Black people persisted in their efforts to leave the dilapidated central city areas where most of them resided in the 1940s. When Black people attempted to secure better housing, White residents responded with court cases, more petition covenants, and violence. In October 1944 an Italian American real estate agent helped a Black home buyer, James Hurd, purchase 116 Bryant Street, NW, in majority-White Bloomingdale. Hurd's White neighbors filed suit, arguing the sale violated the racially restrictive covenant. The DC court upheld the covenant, and the appeals court affirmed the lower court's ruling. Four years later, in 1948, when the case reached the US Supreme Court, the Court ruled that racially restrictive covenants in DC were in violation of the Civil Rights Act of 1866.[45] With this decision, racially restrictive covenants became unenforceable and Black people could purchase homes in previously restricted areas.

In 1950, Petworth and adjacent Sixteenth Street Heights were nearly all-White. The historians at Prologue DC have documented in detail the story of Dr. Clarence D. Hinton, one of the first Black people to move into this area, in oral histories with his children, Audrey Hinton and Diane Hinton Perry. Dr. Hinton purchased 1310 Farragut Street, NW, in 1953. He knew the Supreme Court's decision was no guarantee that he would be able to complete the purchase and move into the house. Thus he found a White person to negotiate the sale on his behalf. When his neighbors learned his identity, they padlocked the doors to try to prevent him from moving in. Dr. Hinton cut off the padlocks and spent the first two nights in his home with his real estate broker to ensure the safety of his family. When nothing terrible happened, Dr. Hinton moved his family into the home. Over the next three years, half the White home owners on his block sold their homes.[46]

By 1960, all the White renters had left the Hintons' block, as had many of the White home owners. By 1970, their block was only 11 percent White. The area around Bryant Street, where James Hurd's neighbors had sued to keep him out, also became nearly all-Black by 1970. As Black people began to move into formerly all-White areas, White people moved out.[47]

Realtors profited greatly by selling houses to Black buyers in neighborhoods that had been restricted to White residents. Many realtors used scare tactics to frighten White families into selling their homes before a neighborhood "turned," claiming property values would plummet. They assailed White residents with junk mail, phone calls, and door-to-door solicitations to sell their homes (Fig. 1). For example, in 1957, the Frederick W. Berkens Jr. & Co. Real Estate Company warned a Mount Pleasant resident that the neighborhood was "fast changing to colored" and suggested a few properties he should consider purchasing in suburban Maryland. In April 1960, a realtor warned a Crestwood resident that "Negroes" were moving in, that the local public schools would soon have Black children, and that property values would fall. Once

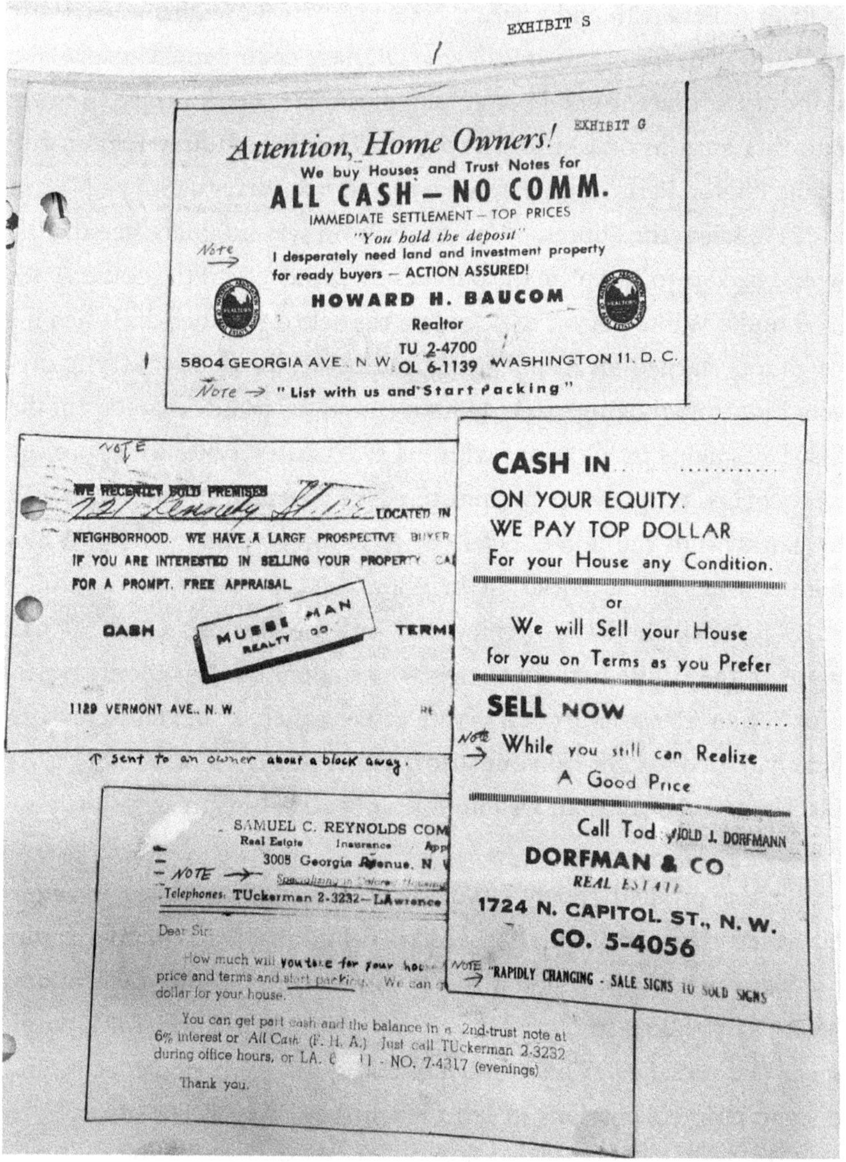

Figure 1. Cards distributed by real estate speculators in the 1950s and 1960s. Neighbors, Inc., Archive, Box 3, US Commission on Civil Rights, May 13, 1962, File Folder #33. Washingtoniana Collection, Martin Luther King Jr. Memorial Library, Washington, DC.

realtors got White home owners to sell their properties and move out of the neighborhood, they sold them to Black people at inflated prices. Between 1950 and 1970, half the White residents of DC left the city.[48]

The Wices were one of the White families that left Petworth in the 1950s. Born in 1942, Paul Wice spent the first fourteen years of his life in a small rented apartment at Second and Hamilton Streets, NW, a few blocks from where I lived as a child. Wice, like me, went to Rudolph Elementary School. When Wice went to Rudolph, legal segregation was in place; the school was all-White, as was the surrounding neighborhood. Once school segregation was outlawed in 1954, Black children began to enroll in Rudolph and other White schools across the city.[49] By the time my older brother Ian enrolled at Rudolph Elementary School in 1977, legal segregation was a thing of the past, yet Ian was the only White student.

Wice graduated from Rudolph in 1954 and transferred to MacFarland Junior High School, which had been a White school before desegregation. MacFarland went from being all-White to 75 percent White when Wice enrolled and then to nearly all-Black within a few years. Paul Wice's family left the city in 1956. Having saved enough money to purchase their first home, this young family, like nearly all White families in Petworth, opted to move to the newly developed suburbs in Montgomery County.[50]

The acceleration of White migration from urban areas in the aftermath of school desegregation was a nationwide phenomenon. The impact this had on DC's racial demographics is shown in Table 2. The city went from 73 percent White and 27 percent Black in 1930 to almost its inverse in 1980: 70 percent Black and 27 percent White.

Although White flight from the city happened at breakneck speed in the 1950s, it would have happened even faster were it not for the efforts of integrationists like Marvin Caplan. When Caplan, who is White, moved into the upper Northwest neighborhood of Manor Park in 1958, he noted that real estate agents were urging White home owners

TABLE 2
Black and White Population in Washington, DC, 1930–1980

Year	Population	Black	White	% Black	% White
1930	486,869	132,068	353,981	27	73
1940	663,091	187,266	474,326	28	72
1950	802,178	280,803	517,865	35	65
1960	763,956	411,737	345,263	54	45
1970	756,510	537,712	209,272	71	28
1980	638,333	448,906	171,768	70	27

SOURCE: US Census Bureau.

to sell their properties. Concerned that his neighborhood would not retain its integrated character, Caplan contacted the Manor Park Citizens Association. Its members demurred, particularly on the question of whether they would admit Black members. Thus Caplan and his neighbors formed an interracial organization of Manor Park residents called Neighbors, Inc., in 1958. Its goal was to establish Manor Park and the surrounding areas as stable, integrated communities. They engaged in several campaigns that urged area residents not to be frightened by "a few unethical real estate operators" who were trying to scare them into selling their homes and leaving (Fig. 2).[51]

Despite the efforts of Neighbors, Inc., the White population of DC declined steadily during the second half of the twentieth century, and the White population of the suburbs expanded rapidly. For example, Montgomery County was a mostly rural area in 1940, with about fifty thousand residents. By 1979, it was a bustling suburb with half a million residents, most of whom were White.

This growth was fueled by low-cost mortgages backed by the FHA as well as the US Department of Veterans Affairs (VA).[52] Between 1934 and 1960, the FHA insured 8,038 mortgages in Washington, DC; 14,702 in Montgomery County; and 15,043 in Prince George's County. Taking population size and mortgage dollar amount into account, Montgomery County home buyers (nearly all of whom were White) accessed

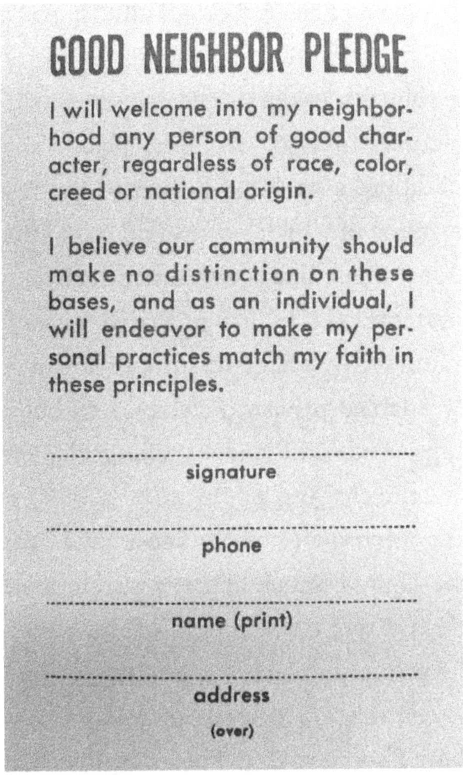

GOOD NEIGHBOR PLEDGE

I will welcome into my neighborhood any person of good character, regardless of race, color, creed or national origin.

I believe our community should make no distinction on these bases, and as an individual, I will endeavor to make my personal practices match my faith in these principles.

----
signature

----
phone

----
name (print)

----
address

(over)

Figure 2. "Good Neighbor Pledge," distributed by Neighbors, Inc., in Northwest DC in the 1960s. Neighbors, Inc., Archive, Box 1. Fundraising / Good Neighbor Pledge Campaign. File Folder #12. Washingtoniana Collection, Martin Luther King Jr. Memorial Library, Washington, DC.

five times as many FHA-subsidized mortgage dollars per capita as did Washington, DC, home buyers. Within DC, nearly all FHA-subsidized mortgages went to the upper northwestern areas of the city, which were also nearly all-White.[53]

Over time, the combination of lending decisions and the unwillingness of White residents to send their children to integrated schools or live in integrated neighborhoods transformed the demographics of the city and its suburbs. The vast majority of federally backed loans during this time went to primarily White suburban areas like the one the Wices moved to.[54] By 1960, the DC suburbs were 94 percent White, whereas the city had just attained a Black majority.[55] In 1974, the funk band Parliament described this trend as "chocolate city" and "vanilla suburbs." By 1980, the White population in Washington, DC, was only one-third of what it had been in 1950. White people had cleared out of almost every neighborhood east of Rock Creek Park, including Petworth.

As White people moved to the suburbs, so did public investments in land development and infrastructure. In 1956, Congress passed the Federal-Aid Highway Act, which appropriated $26 billion to build a 41,000-mile network of highways, many of which led straight out of the cities into the suburbs. In 1957 alone, the federal government invested $1.3 billion in sewer and water systems, $4.8 billion in highways, and $2.8 billion in schools.[56] These public investments disproportionately went to all-White suburbs. They enabled private developers to build shopping centers, office buildings, and subdivisions alongside the newly built freeways that encircled the city and led out of it.[57]

Between 1933 and 1978, federal government policies subsidized over thirty-five million families in the United States in their purchase of homes in new suburban areas. As a direct consequence of these policies, home ownership became the primary vehicle for wealth accumulation. By the early twenty-first century, 60 percent of middle-class Americans' assets were in the form of home equity. These families will pass on trillions of dollars of wealth to their children through accumulated home equity. Nearly all these families are White.[58]

BLACK HOME OWNERSHIP

Although, like many other cities, DC experienced White flight, it stands out as having one of the most prosperous Black populations in the country. In 1969, both the per capita income of Black people ($2,734) and the median household income ($8,488) were among the highest in the country. Notably, in 1969 Detroit and DC were the only two cities in the United States where 40 percent of Black families earned $10,000 or more a year (over $80,000 in 2022 dollars). DC's Black community also had the lowest poverty rate in the country, at 19 percent, less than half the rate of many southern cities.[59] This relative prosperity enabled many Black families to purchase homes, and many did so with the help of the VA.

Although the FHA underwrote very few loans for African Americans, it appears the VA was willing to support African American veterans. And whereas the FHA redlined entire areas of the city and refused to underwrite mortgages in those areas, the VA appraised individual properties and used those appraisals to decide whether it would underwrite the mortgages.[60] Other researchers have argued that Black people were not able to obtain VA loans;[61] my research, however, reveals many Black people in Washington, DC, secured VA loans.

Between 1944 and 1991, the VA subsidized 21,754 mortgages in the city. Race is not reported consistently in the data the VA provided to me after a FOIA request. For example, in the single year 1946, race is reported as "Unknown" for 998 loans; "White," for 42 loans; and "Black," for 17 loans. In each case, the interest rate is 4 percent. Race is reported more consistently after 1970, and the interest rates do not vary by race. Overall, in those instances where race is reported, 70 percent of the VA loans in DC went to Black people.[62]

Many scholars point to the fact that only 2 percent of FHA-underwritten loans went to Black families between 1945 and 1959.[63] This figure is also accurate for DC. The 1960 census shows that Black people received only 2 percent of the FHA mortgages in the DC metropolitan area. However, for VA mortgages the rate is 6 percent.[64] Data from the VA confirm this finding. Between 1943 and 1993, the VA underwrote 14,195,188 loans nationwide. The VA did not record the race of the recipients of over eight million of these loans—more than 58 percent of the sample. Race is recorded in nearly six million cases. Of these six million loans, 574,132, or 9.7 percent, went to Black people. Even if all the missing cases involved White people, this would still amount to 4 percent of VA loans. Despite the missing data, it is clear that over half a million VA loans went to Black people, that the interest rates for these loans were at the prevailing rates, and that Black people were far less underrepresented in VA loans than in FHA loans.[65] VA loans played a significant role in facilitating Black home ownership in Washington, DC.

Although the vast majority of Black home owners had to rely on the private market for their mortgages, there was nevertheless a significant increase in home ownership among Black people in the mid-twentieth century. Between 1940 and 1970, there was a sixfold increase in the number of Black home owners in Washington, DC—from 7,616 to 44,758. The number of home owners increased again in 1980, to 53,534. The increases were marginal until 2010, when the number of Black home owners in DC began to decline steadily.[66]

Although the ability to secure loans from the VA and a handful of Black-owned banks, such as the Industrial Bank and Independence Federal Savings & Loan, had allowed approximately 50,000 Black families to become Washington, DC, home owners by 1980, this did not translate into intergenerational wealth transmission for many of these families. The primary reasons for this are (1) Black communities experienced disinvestment beginning in the 1970s; and, as a consequence, (2) home values in Black neighborhoods stagnated between 1980 and 2000.

CONCLUSION

In cases where Black home owners did manage to carve out residential communities, they were often pushed out to create public housing or parks. The National Capital Housing Authority sited nearly all public housing in Black neighborhoods, and almost all new housing built for Black DC residents during the housing boom of the 1930s and 1940s was public housing. Although public housing met an immediate need for adequate shelter, it also meant many Black families were excluded from the massive, federally subsidized wealth-building project of home ownership. For White families, the homes purchased in new suburban subdivisions would become the foundation of generations of White middle-class wealth.

Anti-Black practices and policies such as racially restrictive covenants and petitions and FHA guidelines institutionalized racial segregation in the DC metropolitan area. The idea that all-White neighborhoods are more desirable and more profitable was cemented in residents' and developers' minds by the 1940s. Federal housing policies in the 1930s and 1940s had also created a scenario in which the home became not only a place to live but also the primary asset for White families in the United States. As housing became increasingly commodified—meaning a financial asset to be exchanged on the market instead of just a place to live—its monetary value gained importance. Realtors, lenders, home buyers, and legislators worked together to create segregationist policies and practices with the goal of preserving this asset for White families. This history is a clear example of the perniciousness of anti-Black racism within a racial capitalist system. It also helps us see how government subsidies enabled wealth accumulation among White families.

Most FHA-financed private housing developments were for White residents only, and federal policies explicitly discouraged subsidizing loans in communities where Black people lived. In this context, neighborhoods like Navy Yard were transformed from integrated working-class communities to neighborhoods dominated by segregated public housing projects for African Americans. Farther uptown, residents of neighborhoods like Eckington and Petworth fought to keep Black people out of their subdivisions. When Black families were finally able to overcome the multiple obstacles to home ownership in neighborhoods built for White occupancy, developers conceived of and built all-White suburbs in Montgomery County and White families abandoned these neighborhoods to move there. The segregation created through these and other practices made it easier for decision makers to unequally distribute public goods along racial lines.

2

THE VIOLENCE OF
DISINVESTMENT

VIOLENCE WAS A PERSISTENT AND PERVASIVE part of my child-hood. At Rudolph Elementary School, my second-grade teacher practiced corporal punishment. Every day, she would require the students in our class to walk around the perimeter of the school for exercise. We were meant to stay in a straight line and keep quiet during the walk. After the walk, she would call any student who had misbehaved to the front of the room. As the students stood with hands out, balled into fists with palms facing down, she would give them a sharp rap with a ruler on each hand. She almost exclusively called boys to the front of the room and never called me.

Although I did not fear the teacher would hit me, the threat of a schoolyard fight was always looming. At Rudolph, I developed a long-standing rivalry with Bonita, who was in my grade, and her younger sister, Theresa. When we argued in school, they would threaten to beat me up at recess. Usually nothing happened. One day, however, the bantering portion of our rivalry had come to a head and there was no getting around an actual fight. When Theresa put her hands up, I did what my friend Trecie had told me girls should do in this situation: I made my hands go in a whirlwind to protect myself and possibly injure Theresa until the teachers came to break up the fight.

The fights got more serious as I got older. As a girl, I didn't have too much to worry about: gendered norms that compelled girls to look pretty and boys to protect their reputation meant that fights between girls were less common and less serious. Nevertheless, I was always mentally ready for the next fight. Throughout junior high and high school, I would spend my mornings rehearsing what I would do if any of the classroom threats to meet my opponent on the schoolyard materialized. I felt as if I had to stay ready for a fight.

Despite my attempts at mental preparation, I was not emotionally ready for the physicality of the blood and bodily injuries a fight between teenage boys entailed. One afternoon, I was hanging out in a friend's basement, and my brother Ian showed up at the front door. I don't know how he made it the two blocks from where he had been beaten up to her house, as blood was pouring out of his head, and he could barely stand. Ian had been jumped, meaning that a group of boys had attacked him. I was able to overcome my shock enough to call an ambulance. As I was riding to the hospital in the front seat of the ambulance, I kept thinking about all the blood and wondering if he was going to make it. Ian was released from the hospital later that day.

Several weeks later, we learned Juice, the boyfriend of my friend's cousin, had been murdered. This was a few days after we had been riding around Georgia Avenue with him and Jay Jay in a hoopty, and Juice had gotten us chicken wings with fries and mumbo sauce for our munchies. Juice was just one of our many friends who lost their lives to gun violence.

As DC's Black population grew in the second half of the twentieth century, public and private investments in public schools, public housing, and community well-being more generally diminished. The city and the federal government built large-scale public housing projects for low-income residents that concentrated low-income people into small geographic areas. This concentration of poverty, however, did not create social problems on its own. It was only after public housing projects experienced disinvestment that these areas became beset with social problems. Farther uptown, majority-Black communities featured good schools, low crime rates, and a thriving business community in the 1960s. It was only when the schools and the community experienced disinvestment that there was a rise in crime and violence. Thus, contrary to arguments that racial isolation and the concentration of poverty lead to a rise in violence, I argue that disinvestment, based in anti-Black and antipoor ideologies, is the root cause of high levels of violence.[1] By the late 1980s, violence had become a defining feature of urban areas across the United States. From 1988 to 1992, Washington, DC, had the highest homicide rate in the country. Like most cities, in DC, the primary targets of gun violence were young Black men.[2] The rise of violence is a consequence of disinvestment in Black communities—most notably in public schools and public housing.

DEFUNDING DCPS

In the 1950s, Anacostia High and Coolidge High were all-White schools that White families fought to keep Black students out of. When the DC Public Schools (DCPS) became majority Black, the level of funding steadily declined. In 1955, when nearly half the students in the public school system were White, 30 percent of the city's budget went to education. By 1964, this was down to 24 percent, even though the school population had increased considerably. In 1978, by which time the schools were only 3 percent White, the public schools received just 18 percent of the city's total budget. And although it is not a direct comparison, in that same year, majority-White Montgomery County spent 45 percent of its budget on the school system.[3]

Black students in DC experienced the ravages of disinvestment both before and after schools were desegregated in 1954. When segregation was legal, DC's Black students attended overcrowded and dilapidated schools, with tattered books held together with strings, desks with deep scars, broken windows, a scarcity of athletic equipment, and inadequate nursing services. In addition, schools were often so overcrowded students attended in two or even three shifts. The poor state of Black schools was the primary reason Black parents organized the Consolidated Parents Group to demand an end to legal segregation.[4]

In the predominantly Black Southeast neighborhood of Barry Farm, children were required to travel several miles to attend overcrowded Browne Junior High, even as the school district opened the brand-new Sousa Junior High for White children right in their neighborhood. One of the children denied access to Sousa was Spottswood T. Bolling. His parents, along with other members of the Consolidated Parent Group, took the president of the Board of Education, C. Melvin Sharpe, to court. *Bolling v. Sharpe* went to the Supreme Court as a companion case to *Brown v. Board of Education*, which ended with a ruling that racial segregation in schools was unconstitutional.

Schools in Washington, DC, became a political battleground in the aftermath of desegregation, with questions of race, money, and leadership at the forefront. Before desegregation could fully take effect, White students (with the support and encouragement of their parents) attempted to undermine the new policy. About 2,500 White students from four schools staged a massive, four-day walkout, refusing to attend their newly desegregated schools (Fig. 3). Nevertheless, four months after the *Bolling v. Sharpe* decision, 97,000 children in Washington, DC, began the school year by attending the public school in their neighborhood, no matter their race.[5] For many students, there were minimal changes. The schools east of the park that had been all-White,

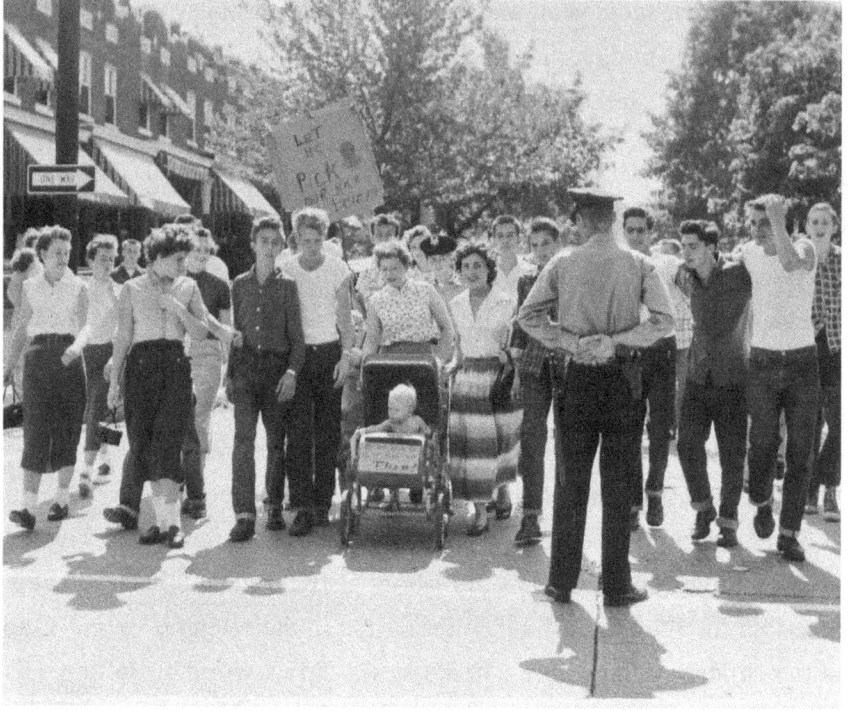

Figure 3. Mrs. Raymond Balderson leads a parade of White Anacostia High School students opposing integration, October 5, 1954. The sign on the stroller reads, "Do we have to go to school with them!" Another sign reads, "Let us pick our KKK friends." Reprinted with permission of the DC Public Library, Star Collection. © *Washington Post*.

however, experienced significant changes, as many of them went from having no Black students to being almost entirely Black in the space of a few years.

The response of many White Washingtonians to desegregation was to abandon the city. Ten thousand White students left the public school system the first year schools were desegregated.[6] In the decade following school desegregation, nearly a third of DC's 500,000 White residents left. By 1974, White enrollment in DCPS had dropped to 3 percent.[7]

A similar story could be told for cities across the country, but the story of school desegregation in DC has a twist. For most of its history, Congress had complete control of DC's laws and finances. This included school financing: the DCPS budget was allocated by Congress, which often granted far less than requested.[8] In 1949, a report by George Strayer of Columbia University Teachers' College had outlined the inadequacy of the DCPS's facilities, teachers, and budget. These problems would only worsen over the next decade, as the number of students in the DC school district increased from 100,000 in 1954 to 150,000 in 1967.[9] In this same period, the school district's population shifted from majority White to nearly all-Black.[10] Turnover was extremely high: the dramatic increase in enrollment happened despite 30 percent of DCPS students leaving the system to study elsewhere. Most of the students who left were White. Most of the new students were Black, and many came from the South, where they often had received inadequate schooling.[11] When DCPS requested funds from Congress to hire more teachers and improve the facilities to accommodate the growing numbers of Black pupils in DC public schools, the requests were denied.[12] Despite funding challenges, the school system was able to make some gains in terms of college enrollment and retention rates after desegregation. For example, the college enrollment rate among graduates increased from 41 to 50 percent between 1957 and 1965. And by 1966, 90 percent of DCPS students completed junior high—up from 67 percent in 1950.

By the mid-1960s, nearly all schools in DC were either more than 90 percent Black or more than 90 percent White. Although de jure segregation was no longer in place, de facto segregation continued, as school enrollments were based on place of residence and residential racial segregation remained entrenched. By 1970, 99.1 percent of Black students in DC attended majority-Black schools, making DCPS the most racially segregated school system in the nation.[13] The small number of White students in the DCPS system primarily attended schools on the west side of the park that were nearly all-White.[14] The greatest disparities in schooling were between the schools west of the park and those east of the Anacostia River, where almost all the students were Black and low-income. In 1971, there were 18.1 students per teacher west of the park, as compared to 22.6 students per teacher in Anacostia. The per-pupil expenditures west of the park were $669, as compared to $478 in Anacostia. The test scores west of the park were 2.4 grades higher than the rest of the city. These disparities led the court to conclude in 1971 that the school system discriminated along racial and socioeconomic lines and to order that DCPS remedy these inequities.[15]

Despite this court decision, the city continued to fail to meet the educational needs of Black students attending segregated schools, particularly in poor neighborhoods.[16] In 1970, a congressional report accused school administrators of incompetence. By 1975, less than one in five city residents who responded to a survey rated their schools as "very good" or "good."[17] In 1978, Conrad P. Smith, president of the DC Board of Education, wrote a column in the *Washington Post* imploring the city council to end the "benign neglect" of DC public schools.[18] In October 1980, the *Washington Post* reported, "There is no question that certain classrooms are suffering from overcrowding, dilapidated or non-existent books and the reduction or elimination of music, art, and foreign language programs."[19]

Parents United issued a report in 1985 that compared Coolidge High, a majority-Black school in Washington, DC, with two schools in the primarily White suburbs, Marshall High in Fairfax County, Virginia, and Rockville High in Montgomery County, Maryland. Despite similar enrollments, Coolidge had fewer teachers, counselors, athletic teams, and library books. Notably, the budget for athletic coaches was eight times higher at Rockville High, and the school spent nearly twice as much per pupil overall as Coolidge.[20] Data from the National Center for Education Statistics show that in 1991, the dropout rate in DC was four times that of the adjacent suburban areas of Montgomery County and Fairfax County and fifteen times that of the wealthy suburb of Falls Church, Virginia.[21] By 1994, DC had the highest dropout rate in the nation, with only 56 percent of students who started the tenth grade earning a diploma. Among those who did graduate, the majority could not pass a test that measured competence at a ninth-grade level.[22] This statistic reminds me of my friend's cousin who graduated from Coolidge in 1989, even though she could barely read the back of a cereal box.

The families Coolidge High served had the highest average income among all the majority-Black high schools in the city.[23] Several of the men we interviewed for this project attended Coolidge High in the 1980s. They all lamented its lack of amenities and educational opportunities. Troy, for example, came from a middle-class family. Both his maternal and paternal grandparents owned homes—in Petworth and farther uptown in Shepherd Park. His mother, a radio journalist, purchased a home in Shepherd Park when he was a teenager. Troy, like many of the Black men I interviewed, did well in school and had food on the table and clean clothes in his closet. At Coolidge, he signed up for the football team. Troy explained that football kept him out of trouble at first: "On the football team, by the time you go to practice, you trying to go home, eat, and go to sleep. There wasn't time to be outside or nothing like that."[24] However, his coach, who was struggling with crack addiction, often failed to show up for practice. Troy explained, "Once the coach stopped showing up," football "fell apart."[25] Troy's father was a drug addict, and his mother's income wasn't enough to buy everything Troy wanted, so when Troy found himself with large amounts of free time after dropping out of the football team, he began to sell drugs, which eventually would lead to ten years behind bars. His narrative and others clearly reveal how disinvestment translated directly into urban violence: as schools and community centers were defunded, young people had few opportunities to play sports or participate in organized after-school activities. For Troy and others, disinvestment in public schools meant that they turned to the streets. And for many, involvement in the crack trade led to their involvement in violence.

LIVING WITH VIOLENCE

Black boys from my neighborhood were murdered at an alarming rate. My friends' boyfriends and brothers were taken from us, leaving behind a heartbreak and longing from which we never would really recover.

My family did not have a television set, so I spent a lot of time in my childhood at my best friend Monique's house, as she had a television set as well as an Atari. We also spent a fair amount of time outside, playing Double Dutch on the corner, hopscotch on the sidewalks, and hide and go get in the alleys that crisscrossed our neighborhood. Monique and I would often walk along Kennedy Street to Rock Creek Park, where we spent many summer afternoons swimming in the cool waters of the creek. On our walk over, we would pass by the carry-out, where we would sometimes get chicken wings with mumbo sauce; the Arcade, where would stop and play PacMan; and the Five and Dime, where we would buy Slim Jims.

This was before Kennedy Street turned into a shooting range, before the son of the owner of the Five and Dime was murdered, and before we attended Erika's funeral on Kennedy Street in 1990. Erika's family lived around the corner from me, in a large home with a manicured yard. The murder of a Black female teenager from a middle-class family barely made the papers. The only mention of Erika Riggings's name in the *Washington Post* was on December 29, 1991, in a list of the names and ages of most of the 3,056 victims of homicide in Washington, DC, from January 1, 1987, through December 28, 1991.[26]

When I was twelve years old, my family moved to Sixteenth and Kennedy Streets. Monique would often come over to my new house, and we made friends with Cydnee and Nmadilaka, who lived closer to Sixteenth Street. The four of us started hanging out on the corner of Fourteenth and Kennedy Streets, often in the small eatery owned by a Black woman named Shay, and Monique started dating Maurice, one of

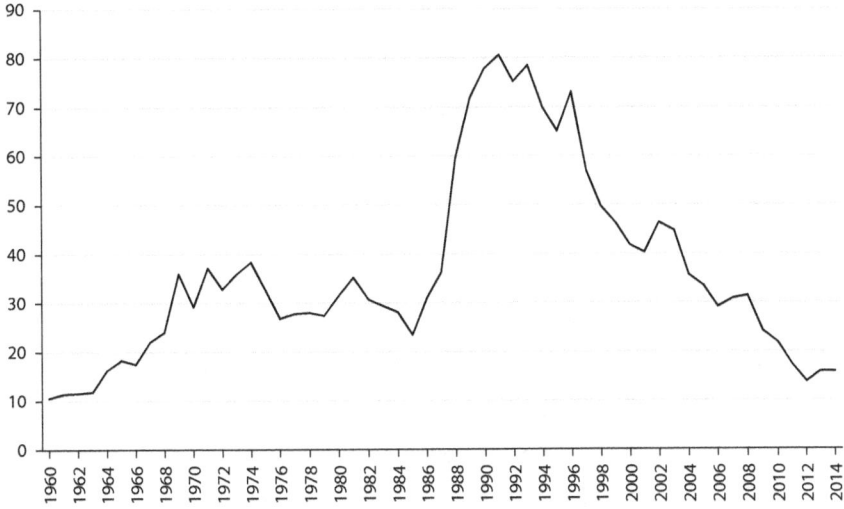

Figure 4. Murder and non-negligent manslaughter rate in DC. Bureau of Justice Statistics data.

the boys who hung out on the corner. People called Maurice "Twin," even though he was actually a triplet. Like many of the boys in our neighborhood, Maurice sold crack. This led to rivalries with other neighborhood crews, which led to violence. First there were fistfights, then knives, and then guns. In my last year of high school, Maurice was shot and killed. We were all devastated, but the other two in the triplet set, Mike and Monica, would never be able to fill the hole left by the loss of their brother.

The number of murders increased steadily beginning in the mid-1980s (Fig. 4). In 1991, the year I graduated from high school, there were 482 murders in the city, and the homicide rate peaked at 80 homicides per 100,000 residents. That was the highest rate for any city in the United States. Detroit was in second place, with a peak of 63 homicides per 100,000 residents in 1987. In the aftermath of the structural violence of racially restrictive covenants, redlining, White flight, and disinvestment, DC experienced a wave of gun violence that would have broad and lasting effects.

This violence hit home when Nmadilaka's brother was killed. In my third year of graduate school, in 2002, I got a call from Nmadilaka that Alo had been killed. Nmadilaka and I were the kind of teenage friends who spent nearly every waking minute together and who wrote letters to each other on Valentine's Day. As I spent nearly all my time at her house, I also became close with her family. Nmadilaka has ten siblings. Kelechi, Ezenwanyi, and Alo are her younger siblings, and OC, Ijeoma, Ugo, Adaku, Oluchi, Sam, and Ben are her older siblings. Kelechi and Ezenwanyi were always underfoot. Nmadilaka's family became my second family; her cousins, Izu and Uzzy, became my cousins. I even went to their parents' country of origin, Nigeria, three times with their family. I was a bridesmaid in Izu's traditional wedding in a small village in Imo State in Nigeria. Alo was a year younger than Nmadilaka and me but always acted like an older brother to us, telling us who we should and should not hang out with and where we should and should not go. Alo had so much potential. He was smart, handsome, charismatic. He could make anyone smile. Like many of the intelligent young men I grew up with, Alo used his skills to build a profitable business selling drugs. Although the circumstances surrounding his death have never been made completely clear to me, and his murder remains unsolved, it seems he lost his life during an armed robbery. I traveled from North Carolina to DC for the wake and the funeral. Nmadilaka and all her sisters wore white. They projected photos of Alo onto the walls. It was unreal. None of us could or wanted to believe what had come to pass. The casket was closed because Alo had been tortured with a sledgehammer. Alo, who had been such a shining light, had spent the last few hours of his precious life being brutalized and tortured. His death merited only a brief mention in the Metro Section of the *Washington Post:*

> The body of a man, apparently beaten to death, that was found in the
> Burke area of Fairfax County was identified yesterday as that of Amaraeg-

bulam Ahaghotu of the District, police said yesterday. Ahaghotu, 26, of the 700 block of Rittenhouse Street NW was last seen Monday, authorities said. His body was discovered Friday near Coffer Woods Road and Burke Centre Parkway, Fairfax County police said. An autopsy determined that the death was caused by blunt force trauma to the upper body. Ahaghotu's car was found yesterday in Southeast Washington.[27]

By the time Alo was killed, I had long left the city. The call from Nmadilaka took me back to a time and place I didn't want to remember. I couldn't believe Alo was gone. Each of Alo's nine siblings believes to this day that their lives would have taken different trajectories were he still with us. His mother has not been the same since the day her worst nightmare became a reality. Each homicide in the city devastated a family and a community. How did DC get to the point where thousands of Black men's lives were ended prematurely?

Public and private disinvestment in Black neighborhoods in the 1970s and 1980s created the conditions in which a crack cocaine market could flourish: failing schools and few well-paying jobs meant there were many young men willing to sell crack to make ends meet. Bleak economic prospects, combined with poor housing conditions, meant there were many people who used crack to escape the drudgery of their lives. The profits and instability that the crack trade introduced to the illegal drug markets in Washington, DC, played a significant role in the violence and turf wars that tormented the city in the 1980s and 1990s.

The majority of people whose lives ended as a result of the rampant gun violence in DC in the 1980s and 1990s were men. Demetrius reflected on the violence during what he accurately termed "the most murderous decade that Washington has ever seen." He explained, "We'd seen people getting killed so much, we were just desensitized to it completely. And, you know, we'd gone through so much trauma because of it all."[28] The shootings of Black men were usually described as *intentional*. And, to be sure, many women were also killed; these incidents were usually described as *accidental* shootings. Young women also witnessed and sometimes enacted violence. Yet conflict between young men was often more serious and more deadly than fights between young women. The sociologist Nikki Jones explains that young women in inner cities can feel pressured to maintain a tough front to survive. However, violence is not a defining characteristic of femininity in the same way it is of masculinity. Jones opines that the pervasiveness of violence in inner-city neighborhoods in the late twentieth century is in part a consequence of the options Black men have for expressing their masculinity in a society that devalues them. Our society values men who express dominance. Whereas upper-class White men can express dominance through their leadership roles at work or in public office, impoverished Black men have fewer options, and the use of physical aggression becomes a critical way for them to express their masculinity.[29] Since our patriarchal society values male dominance, men draw on the expressions of masculinity available to them to garner the esteem and respect they believe they deserve.

Although men are the primary victims and perpetrators of gun violence, men, women, and children all have to live with both the pervasive violence and the deep sense of loss when friends, family members, and neighbors' lives are taken. This sentiment was evident in the oral histories of Women of the WIRE (Women Involved in Reentry Efforts), a network of formerly incarcerated women in DC. One of the participants, Nicolette Williams, who grew up in a neighborhood adjacent to a housing project in Southeast, described the normalization of violence in her neighborhood in the 1980s and 1990s: "You seeing violence . . . You seeing people selling drugs. You seeing things that no child has no business seeing when you live in that environment. It's like, it kind of becomes your left arm. And it's nothing to you. You don't feel anything when you see those things."[30]

In addition to experiencing child abuse at home and witnessing and experiencing violence on the streets, Nicolette endured loss and state violence. As she explained:

> I have friends that's never getting out [of prison]. And I have friends that I ain't never gonna see again. It ain't because they locked up. It's because they dead. Half of my friends and stuff that I grew up with, when I came home from prison from doing sixteen years, like 85 percent of them are dead.[31]

This feeling that "all my friends are dead or locked up" was pervasive in my interviews with formerly incarcerated Black men and in the oral histories of Women of the WIRE. With over four thousand Black people murdered in Washington, DC, between 1988 and 1998, and half of Black male youth under the purview of the criminal legal system in 1997, these feelings were not far from the truth. Violence as the norm was nowhere more evident than in public housing.

DISINVESTMENT IN PUBLIC HOUSING

The National Capital Housing Authority began building segregated public housing in the nation's capital in 1937. Black public housing in Black neighborhoods. White public housing in White neighborhoods. In many cases, these housing projects started off doing what they were designed to do: provide safe and comfortable homes for low-income residents, albeit in a segregated setting. But by the 1960s, virtually all public housing units in DC became occupied by Black residents, and the government began withholding funds for repairs and upkeep.

President Nixon declared an end to antipoverty programs in the 1970s and froze the funding for new public housing at a time when tens of thousands of Black families in DC needed affordable places to live. In 1981 Congress passed an amendment to the US Housing Act of 1937 that gave priority to low-income families in housing projects. Since people made rental payments based on their income, this amendment reduced the amount of money the public housing system collected in rents, but it did not provide any new sources of revenue that could go toward repairs.[32] Moreover, during Reagan's two terms as president (1981–1989), the federal government cut the budget of the public housing program by 76 percent.[33] Reagan's cuts were not limited to public housing: the federal government slashed school lunch programs, food stamps, medical assistance, cash transfers, and job training programs, sinking large numbers of people into poverty and producing real and tragic consequences in people's lives.[34] By 1983 the national budget for public housing was just a quarter of what it had been five years earlier. The failure of the local and federal governments to continue to invest in and improve public housing, combined with a discriminatory and difficult job market, created deplorable conditions for Black people living in and around housing projects.

Alonso was born in 1974 and grew up in Lincoln Heights, a large housing project in Northeast DC. He explained that drug addiction was a problem in the complex for as long as he could remember but that both drug addiction and violence became worse with the arrival of crack in the early 1980s.

> Lincoln Heights has always had drugs. Ever since I was small. The first dead person I ever seen was a heroin addict who OD'd on the side of the building. I had to be seven or six. It always had drug problems, but it was a different element when it came to crack. I think it just got more violent around that time.[35]

It is worth noting that Alonso said that he saw a dead body for the first time when he was a young child, which implies that he saw other dead bodies later. These sorts of traumatic childhood experiences were common among the Black men we interviewed who grew up in DC in the 1980s.

The Capper and Carrollsburg Dwellings in Navy Yard, the Barry Farm Dwellings in Anacostia, and the East Capitol Dwellings and Capitol View Plaza in Capitol View reveal a clear pattern: disinvestment in public housing set the stage for a rise in violence.

Navy Yard

The public housing projects in Navy Yard had opened in the 1950s with much fanfare and promise. By the 1970s, this waterfront neighborhood was occupied almost exclusively by low-income Black families and had become a classic case of post-1970s disinvestment. A 1977 US Department of Housing and Urban Development (HUD) report states that the six-story Arthur Capper building had "stench-filled hallways" and "dilapidated play equipment," as well as several broken interior and exterior doors.[36] The neighborhood also experienced private disinvestment, such as the closure in 1979 of Navy Yard's Safeway.[37] With the closure of the grocery store, the remaining businesses included warehouses, nightclubs, auto shops, and carry-out restaurants.[38] To be sure, nightclubs provided entertainment for people across the city, particularly working-class Black gay men who were not welcome elsewhere, and carry-out restaurants provided a cheap and quick source of food.[39] Nevertheless, the prevalence of these types of businesses instead of bookstores, sit-down restaurants, coffeehouses, and grocery stores is indicative of private disinvestment in the everyday life of the community. Private investment would not return to Navy Yard until White people began to move into the area in the second decade of the twenty-first century.

Navy Yard was overcome with violence in the 1980s. On June 23, 1988, Brandon Terrell was shot and killed outside the Chapter III nightclub. A few months later, on October 27, there were two separate shooting incidents in one night. First, the outside of the Chapter III club was sprayed with gunfire. Then, a few hours later, nineteen-year-old Vondalia J. Robinson, was killed when a stray bullet struck her head as she was leaving the nightclub.[40] In 1989, a large open-air cocaine market was operating at one of the entrances to the Capper housing project.[41] The city responded by installing chain-link fences around the buildings and requiring residents to show ID cards to enter. Instead of addressing the root causes of the drug trade and spikes in violence, the city responded by adding security measures instead of investing in community programs, job opportunities, drug treatment programs, and better schooling.

Capitol View

Although created as an elite subdivision for Black residents, the Capitol View community of Black home owners, with well-kept brick homes and manicured lawns, received few of the amenities available in a place like Chevy Chase, home to a beautiful public library, a recreation center, large green areas, and several schools with unique floor plans and elaborate playgrounds. Despite community protest, public housing was built in the heart of Capitol View, and in 1955 East Capitol Dwellings opened to 577 Black families: 391 on the south side and the remainder on the north side of East Capitol Street. The legendary singer Marvin Gaye and his family were among the first residents. Like many others, the Gaye family left dilapidated housing in the Southwest quadrant to move to the complex. Gaye and his family lived in this public housing complex until about 1962.[42]

Faulty construction and soil erosion issues led to disrepair from the very beginning.[43] An inadequate heating system left many families cold all winter.[44] Nevertheless, social problems did not manifest immediately, and the area had one of the lowest crime rates in the city from 1952 to 1965.[45] However, the significant maintenance issues in East Capitol Dwellings were never adequately addressed, and twenty years later, public disinvestment meant the original heating issues persisted, and residents now also complained about the lack of hot water.

In 1971, the housing authority sited a second major public housing project in Capitol View. This project, Capitol View Plaza, comprised thirteen-story high-rises and townhouses. The new construction brought the number of families in public housing in this relatively small area to over a thousand. The construction of this public housing met an important need for low-income residents. Nevertheless, a year after its completion, there were still five thousand families on a waiting list for public housing,[46] and as the number of low-income Black residents in Capitol View increased, the neighborhood experienced private disinvestment. There had been several small grocery stores and drugstores in the area in the early to mid-twentieth century, but most of them had closed by the 1970s.

Shortly after the completion of Capitol View Plaza, the neighborhood began to see high rates of crime—a problem that would worsen in years to come.[47] In 1978, a woman's home was firebombed after she confronted youths about selling drugs.[48] In the early 1980s, open-air drug markets emerged near East Capitol Dwellings.[49] With the youth unemployment rate at 50 percent, selling drugs was a way for young men to earn cash.[50] By 1986, many had begun to deal crack cocaine. In 1993, there were seventeen homicides in East Capitol Dwellings alone—making it one of the most violent areas in the world.[51]

To this day, there are no sit-down restaurants in majority-Black Capitol View and the closest full-service grocery store is miles away.[52] Tellingly, the issues in Capitol View Plaza became so overwhelming that just thirty years after the high-rises were built, the DC housing authority decided demolition was the best solution.

Barry Farm

Barry Farm Dwellings, once the pride of public housing in the city, fell into disrepair when the government defunded public housing. A 1966 article in the *Washington Post* reported that tenants had organized to demand better housing conditions.[53] The tenants reported overdue repairs to electricity and water systems, rats and roaches, bursting pipes, and inadequate maintenance personnel. By 1981, these problems had only worsened. The public housing authority had stopped fixing holes in screen doors, canopies, walls, and ceilings. When refrigerators, gas ranges, and ovens broke, no one came to repair or replace them. Rodents roamed the premises, and the city did little to manage this problem or even to ensure adequate trash removal.[54]

This neglect, concentrated poverty, and the arrival of crack cocaine translated into violence. In 1993, Troy Perry, Anttwon Rivers, and James Dunston began their day playing basketball at Barry Farm Dwellings.[55] By the evening, all three teenagers had been gunned down. Perry and Rivers were both new fathers, and Dunston had recently finished high school and had a clerical job with the US Navy.[56] High rates of crime and violence continued in Barry Farms, even as the homicide rate declined in other parts of the city in the late 1990s and early 2000s.[57]

Although Barry Farm Dwellings had become dilapidated by the 1980s, it remained a strong community. Its large yards meant it was a community where people spent a lot of time outside, where children played together, and where neighbors got to know one another and relied on one another for support and survival. In her interview for the Barry Farms Oral History Project, Detrice Belt, who moved to Barry Farm Dwellings in 1995, when she was eleven years old, and lived there most of her life, described the place this way: "It was a community. We got along, we knew each other, we could go knock on people's doors and ask for things."[58]

In each of these public housing projects, it was not the low-income projects themselves that created problems but the failure to invest in their upkeep.[59] Barry Farm Dwellings and Carrollsburg Dwellings thrived initially. East Capitol Dwellings had structural problems from the beginning but was nevertheless a stable, low-crime community for decades. It was only when these housing projects experienced disinvestment that they suffered a rise in violence and drug addiction.

DISINVESTMENT UPTOWN

The grandparents of many of our interviewees went to extraordinary lengths to purchase homes uptown in all-White neighborhoods in the 1950s. This investment, however, would not ensure a safe haven for their grandchildren, who would confront the violence of disinvestment directly. As these neighborhoods transitioned from all-White to majority Black, there was a slow but sure shift from public and private investment to disinvestment. Let's take a close look at what happened in Petworth, where Roosevelt High School is located, and in Eckington, home to McKinley Tech High School.

Petworth

Theodore Roosevelt High School is the public high school most Petworth residents are zoned to attend. Roosevelt High was desegregated in 1954 and became majority Black within a few years. An excellent school before desegregation, it continued to provide a first-rate education at least until the 1970s. When Bonnie Benson, daughter of Ezra Taft Benson, secretary of agriculture, enrolled there in 1955, it was a "blue-ribbon" school, "noted for high standards of scholarship" and its record of sending a large percentage of its students to college. Bonnie Benson took the school's yearbook on a trip with her father to Europe, Asia, and the Middle East and proudly showed off the photos of Black and White students playing and working together. Each year Bonnie attended Roosevelt, however, more White students left the school. By the time Bonnie was preparing for graduation in 1958, the school had become nearly 80 percent Black, and she was one of a handful of White students.[60]

Petworth, the same neighborhood that White residents fought to keep Black residents like Dr. Clarence Hinton out of, underwent an extended period of decline and disinvestment beginning in the 1970s. This disinvestment did not immediately follow desegregation, as the neighborhood continued to boast excellent schools and an array of small businesses in the 1960s. Dr. Hinton's daughter Audrey Hinton went to Roosevelt in 1961, seven years after the school was first integrated. Audrey has fond memories of her social and academic life at Roosevelt; in her oral history interview, she described going to the Safeway at Fourteenth and Colorado Avenue, the Colony Theatre on Georgia and Farragut, a bakery, a Hot Shoppes, a Little Tavern, and drugstores with frozen custard, all within walking distance of her house.[61] In the 1960s, Petworth had two theaters, the Colony and the Kennedy, as well as ice cream shops, grocery stores, and clothing stores. Both Kennedy Street and Georgia Avenue were home to a variety of thriving small businesses. But by the 1970s, the theaters had closed, as had most of the grocery stories and delis and other eateries.

While the median income and home ownership rates in Petworth remained steady between 1940 and 2000, beginning in the 1970s, other aspects of the neighborhood began to change: one-third of the Black residents of Petworth left between 1970 and 2000; the unemployment rate increased from 3.7 percent in 1970 to 6.4 percent in 1980; and the poverty rate peaked at 15.1 percent in 2000 (Table 3).[62] As White families, middle-class Black families, and employment opportunities moved out to the suburbs, primarily Black areas of DC began to experience increases in the rates of joblessness and poverty. This disinvestment, along with the availability of handguns from neighboring Maryland and Virginia suburbs and the arrival of crack cocaine, created the conditions for an unprecedented wave of gun violence. Between 1986 and 1991, there were fifteen homicides in the census tract where Rudolph Elementary School is located, with seven in 1991 alone. That year, this census tract ranked 14 among the 179 census tracts for homicides in the

TABLE 3

Petworth: Unemployment, Poverty, Income, 1970–2000

Petworth Population by Race, 1940–2000

	1940	1950	1960	1970	1980	1990	2000
Total	34,346	33,826	35,275	30,662	26,849	24,553	22,957
White	34,073	32,650	11,812	1,687	716	696	1,012
Black (Negro)	271	1,092	23,256	28,780	25,824	23,279	19,691
Asian (AAPI)	—	—	—	—	64	98	127
Latinx (Hispanic/Spanish)	—	—	—	—	336	926	2,519

Petworth Home Ownership by Race, 1940–2000

	1940	1950	1960	1970	1980	1990	2000
White home owners	4,889	—	1,680	549	233	182	180
Black (non-White) home owners	4	146	3,463	4,431	5,007	5,013	4,645

Petworth Socioeconomic Characteristics, 1940–2000

	1940	1950	1960	1970	1980	1990	2000	2010	2019
Household income*	—	—	—	—	58,007	62,333	58,081	61,724	95,528
Unemployment (%)	—	2.6	3.1	3.7	6.4	8.1	9.1	12.8	7.8
Poverty (%)	—	—	—	9.2	10.7	10.0	15.1	11.4	7.4

SOURCE: Steven Manson et al., IPUMS National Historical Geographic Information System: Version 17.0 [dataset]. Minneapolis, MN: IPUMS, 2022. http://doi.org/10.18128/D050.V17.0.

NOTES: *Adjusted in 2019 dollars. Averages for the tracts. Income data for 1940, 1950, 1960, and 1970 available only using ranges.

city. In 1991, there were 19 homicides, yielding a rate of 70 homicides per 100,000 residents. This number was just below the city's average, yet nevertheless made Petworth, a middle-class Black neighborhood with relatively low poverty and unemployment rates, one of the most violent places in the country.

Black people who purchased homes in Petworth in the 1950s and 1960s constitute the first wave of Black residents into this neighborhood. Their children had access to excellent schools as education in Petworth in the 1950s and 1960s remained top-notch. In addition, they were the first generation of Black people to experience the benefits of affirmative action. Many of the children of this first wave of Black residents have done very well, but many of them have left the neighborhood.

Phylicia Fauntelroy (now Dr. Bowman) was in the Honors track at Roosevelt.[63] Over lunch at a Mexican restaurant in August 2022, Dr. Bowman explained to me that Roosevelt not only prepared her very well for her education at Oberlin College; it also provided a first-rate education to all students. Many of Dr. Bowman's fellow alumnae have done very well. Shirley Ann Jackson, who graduated from Roosevelt in 1964, went on to become the first Black woman to earn a PhD at the Massachusetts Institute of Technology. As of this writing, Dr. Jackson is the president of Rensselaer Polytechnic Institute. Other notable alumnae are Sharon Pratt (Class of 1961), who became the mayor of DC, and Charlene Drew Jarvis (Class of 1958), who became a city council member as well as the president of Southeastern University. Isabel Wilkerson, a 1978 graduate and author of *The Warmth of Other Suns*, was the first African American woman to win the Pulitzer Prize in journalism. In a radio interview, Wilkerson recalled that in the 1970s Roosevelt High School was filled with Black students who had high hopes and dreams as their parents came North during the Great Migration seeking out better opportunities, but she pointed out that the school did not have the resources students needed to succeed by the time she graduated.[64] Dr. Bowman also lamented the decline in the educational quality at Roosevelt since her graduation.

The Roosevelt High that Carl attended in the 1980s bore little similarity in terms of curriculum and atmosphere to the school Phylicia and Audrey attended two decades earlier. When Carl enrolled in Roosevelt in 1984, the school had become unsafe, and the educational quality had spiraled downward. Carl's grandparents lived in a home they owned in Petworth, but his parents—like most Black professionals—moved to the suburbs, until divorce brought Carl and his mother back to Petworth to live, once again, in his grandparents' home.[65] By the time Carl graduated from Roosevelt High School in 1988, Petworth was on the verge of an epidemic of gun violence. In 1991, a senior at Roosevelt High was kidnapped and killed while on his lunch break.[66] On New Year's Eve in 1993, Michael D. Williams, age thirty-seven, was the last homicide victim of the year. He was shot a few blocks from Carl's grandparents' home. Two hours earlier, two men were shot, yet not killed, a few blocks in the other direction. On the last night of 1993, six people were shot and killed in Washington, DC. The year finished with 467 homicides, the third-highest annual number since the record was set in 1991 with 489 homicides.[67] These homicides happened all over the city, primarily in Black neighborhoods. Notably, they happened in Black neighborhoods that were poor and working class and in the more well-off Black neighborhoods of the city. Although Petworth was not poor, it was near neighborhoods that were bearing the brunt of the end of antipoverty programs, failing schools, and pervasive joblessness—all of which created the conditions for the rise in violence.

Eckington

Eckington is mostly a residential neighborhood, although it has some light industry. Judd and Detweiler had a printing shop at Florida Avenue and Eckington Place from 1912 until 1986, where they printed both

National Geographic and *Newsweek*.[68] Before 1954, the schools, parks, and swimming pools in Eckington were for White residents only. Most White residents, however, left in the aftermath of school desegregation. By 1958, only one White child remained in Eckington School.[69] In 1965, Eckington Presbyterian Church closed its doors. The *Washington Post* reported that "prejudice killed" the church: its White congregation disbanded in response to the arrival of Black parishioners.

The Eckington neighborhood transitioned from working- and middle-class White to working- and middle-class Black in the 1970s. Later in the 1970s, the socioeconomic profile of the neighborhood changed again as middle-class Black residents left. In 1976, McKinley Tech High School, which sits on a hill in the heart of Eckington, had a stellar reputation. Over half its graduates went on to colleges and universities, including such prestigious schools as Howard, UCLA, and Harvard. The guidance counselor, Mrs. Corley, explained to a *Washington Post* reporter, "McKinley teachers teach with the expectation of college." Mrs. Gilkes, chair of the music program, spoke proudly of former students who had studied at Oberlin, Juilliard, and Carnegie Tech. Many of the students came from the Black middle class and participated in the school's magnet programs, which included arts, music, and engineering. The school's 2,302 students represented the largest enrollment in the city.[70]

Things began to deteriorate soon thereafter. Funding challenges led to classes being canceled because of teacher shortages and lack of supplies. These annoyances became more pronounced over the next decade, as the school fell into disrepair and the city failed to address the growing maintenance issues. By the mid-1980s, both the school's building and its educational offerings were in a state of decline. The school became a shadow of its former self.[71]

It is worth noting that Eckington, like Petworth, was not a poor neighborhood at the turn of the twenty-first century. Its median household income in 2000 was at the citywide median, and one in five of its residents had a college degree. Just 13 percent of the residents were poor in 1990, and only 9 percent were unemployed. Nevertheless, Eckington experienced a wave of violence. The census tract that includes most of Eckington counted only 2,814 residents in 1990; between 1986 and 1991, the area recorded twenty-one homicides.

In the early 1990s, there were several violent incidents on the campus of McKinley Tech High School, leading school officials to issue an order that students would no longer be allowed to leave campus for lunch.[72] This order came after there were four shootings in or near Eckington in the first two weeks of September 1991.[73] Nevertheless, the violence continued unabated: in 1994, a student at McKinley Tech High school stabbed another student after a basketball game. In the aftermath of that incident, Ellen Carter-Davis, an advisory neighborhood commissioner who had lived in Eckington for forty-three years, told the *Washington Post* that the neighborhood had become a "lot like a war zone."[74]

Not all residents shared Carter-Davis's perspective. In 1989, Catrina, a high school student, told a researcher, "When the media does a story in our neighborhood, . . . they usually fail to cover the good things. They don't recognize those who are doing good." She added, presciently, "A number of Caucasians are moving back into the city and doing things to accommodate themselves, like fixing up streets and old buildings, and trying to get the drug dealers off the corner, whereas Black people in this city have been complaining for years and nothing has been done about it."[75]

In the 1980s, Eckington was home to working- and middle-class Black families who had to endure both the violence of the streets and that of the state. This became clear in our interviews. For example, Antwan's parents purchased a home in Eckington in 1981. Antwan's mother was a secretary, and his father worked at St. Elizabeths Hospital. Antwan's parents worked long hours to ensure their kids had what they needed. Despite their efforts, Antwan and his three brothers all ended up behind bars—a story discussed in the next chapter.[76]

Marcus grew up in a home his grandmother owned in Bloomingdale, which is adjacent to Eckington. He described Bloomingdale in the 1980s:

> I viewed [my neighborhood] as normal as a child. But . . . I know now that it was very chaotic. It was plagued with violence, drugs, drug using, drug selling. . . . A lot of neglect of children based on drug use. Crack really hit and that took on, I would say a downward slope of how people cared for their children as well as how they cared for themselves. It had an adverse effect on individuals whether children went to school on a daily basis, being fed on a daily basis, being clothed as well. . . . I had four cousins; two ended up started smoking crack cocaine, one became a PCP addict and another one, he became a combination of all three. So, that had an effect on my family seeing that daily.[77]

As Marcus explained, drug use, drug selling, and crime became features of the neighborhood in the 1980s. In this way, Eckington was strikingly similar to much poorer Barry Farms and Navy Yard.

CONCLUSION

Neighborhoods with high levels of concentrated poverty and racial isolation often have high levels of violence. The analyses in this chapter make it clear that it is not simply the presence of poor people or of Black people that leads to high levels of violence. The housing projects in DC were built to provide safe and affordable housing to low-income residents. They originally served this purpose and only became overrun with violence in the aftermath of disinvestment. Similarly, Petworth and Eckington became majority Black in the 1960s. The neighborhoods did not immediately become violent when White people left. Instead, violence became a social problem in the 1980s, as the community experienced public and private disinvestment.

In 1980, the majority-Black neighborhoods of Brightwood Park, Eckington, and Bloomingdale all had median household incomes around the citywide median. The median income in Eckington was more than double that of Barry Farm and Navy Yard. Despite this, Brightwood Park, Eckington, Bloomingdale all had homicide rates comparable to the rates in the much poorer neighborhoods of Capitol View, Barry Farm, and Navy Yard.[78]

By the time I was in high school, we had moved to Sixteenth Street, which meant I was zoned to attend Wilson High School, west of Rock Creek Park, one of two integrated public high schools in the city. The only other public high school in the city that had a significant number of students who were not Black was an experimental school called School Without Walls. Wilson High is in one of DC's wealthiest and Whitest neighborhoods. When I attended Wilson, most of the students were either Black or White, with smaller numbers of Asian and Latinx students. The school's location, however, did not protect it from the wave of violence that swept over the city in the 1980s.

On January 27, 1989, two young men with guns showed up at 2:25 p.m. and launched a barrage of gunfire into the crowd of students leaving school. Four students were injured and rushed to Children's Hospital. Fortunately, they survived. They would not be counted among the 434 people murdered in the city that year. City officials viewed this school shooting as a case of street violence seeping into the schools. School Superintendent Andrew Jenkins stated, "I don't think our schools are safe, but neither are any other places in the city now."[79]

I had chosen to skip school that day and thus watched the incident on television. Unfortunately, I would have other opportunities to witness gunfire. When I was sixteen, Nmadilaka and I were walking along Kennedy Street when someone began shooting. I didn't see a gun or the shooter, but I knew they were gunshots because I could hear the bullets coming toward us. The sound wasn't going up in the air like a firecracker does; it went sideways. When we heard the gunshots, we instinctively dove to the pavement and laid on the ground until the shooting was over. The gunman left, and it was over quickly. We ran down the street, glad to have emerged unharmed.

As Kennedy Street was slowly transforming into a shooting range and even Wilson High School experienced the direct effects of the violence of disinvestment, the city and federal government's response was singular: enhance the criminal legal system.

PART TWO

CARCERAL INVESTMENT

BY 1990, TWO-THIRDS OF THE JOBS in the DC metropolitan area were in the suburbs. Half of all Black youths were unemployed. Enter crack cocaine. With high unemployment and failing schools, young men began to sell crack in open-air drug markets to make ends meet. Crack was lucrative. Turf wars and gun violence ensued.

By 1991, Washington, DC, had the highest homicide rate in the country. The city's response to this tragedy was to double the police force. At the end of the twentieth century, Washington, DC, had the highest incarceration rate in the world. The capital of the nation became a world leader in incarceration.

The Black community in DC is still dealing with the consequences of this decision to invest in policing and prisons instead of schools and community centers.

3

CRACKING DOWN

The War on Drugs and Downward Mobility

⁣

BOTH SETS OF EARL'S GRANDPARENTS came to Washington, DC, during the Great Migration. After securing employment and attaining financial stability, his maternal grandparents purchased a row house in Petworth and his paternal grandparents, a home in Southeast. This financial stability did not pass to the next generation. Earl's mother became a hairdresser and moved into a public housing project in Park View. His father sold drugs for a living. In 1985, when Earl was fourteen years old, a serial killer murdered his mother in her home, which left him practically orphaned as his father had been in prison since Earl was six years old.[1]

Despite these challenges, Earl did well in school. He took the city bus every day up Georgia Avenue to Rabaut Junior High School, where he was in the gifted and talented program. A few months after his mother's death, one of the neighborhood boys made fun of Earl for heading to school, so Earl stopped going. Earl explained:

I still remember the last day I went to school. It was early in the morning. I had a neon green notebook. I was walking up Morton Street. You remember Lil' Man? Lil' Man saw me with a notebook and was like, "Where you goin' at?" I was like, "Nowhere." He was like, "Nah, you gettin' ready to go to school." That's the last day I went to school.[2]

Earl's uncle introduced him to the drug trade when he hired him to carry a backpack full of drugs for a few dollars. From there, Earl quickly graduated to selling drugs. By the age of fourteen, he was selling crack cocaine on the corner in Park View. Two years later, he was sentenced to sixteen to eighty years in prison.

When Earl was on the streets, his friends called him a "square" for going to school. Ironically, in prison he found a different kind of peer pressure. Earl perceived there were two types of inmates, "smart inmates and dumb inmates." "The smart inmates had influence," he said. Earl decided which group he wanted to be in. When a fellow inmate handed him *The Autobiography of Malcolm X*, Earl read it, and then he read *The Confessions of Nat Turner* and *Blood in My Eye*. Although he had only completed the seventh grade on the streets, Earl got his GED and associate degree while incarcerated.

Crack cocaine first appeared in Washington, DC, in the early 1980s, and many blame it for the devastating rise in crime, violence, and policing and for the downward mobility of Earl's generation. However, crack is not the primary reason for the trajectory Earl's life took. In Earl's case, the intergenerational downward mobility began with his parents—both of whom were unable to achieve the financial stability *their* parents had attained—and long before crack arrived in the city. The deflated economic prospects for Earl's parents are part of the story of why crack use and selling became widespread. Another part of the story is that many boys, like Earl, sold drugs to acquire material goods like designer shoes and clothes they needed to garner respect and attract girls.

The 1980s, known as the "Decade of Greed," celebrated "champagne wishes and caviar dreams."[3] *Lifestyles of the Rich and Famous* won an Emmy. We all watched Tony Montana stick his face into a hill of cocaine in the acclaimed film *Scarface*. According to Reaganomics, wealth, generated from tax cuts, was supposed to "trickle down" to the 99 percent. Although wealth never trickled down, materialism did.

In DC high schools in the 1980s, kids who did not wear brand-name clothes were teased for being "off-brand." If your clothes weren't new, you risked being called "dirty." Girls wore large earrings made of real gold and carried expensive leather bags made by Coach, MCM, Gucci, Louis Vuitton, and Mark Cross. Boys wore brand-new designer tennis shoes, Timberland boots, and Fila sweatsuits and often drove Nissan 300 ZXs or Pathfinders, Toyota 4Runners, and Lexuses. In the teenage dating market, girls expected boys to have fresh clothes and new shoes and drive a nice car. Selling crack provided a way for boys to attain them.

Decades of disinvestment in Black neighborhoods in Washington, DC, left poor, working-class, and middle-class Black neighborhoods with failing schools, a paucity of income-generating opportunities, few activities for youth, and limited access to the economic boom of the 1980s.[4] Disinvestment set the stage for the crack trade in poor, working-class, and middle-class Black neighborhoods. The city's response was to reinvest in these neighborhoods, but instead of investing in schools, employment, and community well-being, the city chose the path of carceral investment. This created a scenario whereby many Black people who grew up middle class fell into poverty.

JOBLESSNESS IN THE CITY

During the 1970s, the uptown high schools in Petworth and Eckington became majority Black and slowly lost the staff and resources that had made them excellent schools in the 1950s and 1960s. At the same time, the exodus of jobs to the suburbs left the city with a declining tax base, which in turn limited the city's ability to provide basic services such as transportation, street cleaning, garbage pickup, and street lighting. In a study conducted in the 1980s in an inner-city neighborhood in Washington, DC, a focus group participant told researchers there were no streetlights in his neighborhood.[5] Disinvestment in cities had significant consequences. When President Nixon declared an end to antipoverty programs, low-income urban residents lost the support that had once provided them with food, daycare programs, legal services, and even arts workshops that kept young people engaged in constructive activities.[6] Many of my interviewees' parents came of age in the 1970s, a time when joblessness became a significant problem for Black men.

When Elliot Liebow spent eighteen months between 1962 and 1963 conducting ethnographic research among a group of Black men who hung out on a street corner in the Shaw area of Washington, DC, nearly all the men worked.[7] Within a generation, most men hanging out on street corners would be jobless.

Liebow did not include neighborhoods like Petworth in his acclaimed book, *Tally's Corner*. If he were to have traveled uptown to this neighborhood in the 1960s, he would have found that the majority of residents were home owners and the unemployment rate was low—about 3 percent in 1960. Over the next decades, the unemployment rates both uptown and downtown went up: by 1980 the unemployment rate in Petworth had doubled, and by 1990 it had reached 8.1 percent. This doubling of the unemployment rate in a generation reflects national trends and provides an indication of how economic precarity affected Black middle-class neighborhoods. The effects in poor neighborhoods were even more devastating.

As factories moved out of cities such as Detroit and Chicago, many working-class people were left without work.[8] Deindustrialization—

the process of manufacturing plants shutting down in major cities—created unemployment crises nationwide. This crisis had particularly pernicious effects on Black men. By 1980, only three-quarters of Black men in working- to middle-class neighborhoods in the United States were employed. In poor neighborhoods, there were as many Black men without jobs as there were with jobs.[9]

Having never had a large industrial economy, Washington, DC, did not experience deindustrialization in the same way as other US cities. Nevertheless, there was a redirection of public and private investment to the suburbs as White people began to leave the city. The federal government set up major defense, health, and intelligence offices in the suburbs. Between 1963 and 1968, the federal government moved over forty thousand jobs from Washington, DC, to the suburbs. Major companies like AT&T and IBM set up shop in suburban industrial parks, where they expected they would find the skilled workers they needed for the new high-tech industries.[10] Between 1970 and 1990, job growth in the suburbs far outpaced that in DC. By 1990, only one in three jobs in the DC area was inside the city limits—down from half of all jobs two decades earlier. In Washington, DC, decades of disinvestment in the public school system meant that many Black DC residents were not qualified for the new high-tech jobs.[11]

DOWNWARD MOBILITY

The Opportunity Atlas provides data on a cohort that overlaps with the cohort in my study—children born between 1978 and 1983. These data provide strong quantitative evidence to support my finding that many people raised in Black working- and middle-class neighborhoods in DC did not achieve intergenerational upward mobility, yet did experience high rates of incarceration. The data are similar across the board, whether one compares Petworth to Barry Farm or Eckington to Capitol View. Boys who grew up in Black neighborhoods in Washington,

DC, in the 1990s have relatively low incomes and relatively high likelihoods of incarceration. In Bloomingdale (a neighborhood adjacent to Eckington), which had a median household income of $62,000 (in 2015 dollars) in 1990, 11 percent of boys were behind bars in 2010; their average income was $19,000 in 2015, and 69 percent were employed. Remarkably, Bloomingdale was not doing much better than Navy Yard, which had a median household income of just $11,000 in 1990. Among boys who grew up in Navy Yard, 7 percent were behind bars in 2010, their average income was $19,000 in 2015, and 62 percent were employed. Even in tony Shepherd Park, 2.2 percent of the Black boys in this cohort were incarcerated in 2010, more than double the percentage of boys who grew up in the primarily White neighborhoods west of the park.

These findings are not unique to Washington, DC. In a 2007 study funded by the Brookings Institution, Julia Isaacs matched the family income of parents in the late 1960s to their children's family income in the late 1990s to early 2000s. Isaacs explains her findings: "Whereas children of white middle-income parents tend to exceed their parents in income, a majority of black children of middle-income parents fall below their parents in income and economic status."[12] This national study thus found that most Black children from middle-class families did not attain the economic security their parents had. Moreover, Isaacs found that almost half of Black people whose parents were solidly middle class were poor.

My interviews with Black men born between 1965 and 1980 who were sentenced to prison at the height of the War on Drugs also help us understand the trend of intergenerational downward mobility that Isaacs identified. In the 1950s, many Black families were able to purchase homes in neighborhoods experiencing White flight. To many, particularly those who had escaped the brutality of the pre–Civil Rights South, this achievement must have felt like a version of the American dream. However, my research has made it clear that buying a home did not translate into intergenerational wealth for many of these Black families, particularly for those that stayed in neighborhoods that experienced disinvestment.

The parents in Isaacs's study represent the first generation of Black residents to move to neighborhoods like Petworth, Eckington, and Bloomingdale. In the 1950s and 1960s, many Black people in DC purchased homes in areas experiencing White flight. These Black families had children (the second generation in this study) who grew up in these homes in the 1960s and 1970s.

The trajectories of the second-generation children varied dramatically. Some of them graduated from the excellent majority-Black high schools in Petworth, Takoma Park, and Eckington. Most did not return to these neighborhoods, opting instead to move to the suburbs or out of the area completely. The children of this first wave of Black home owners who enrolled in university nearly all left the neighborhood and never returned.[13] If they stayed in the DC area, they either moved to DC suburbs like Fort Washington or Bowie or to upper-class Black neighborhoods like North Portal Estates or Shepherd Park instead of their parents' neighborhood.

Of the second-generation people who stayed in the city, some moved out of their parents' home and into rented apartments or public housing. Others stayed in their parents' home, and many of their children—the third generation and the interview cohort born between 1965 and 1980 in this study—were raised in their grandparents' homes. Some of the second generation who did not enroll in college were drafted during the Vietnam War, and some returned from the war with heroin addictions. Others who did not enroll in college found it difficult to secure stable work as the labor market was changing, leaving many unskilled workers behind. The unemployment rate in Petworth and other Black middle-class areas began to rise in the 1970s.

By the 1980s, unemployment had reached a crisis level. It was becoming increasingly difficult for the third generation to get a good education in majority-Black DC public schools. When crack arrived in the

1950–1960	1960s–1970s	1970s–1980s	1990s–2000s
Home Ownership	**Intergenerational and Public Housing**	**Intergenerational, Insecure Housing**	**Intergenerational Home Loss**
First Generation (GI) of Blacks purchase homes and raise Second Generation (G2) in middle-class White Flight neighborhoods with quality schools.	Businesses move to the suburbs. G2 unable to procure secure jobs stay in G1 homes, move to public housing, or leave neighborhood. Some G2s return from Vietnam addicted to heroin.	Some G2s addicted to crack and/or incarcerated for heroin. Third Generation (G3) raised in G1 homes, unable to procure quality education or employment, sell crack.	50% of Black male G3s incarcerated for drugs, long sentences—upwards of 20 years, homes sold or confiscated; others priced out of new home purchases.

Figure 5. Timeline: Intergenerational downward mobility, 1950s–2000s.

mid-1980s, some in the second generation became addicted and many in the third generation began to sell crack. By the 1990s, half of all Black men in the third-generation cohort in DC were caught up in the criminal legal apparatus (Fig. 5).

The story of Travis—one of the many grandchildren of people who bought homes in neighborhoods experiencing White flight in the 1950s—makes this timeline clear. In his case, however, it was his great-grandparents who purchased a home, in Mount Pleasant in 1959. This brick row house has been home to several generations of his family. His grandmother, his mother, then Travis grew up there. In October 2022, Travis's grandmother and aunt still lived in the home, which is currently worth over $1 million.

Travis's mother gave birth to him when she was a teenager. She worked at an insurance company when Travis was small and then got her cosmetology license when the insurance company shut down. Living in her family home ensured she was able to weather financially difficult times. It also made it easy for Travis to stay close to his father's side of the family, who lived just a few blocks away in Mount Pleasant. When Travis's mother moved out of her parents' home after Travis was incarcerated, she rented an apartment in a Maryland suburb.

Travis's great-grandparents were able to gather the resources to purchase a home in Columbia Heights in 1959, but subsequent generations of his family have not been able to purchase homes anywhere in DC. This means that this home is the primary source of wealth for Travis's parents, uncles, aunts, and cousins. If the family were to sell the home, the inheritance would be divided up between more than a dozen people, and his family could be priced out of that neighborhood permanently. The only way this home will stay in Travis's family is if his grandmother signs the deed over to one person, as no single person in his family is currently able to buy the others out and keep the home.[14]

Understanding how and why this happened requires taking a step back and looking at the War on Drugs, which began to unfold in the 1970s.

A WAR ON DRUGS

Until the 1970s, the drug laws in DC had been relatively lax, with a one-year maximum sentence for first-time drug offenders and a ten-year maximum sentence for a second offense. The local law did not distinguish among substances, nor did it distinguish between possession and sale.[15]

But in June 1971, Richard Nixon declared that drugs were "public enemy number one."[16] A writer for *Harper's*, Dan Baum, later interviewed Nixon adviser John Ehrlichman on the politics of drug prohibition. When Baum asked him about Nixon's War on Drugs, Ehrlichman responded:

> You want to know what this was really all about? The Nixon campaign in 1968, and the Nixon White House after that, had two enemies: the antiwar left and black people. You understand what I'm saying? We knew we couldn't make it illegal to be either against the war or black, but by getting

the public to associate the hippies with marijuana and blacks with heroin, and then criminalizing both heavily, we could disrupt those communities. We could arrest their leaders, raid their homes, break up their meetings, and vilify them night after night on the evening news. Did we know we were lying about the drugs? Of course we did.[17]

Ehrlichman's statement that the Nixon administration criminalized drug dealers to maintain control of the Black community constitutes a rare admission of an underlying purpose of the criminal legal system.

Understanding how the War on Drugs played out in DC requires keeping several factors in mind. Before the implementation of Home Rule in 1975, the federal government had legislative and budgetary control of the city. Even after Home Rule was implemented, the federal government continued to maintain important powers, including the right to veto legislation and budget proposals.

In this context, the Nixon administration initiated the District of Columbia Court Reorganization Act in 1970, which introduced mandatory minimums as well as life sentences for third criminal convictions, precursors to the mandatory minimum and "three strikes" laws later enacted in California and New York. The act also broadened the grounds for "no knock" raids and wiretapping, both of which became common police tactics during the War on Drugs.[18] DC was, in many ways, a test case for aggressive drug and policing tactics.

The harsh provisions of the 1970 District of Columbia Reorganization Act, including mandatory minimums, were implemented at the federal level by the Crime Control Act of 1984—the culmination of several anticrime measures introduced by Sen. Joe Biden and Sen. Ted Kennedy and the first significant revision of the federal criminal code in several decades. The Crime Control Act of 1984 enhanced sentencing provisions and expanded pretrial detention—which would lead to thousands of legally innocent people spending days, weeks, or months behind bars.

By 1980 DC was a majority-Black city, and most of the city's leadership and police force were Black. The rise in illegal drug use, particularly heroin, was devastating Black communities. The Reagan administration cut off welfare for half a million families, cut food stamps for one million families, and removed 2.6 million children from school lunch programs. By the end of the Reagan presidency (1989), 33 million people in the United States were living in poverty, several million more than when he took office.[19]

Part of this broader trend of disinvestment in cities was the defunding of drug treatment centers, which were overcrowded and had long waiting lists. Given the insufficiency of drug treatment programs in Washington, DC, the only other perceived solution was criminalization. Thus, in 1982 three-quarters of DC voters voted in favor of Ballot Initiative 9, which instituted mandatory minimums for several drug offenses. These included four years for selling heroin, two years for selling cocaine, and one year for selling large quantities of marijuana. Support for this initiative was strong across the city, yet support was strongest in low-income Black communities, which were hard-hit by drug addiction and its attendant problems. In Ward 8, where Barry Farm Dwellings is located, 75 percent of voters voted in favor of the ballot initiative, as compared to 67 percent in majority-White Ward 3.[20]

The number of drug-related deaths in DC increased from 105 in 1977 to 276 by 1986. In just one year, between 1986 and 1987, emergency room admissions involving cocaine doubled, as did those involving PCP. The rates of PCP use and the harms associated with it were particularly high in Washington, DC, in the 1980s. Los Angeles was the only other city with a significant PCP problem, but the abuse rates in DC were far higher. By 1987, the city was spending about $14.5 million a year on drug treatment, but, again, the treatment programs were full and had long waiting lists. In that same year, the budget for the Metropolitan Police Department was $163 million.[21]

A media frenzy around drugs ensued after the deaths in 1986 of basketball Hall of Famer Len Bias and football All-American Don Rogers. Both had died of powder cocaine overdoses. Bias died just two days after being signed to play for the Boston Celtics, and Rogers, who was playing for the Cleveland Browns, died just one day before his wedding. Drugs became the center of national attention, and shortly after these two tragic overdose deaths, Congress passed the Anti-Drug Abuse Act of 1986, which set a five-year mandatory minimum sentence for offenses involving 100 grams of heroin, 500 grams of cocaine, or 5 grams of crack cocaine.

Crack is a form of cocaine that can be smoked. It is made by boiling cocaine with baking soda and allowing the mixture to cool into a solid. This solid is then broken up into small pieces, known as rocks. People have been making crack from powder cocaine at least since the 1970s, but the trade didn't take off until the 1980s when the cocaine dealer "Freeway Ricky" Ross connected with Daniel Blandón, a Somoza supporter and cocaine trafficker from Nicaragua. Ross began to wholesale cocaine at $125 a gram, but it was still an expensive drug. Crack could, and did, reach a much wider market.[22]

Crack cocaine soon became the focal point of the War on Drugs. The 100-to-1 disparity in the quantity of crack versus powder cocaine requiring a mandatory sentence has become notorious as an example of thinly veiled institutionalized racism: low-income Black people are more likely to use and sell crack than powder cocaine. This law meant that they were much more likely than White people to go to prison for having a much smaller quantity of narcotics. Drug arrests in DC doubled between 1982 and 1986. Drug arrests of juveniles quadrupled. By 1986 DC's arrest rate was ten times that of its Virginia suburbs. The average federal prison sentence also increased from forty-six months in 1980 to sixty-one months in 1986.

Two years later, the Anti-Drug Abuse Act of 1988 implemented a five-year mandatory minimum sentence for simple possession of crack cocaine, with no evidence of intent to sell. Before 1988, the maximum penalty that one might expect to receive for simple possession of any amount of any drug in federal courts was one year.[23]

In a 1989 congressional hearing on appropriations, Mayor Marion Barry referred to the War on Drugs as the city's "number one priority." This was not just a verbal commitment. In that same hearing, Mayor Barry explained that this prioritization meant the city had funneled more money to law enforcement and corrections. To do this, the city had to redirect nearly $80 million from other agencies, including the Department of Public Works, the Department of Housing and Community Development, the Department of Recreation, the Department of Employment Services, and the University of the District of Columbia. In his remarks, however, Barry made a point of explaining that drugs were not cultivated in Washington, DC, and thus that the city could not solve the problems associated with the drug trade on its own. Moreover, he opined that "poor housing, poor educational opportunities, lack of job-related skills, loss of home and low esteem have made many families vulnerable to the current drug scene."[24]

When President George H. W. Bush took office in 1989, he appointed William J. Bennett the federal "drug czar," a cabinet position created by the Anti-Drug Abuse Act.[25] Bennett staged a drug deal in Lafayette Park, a small green space just across from the White House,[26] as a prop for a televised speech about drugs in the capital city in which Bush held up three ounces of crack cocaine—worth $2,400 on the streets—and said, "This is crack cocaine, seized a few days ago by drug enforcement agents in Lafayette Park." It would have been shocking if it were true, but there were no crack dealers near the White House. Although the deal was staged, the dealer, eighteen-year-old Keith Jackson, was sentenced to ten years in prison.

And Bush made his point: crack cocaine justified the intense incarceration policies that would continue through the 1970s and into the

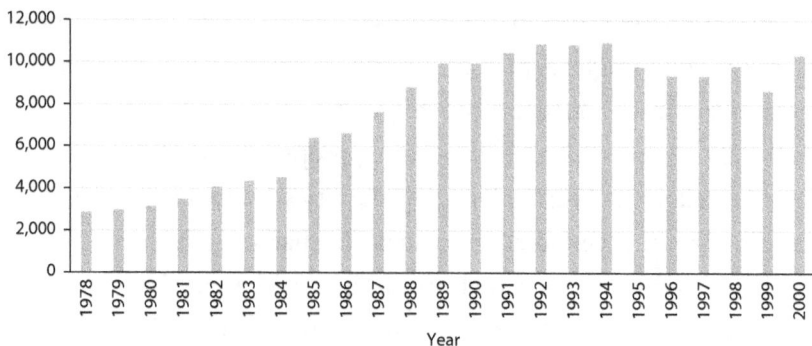

Figure 6. Count of DC inmates by year, 1978–2000. Bureau of Justice Statistics data.

1990s. As a result of changes in federal laws as well as local laws, the increase in the incarceration of DC residents between 1978 and the turn of the century was significant (Fig. 6).

Crack gave proponents of the War on Drugs legitimacy, and the criminal legal apparatus expanded even more dramatically after 1986. This expansion represents a significant investment in punishment: The Bureau of Prisons (BOP) budget grew from $317 million in 1980 to $952 million in 1989. By 2002, the BOP budget was nearly $4 billion dollars. After taking inflation into account, this represents a nearly eightfold increase in spending on federal prisons between 1980 and 2002.[27] Thus the overwhelming response to problems associated with the drug trade was to strengthen the coercive arm of the state.[28]

POLICING THE CITY

With the arrival of Home Rule in 1973, the city elected its first mayor in over a century, Walter Washington. In 1978 Mayor Washington, a Black man, swore in DC's first Black police chief, Burtell Jefferson.[29] This was a momentous occasion. Twenty years earlier, the highest-ranking Black police officer was a corporal; none of the department's sixty-nine sergeants, eighty lieutenants, twenty-nine captains, thirteen inspectors, or eight deputy chiefs were Black.[30] With Home Rule, the police force as well as its leadership became majority Black.[31]

When Marion Barry, a civil rights activist, took office as mayor in January 1979, he hired a team of Black employees to run the city. He was explicit about his desire to serve the Black community in a city that was about 70 percent Black. In 1978, only 7 percent of city contracts went to minority-owned businesses. By 1985, 35 percent of city contracts, worth over $150 million, were going to minority-owned businesses. This focus on minority issues had enduring effects not only for the Black middle class but also for the Black elite. Both Black Entertainment Television (BET) and the Black-owned Peebles Real Estate Corporation got their start in DC during this time, and each eventually grew into a powerful national corporation. Barry's initiatives also helped pull some Black people out of poverty—mostly by giving them jobs. He added four thousand workers to the city's payroll, making the city's government the largest per capita public employer in the country.[32] Many DC residents, including me, will proudly tell you that Marion Barry gave them their first job.

In August 1986, Mayor Barry celebrated the launch of Operation Clean Sweep, a program conceived by the Metropolitan Police Department's Black leadership that aimed to arrest as many drug dealers as possible. Teams of over one hundred officers would arrive en masse at the city's open-air drug markets, where they would arrest everyone they perceived to be involved in the drug trade. Washington, DC, led the nation in drug arrests in 1986.[33] Nearly half of the arrests, however, did not lead to charges being filed, meaning that police officers spent their time and resources taking people to police stations across the city only to release them after a few hours. This is not only a waste of resources; at the least, it is extremely inconvenient, and at worst, it traumatized those who were arrested. The program did not make a lasting difference in the rates of drug use or sales in the city.[34]

After spending over $6 million on police overtime, in 1988, Marion Barry announced an end to police overtime and thus to Operation Clean Sweep. Public authorities often launch intensive law enforcement operations in the hope of decreasing drug use and drug-related violence. Unfortunately, these operations usually have the opposite effect.[35] Looking back at the specific case of Operation Clean Sweep, the investigative journalist Christian Parenti argued that the "mass arrests and constant police pressure merely fueled violence by stirring rivalries, destabilizing dealers' business networks, hierarchies, and turf arrangements, and setting off bloody power struggles, suspicions, and turf feuds."[36]

A few months after Mayor Barry announced an end to police overtime, Congress mandated that Washington, DC, hire more police officers. In 1989 Congress voted to withhold the $430 million federal payment to Washington, DC, unless the city hired 1,800 more police officers. This vote was in response to the rising fear of crime and the fact that over half the police force was about to become eligible for retirement.[37]

Thus in 1989, the police force embarked on a hiring spree that led to the recruitment of 1,471 officers in less than two years. In this hiring rush, the city loosened its requirements and background checks and fast-tracked police training.[38] By 1994, new recruits made up one-third of the police force, yet accounted for more than half of DC police officers arrested on criminal offenses or in disciplinary proceedings in subsequent years.[39] By 1997, DC had more police officers per capita than any city in the country.[40]

Police officers routinely seized not just drugs but also cars, houses, furniture, jewelry, and cash, as part of what the legal scholar James Forman Jr. describes as "perhaps the most robust asset forfeiture protocol in the country."[41] The forfeiture provisions of the 1985 Crime Control Act allowed local law enforcement to seize cash and property from people accused of drug offenses and allowed police departments to keep most of the proceeds for themselves. Thus forfeiture laws created an opening for officers to skim money off the top, and sometimes police officers seized the money without handing it over to the police department. When I was a teenager in Washington, DC, my Black male friends would often share stories about police officers shaking them down and taking their cash. Of course, this did not happen only to people involved in the illegal drug trade. One of our interviewees, Edward—to be sure, just one person's account—described how police officers took his money in 1988:

> I was in the process of getting ready to go meet a lawyer to give him some money. . . . I got out of the car and stopped to speak to someone. And the police jumped out around there, I guess [they were] doing a drug bust. . . . They were locking up people, and they grabbed me, and one of them said, "Let him go. He wasn't doing nothing." They said, "Search him first and then, if he's clean, let him go." But I had like, $8,000 on me. . . . After they searched me down, they found I had this money on me, they went back and had like this huddle and, um, came back and said, "You're under arrest." And I said, "For what?," and they said, "Possession of drugs with the attempt to distribute." The whole thing was just to take the money. . . . From the time they arrested me to the time we got to the precinct that $8,000 went to $800. So they took the money and gave me this bogus charge just to take the money.[42]

Operation Clean Sweep played a role in exacerbating a culture of impunity in the Metropolitan Police Department and helped entrench specialized units in the police force, many of which specialize in aggressive policing tactics. One example is the Rapid Deployment Unit, which uses techniques that Forman calls "warrior policing" because of their forceful nature. Introduced in response to the presence of illegal drugs and high rates of violence, the aggressive tactics reduced neither. In the early 1990s, DC paid out about $1 million a year to victims of police misconduct.[43]

As a White girl growing up in DC, I mostly escaped the routine harassment and brutality that Black boys and men faced from police. Police generally left me and my female friends alone, except at the checkpoints. Overstaffed and pressured to demonstrate their vigilance against drugs, the DC police set up checkpoints where anyone entering a designated area automatically became a suspect. When I was sixteen, my friends and I drove up to a basketball court near the Montana Terrace public housing projects to watch our boyfriends play ball. Nmadilaka, Ijeoma, and I were each going out with boys from the Montana Crew, as the boys who hung out there were called. Nmadilaka was seeing Kaos, Ijeoma was seeing Taco, and I was seeing Yogi. After watching them play ball and chatting, we went back toward our car. Two police officers approached us and said they wanted to search our car, because—as one of the officers stated—he had seen one of us exchange something with the boys and that it could have been crack. We were infuriated by the insinuation that we might be there to buy crack. We had on clean new clothes and wore fresh makeup and hairdos and did not, in our minds, look anything like people who smoked crack. I told the police officers that that they did not have the right to search our vehicle without our consent. The officer responded that we were in a "red zone" and that our constitutional rights were suspended. I have not found any evidence that these "red zones" actually existed, but I did find this tidbit published in 2008 in the *Washington Post:*

> D.C. police have used various forms of checkpoints for years. In 1988, for example, they blocked streets and searched courtyards in a pair of apartment complexes in Northeast Washington in a bid to drive out drug dealers. That move came during the crack cocaine epidemic, in a year when the city recorded 372 homicides. [In 2008], the city had 181 killings.[44]

The police performed a cursory search of our car and let us go, as we did not have any illegal drugs.

In addition, the abundance of police officers meant that police often overresponded to minor events. I remember a summer afternoon in 1990. I was enjoying a two-piece fried chicken meal at the Popeye's near my house when a shouting match broke out between two customers near the cash registers. Someone called the police, and four police cars soon arrived in the parking lot. Eight police officers were deployed to deal with an argument over fast food.

I was fourteen in 1988. By the time I graduated from high school in 1991, my hometown had become the murder capital of the world. The response to the spread of crack and the rise in murders was carceral investment in policing and prisons. The response reverberated across the Black community in DC.

On January 18, 1990, Mayor Barry got caught up in his own net, arrested on charges of cocaine possession. Crack not only ravaged the city; it ousted its beloved "Mayor for Life."

CRACK IN THE NEIGHBORHOOD

In a nationwide, longitudinal study, Steven Alvarado found that children who grow up in disadvantaged neighborhoods are more likely to be incarcerated than those from middle-class neighborhoods. However, this is truer for White or Latino boys than it is for Black boys. Alvarado found that Black boys from both disadvantaged and advantaged neighborhoods have relatively high likelihoods of incarceration.[45] Alvarado's findings resonate with the relatively high rates of incarceration of Black boys from Bloomingdale. My interviews with formerly incarcerated Black men who grew up in a wide variety of neighborhoods help us understand why class is less of a protective factor for Black boys.

Most research on why Black youth became involved in the crack cocaine market in the 1980s and 1990s focuses on poor youth with limited options in the formal labor market.[46] For example, Philippe

Bourgois argued in *In Search of Respect* that selling drugs provided youth in a disadvantaged neighborhood with the opportunity not only to earn money but also to garner respect—something largely unavailable to them in the formal labor market.[47] There is far less research on why youth who are not poor engaged in drug selling. Selling drugs was often a survival strategy for youth from poor families. For those from middle-class families, selling drugs allowed them to fill in the gaps created by disinvestment in their neighborhoods.

Youth from Poor Families: Selling Drugs as an Escape from Poverty

Some of the Black men we interviewed grew up in the 1980s in families where food was scarce, and their clothing or shelter was inadequate. Notably, their poverty was rarely intergenerational as their grandparents were often financially stable.

When Earl's mother was murdered, he could have gone to live at his grandmother's house and focused on his studies. "After [my mother] got killed," he said, "I went for probably a month saying, 'I ain't going to hustle no more. I'm going to make my mother proud of me, get my life together. I'm going to do the right thing.'"[48] But by that point his local school offered few extracurricular activities to keep an energetic teen engaged. He worried about getting teased by other kids if he didn't have the latest styles. Earning money to buy whatever he wanted was also a way to ease the pain of his father's imprisonment and mother's murder.

Hustling, however, came with a great cost. Earl explained, "When you're selling drugs, you got to protect your territory. If somebody owes you money, you've got to deal with them. You've got to know who to deal with, who not to deal with. Does this person warrant getting shot? Stuff like that. That comes with just being out there."[49] Earl ended up doing seventeen years in prison for protecting his territory, as he put it.

One day, one of Earl's friends interrupted their card game to tell them that Frank, who was not from Park View, was selling crack on their corner. Earl and his friends went outside to let Frank know he couldn't work their corner. When Frank saw their guns, he agreed to leave. One of Earl's friends suggested that instead of letting Frank go, they should follow him and rob him of his cash and drugs. They followed Frank to his car and demanded Frank give them his money and stash. When Frank resisted, Earl's friend shot and killed him. Earl and another friend were charged and convicted of armed robbery and possession of a firearm; the one who pulled the trigger was convicted of murder. The prosecutor tried sixteen-year-old Earl as an adult. He was found guilty of charges related to this crime and sentenced to sixteen to eighty years in prison. He was released in 2009, after serving seventeen years.

Marcus, who spent over two decades in prison on drug and firearm charges, gave a similar explanation for his involvement in the drug trade:

> At the end of junior high school, I had started selling drugs [because] I wanted the more fancy tennis shoes, outfits, clothes—various things that my mother and grandma really couldn't afford because they were on limited income of paying bills and providing groceries and all those types of things. . . . They used to buy me the shoes that cost like $40.[50]

In DC in the 1980s and 1990s, other kids would tease you if you wore $20 shoes from Payless instead of the more popular and expensive Nike, Adidas, and New Balance sneakers. It seemed like most kids were selling crack to get these goods, and as Earl explained, that made it hard to resist getting into the crack trade.

Darnell sold drugs to buy stylish clothes, which led to him doing five years in prison. He began selling drugs at the age of fourteen. Darnell explained, "My mother didn't make a lot of money. So I didn't have all the designer jeans and all the designer clothes back in the day, I had some real corny stuff. I mean, like Goodwill type of stuff. . . . I needed to change my image. People thought I was dirty, and I wasn't. It was just because of my clothes."[51] Darnell and other people we interviewed told us they sold crack because they did not want to be teased for wearing "off-brand" clothes or called "dirty" for not having new clothes.

Andre spent seventeen years in prison on drug distribution charges. He was raised by a disabled single mother who relied on meager government assistance. He washed car windows and did odd jobs to earn extra cash. Andre described his community growing up as close-knit but explained that crack changed everything: "First of all, my neighborhood was plagued with crack. In the nineties coming up, guys used to drive the cars and wear the flashy clothes and the jewelry and things of that nature. And those were my idols. I wanted what they had."[52]

Mustafa S. F. Zulu lived with his mother in his grandparents' comfortable River Terrace home. He did well in elementary school and loved math and science. But when his mother moved into a public housing project in Potomac Gardens, he went from a life of comfort and love to one where his mother, who fell into drug addiction, neglected him, and his stepfather, who was also addicted to drugs, was abusive.

He dropped out of school in the seventh grade, and a neighborhood drug dealer, Michael Graham, employed the twelve-year-old to work as an enforcer for Graham's drug business. Mustafa describes himself as a child soldier. Graham put a gun in his hands and taught him to use it to protect himself and members of the organization. In 1993, at the age of sixteen, Mustafa was arrested for the murder of his employer.

In April 2017, Mustafa requested a resentencing hearing under the DC Incarceration Reduction Amendment Act, based on the fact that he was sixteen when he committed the crimes that led to his incarceration. The court ruled against his request, and although Mustafa has filed multiple appeals, as of this writing in January 2023, he remains behind bars.[53]

Drug selling allowed Earl, Marcus, Darnell, Andre, and Mustafa to buy the clothes and shoes they wanted to fit in with their peers. Selling drugs also allowed them to have their basic needs met when their families fell into crisis. In Washington, DC, in the 1980s and early 1990s, the social safety net for these families was thin and full of holes, and each of these young men fell through. The coercive arm of the state was, however, robust, and each of these young men was eventually incarcerated.

Although their parents struggled to attain financial stability, these were cases of intergenerational downward mobility more than intergenerational poverty. Earl's maternal grandmother owned a home in Petworth. Marcus's grandmother owned a home in Bloomingdale. Mustafa's grandparents owned a home in River Terrace. Darnell's great-grandmother owned a home in Park View, and Andre's great-grandfather owned a home in Northeast. These men grew up impoverished because their parents struggled to attain the financial stability *their* parents had attained—which was often exacerbated by their addictions.

Youths from Middle-Class Families: When Teenagers Can Earn a Thousand Dollars a Day

There is another group of men who grew up in more financially stable homes, yet still ended up getting into trouble with the law. They had food on the table and clothes on their backs, but they wanted more.

Milton, who is from Mount Pleasant, explained, "I come from a household where I had food on the table. My mother clothed me. . . . She gave me the things that I needed to live." He elaborated, "[None of my friends came] from a dire situation where you had to sell drugs or be on the street, but [I had] to sell drugs to have a car. I probably could have worked at two jobs and got it. But that's just the world we lived in."[54]

This world of fast cars, designer clothes, and beautiful young women carried a much higher cost than Milton imagined as a teenager. Milton was charged with a host of drug and murder charges that led to a sentence of life without parole. He served twenty years in prison. I interviewed him after his life sentence was overturned.

When asked why he began to sell drugs, Carl, who spent thirteen years behind bars on drug and car theft charges, responded:

> I can't even say peer pressure because I know a lot of people that actually, they were hungry out here, and they were doing it for a reason. Their mother and father were away from home, and they had siblings to take care of. I didn't really have that dynamic at home. I think I did it more or less to fit in, in the beginning. And then, once the money started getting good, then I just kept it moving.[55]

While Carl started selling drugs to fit in, other interviewees started selling drugs to fill the void left by the lack of enrichment activities in their neighborhoods. One of our interviewees for this project, Kwame, who grew up in a middle-class home owned by his parents in Petworth, dropped out of Coolidge High School in the tenth grade because he found school boring. He believed school was not teaching him what he needed to know. His father, who is originally from West Africa, taught him a lot of Black history, and the school's curriculum did not reflect that. He explained that he did not perceive many viable options:

> I think young men need something that can hold their attention and their energy, they're constantly looking for something. They're looking for adventure. But at the same time, you're looking for adventure, you're also looking for income. You're so young and dumb, and you make a lot of mistakes. . . . Even if you're a young man that's interested in, say, being a scientist or being an astronaut, it's really no programs in this area for something like that. You would have to travel, especially at that time. You could go to the Air and Space Museum and you see something, and you're

like, "Oh, shit, I would love to do this." But your parents would need money to send you to somewhere out of state to do it. Then after a conversation with your parents, you realize that's not going to happen. They're working hard to pay the mortgage, take care of children. So eventually you kind of wade out into the wilderness.[56]

To a bored fourteen-year-old boy, the possibility of making hundreds of dollars a day selling drugs is deeply attractive. The people I interviewed agreed on one thing: the money was good. Arthur, also from Petworth, explained that crack was very popular when it first arrived in Petworth. He could make $200 walking the five blocks from his house to the corner where he and his friends sold drugs, and few hundred more once he got there. For Arthur, both the profits and the camaraderie made selling crack hard to resist. He told me that his goal as a fourteen-year-old was to make $1,000 a day.[57] A lot of money for anyone, this was a tremendous amount for a teenage boy.

Arthur and Kwame grew up a few blocks from one another and refer to each other as "sandbox friends." Arthur would spend six years behind bars on drug charges. Kwame spent twenty-three years incarcerated on a variety of charges.

A GENDERED DRUG BUSINESS

The majority of the drug dealers in DC in the 1980s and 1990s were men. However, women sometimes also got involved in drug distribution. A common route for women into the drug trade was through dating drug dealers, as was the case for Lashonia Thompson-El, who grew up in Southeast DC in the 1980s and served eighteen years in prison on homicide charges. Lashonia, whose story was recorded for the Women of the WIRE oral history project, told the interviewer that she was raised by a single mother who worked for the federal government.

Lashonia did not grow up in poverty, but her family's home was adjacent to public housing, in an area of the city that became particularly susceptible to the ravages of disinvestment.

When Lashonia talks about her experiences before being incarcerated, she describes her life as a strange mix of violence alongside glitz and glam. Lashonia got involved in the drug business while dating a drug dealer when she was fifteen. But she soon began to sell drugs herself, so that she could make her own money. Once she started selling drugs, Lashonia carried a gun with her nearly all the time and used her earnings to buy "big bamboo earrings and Gucci sneakers." She explained:

> Gun violence was so normalized that I don't think it had really dawned on me, like, the finality of death, if that makes sense, because it was like, we was going to a funeral every weekend, like we would go shopping, to get a fly outfit, because somebody important in our community has been killed, and most likely they probably somebody that's somebody to us, right? So we was literally going to funerals like every weekend.[58]

Lashonia, like many others, got caught up in the glamorous lifestyle that selling crack afforded her. This came at a great cost, but it was a cost many teenagers were willing to pay for a route out of poverty or even to alleviate boredom.[59]

The illegal labor market is gendered, just like the formal labor market. Men controlled access to the supply of crack cocaine into the city and onto the streets. Some of these men would include their female relatives in the business, but in most cases crack dealing was an all-male enterprise.

In contrast, both men and women purchased and smoked crack. The divide here was primarily generational. When I was a teenager in Washington, DC, the drugs of choice among my friends both from my school and from my neighborhood were marijuana and alcohol. A few people my age would occasionally put crack in a marijuana cigarette to create a "Woodie" or PCP in a marijuana cigarette to create "Love Boat," but this was the exception; smoking blunts and drinking St. Ides were far more common. For my generation, crack use was heavily stigmatized, and we grew up knowing we would be ridiculed for smoking crack.

Criminologists sometimes refer to people born between 1955 and 1969 as the "crack generation" and to those born since 1970 as the "marijuana/blunt generation."[60] Accordingly, relatively few of our interviewees, Black men born between 1965 and 1980, had used crack themselves. Nevertheless, many of them had sold crack, and many of their parents had become addicted to crack.

In our interviews with both Black men who grew up in middle-class neighborhoods and Black men who grew up in poor neighborhoods, we learned of cases of parents becoming addicted to drugs as well as of parents selling drugs. The gendered nature of the drug trade meant that we heard more often of mothers having become addicted to drugs and of fathers having sold drugs. Several of our interviewees became practically orphaned as a result of drug use and dealing.

Malik, for example, explained that his father was incarcerated and that his mother did not properly care for him after becoming addicted to crack. Malik went to live with his grandmother, who had a steady job working for the federal government and owned a house in Southeast. Like many grandparents, she took Malik in when she was able to.[61] But decades of disinvestment and carceral investment in Black communities meant that many Black families were "economically and emotionally worn down by long-term unemployment, punitive criminal legal policies, and the ravages of HIV/AIDS," a combination of circumstances that made it difficult for many Black grandparents to keep their grandchildren out of the clutches of the criminal legal system.[62] When Malik was kicked out of junior high school for fighting, his grandmother sent him back home to live with his mother. Two years later, at the age of sixteen, Malik was arrested on murder charges.

Stories of Black boys raised by single mothers in poverty who become embroiled in the criminal legal system abound. However, Malik's story—as well as that of many of the Black men we interviewed—has a twist insofar as their grandparents were home owners. It is difficult to know how common intergenerational downward mobility is, as few studies of poverty or of incarceration include questions about the financial portfolio of grandparents. In our study, nearly all of the thirty-seven formerly incarcerated people we interviewed came from families with a history of home ownership.

CONCLUSION

Buying a home in the 1950s did not translate into intergenerational wealth for many Black families because their neighborhoods experienced disinvestment and then carceral investment. This is what happens in the context of racial capitalism and anti-Black racism. Under racial capitalism, properties are imbued with value according to the racial composition of the population. Anti-Black racism meant that when these disinvested neighborhoods began to experience social problems, the only perceived solution was carceral.

Disinvestment in majority-Black schools and neighborhoods occurred despite Black leadership in a majority-Black city. On the one hand, an important legacy of Mayor Marion Barry is the establishment of a path to the Black middle class for many DC residents. Many Black people who graduated from Coolidge, Roosevelt, and McKinley Tech High Schools in the 1960s returned to the city with undergraduate and graduate degrees that allowed them to secure top positions in the city government and in the public schools. The rolls of city workers grew during Barry's administration, and this growth in city employment created stable jobs for Black DC residents who had completed high school or more.

At the same time, many Black DC residents, particularly those who had not finished high school or who were struggling with drug addiction, were left behind. By the late 1970s, unemployment was a growing crisis, and the city's primary response to the rising problem of drug addiction was punitive. As the city's schools failed and its public housing collapsed, Marion Barry, like his counterparts around the nation, turned his focus to the War on Drugs. This decision would have significant consequences for the children of people who graduated from DC public schools in the 1960s.

Instead of paying for parks and libraries, the city took the path of carceral investment, expanding the criminal legal apparatus.[63] Instead of addressing the root problems of failing schools and widespread economic precarity, the city focused on the symptom—the spread of crack and its attendant violence. These decisions put large numbers of Black people behind bars.

By 1991, 40 percent of African American men aged eighteen to thirty-five in the nation's capital were ensnared by the criminal legal system—either in prison or jail, on parole, out on bond, or wanted on a warrant. Six years later, despite declining crime rates, fully half of Black men were under the control of the justice system. Black men in DC had an incarceration rate thirty-six times that of White men.[64] The rate of incarceration in DC rose steadily from 378 persons per 100,000 residents in 1978 to a peak of 1,712 per 100,000 residents in 1994. This was 4.4 times the national rate and the highest incarceration rate in the world.[65]

On a weekend morning in the summer of 2021, my sister and I were walking through our neighborhood and passed by a corner café full of White folks sitting on the terrace having brunch. My sister, who has lived in our neighborhood all her life, commented that there were so few Black people on a corner where you used to see Black boys and men hanging out at all times of day or night. She added, "They're all in jail, dead, or in Maryland." There is some truth in this observation. The combination of drug addiction, homicide, and mass incarceration reduced the Black population of Washington, DC, during the 1990s. And many people who lost family members to these multiple crises moved to Prince George's County, Maryland.

Each of the thousands of homicides and tens of thousands of incarcerations had a ripple effect. Some family members lost their homes through foreclosures or evictions due to the loss of income from an incarcerated or murdered relative. Some family members left for Prince George's County or the South to protect their remaining relatives from violence and incarceration. Some people left so they would no longer have to be reminded of their losses.

4

BRINGING IN THE FEDS

Targeting Black Middle-Class Neighborhoods

IN MAY 1993, A JUDGE told nineteen-year-old Donnie Strothers he was going to spend the rest of his life in prison for selling drugs. Donnie Strothers had been caught selling 14 grams of crack cocaine to an undercover agent near his home in Mount Pleasant.[1]

Just one year before, the *Washington Post* had named Donnie one of the five most talented basketball players in the city.[2] Donnie's brothers and sisters had all graduated from high school and moved on to university, and his parents expected him to do the same. However, shortly after high school graduation, Donnie was convicted of one count of conspiring to distribute more than 50 grams of crack cocaine and one count of distributing more than 5 grams of crack cocaine. The conspiracy charges were a result of his low-level affiliation with the Newton Street Crew in Washington, DC. He was sentenced to concurrent prison terms of life and forty years.[3] This was his first conviction.

Federal and local authorities worked together in the 1980s to depose drug kingpins using Continuing Criminal Enterprise (CCE) statutes (also known as the Kingpin Statutes). These highly lauded operations led to the convictions of three drug kingpins: Cornell Jones, James Smith, and Rayful Edmond. Just after the kingpin cases, the task force began to use Racketeer Influenced and Corrupt Organizations (RICO) statutes in drug cases—legal tools originally designed to take down large-scale criminal organizations such as the Mafia. There were six RICO cases in DC between 1991 and 1995.[4] However, these cases were not of the same magnitude as the kingpin cases. A close analysis of the six RICO cases makes it clear they did not target the major drug sellers in the city. Although both open-air drug markets and homicides were happening all over the city, the task force targeted six crews in very specific areas: Black middle-class neighborhoods (Maps 3a and 3b).

These neighborhoods were likely the focus of joint federal-local operations because these were the communities most ardently demanding that *something* be done to address the drug trade and addiction. The city and federal government answered these calls with a show of force. The availability of federal statutes and the creation of the federal-local Operation Violent Gang Safe Streets in DC allowed law enforcement agents to arrest alleged members of drug crews on trumped-up charges and sentence them to life in prison.

Donnie's arrest was part of a sweep of arrests of young Black men that resulted from Operation Violent Gang Safe Streets, but he is not the only person I knew who was targeted. I knew people in three of the six cases: my close friend's brother was in the same case as Donnie; my college roommate's boyfriend was in the Fern Street case; and one of my elementary school classmates was in the First and Kennedy case. I did not know the young men in the other three cases that were in the area around North Capitol Street that conjoins the Bloomingdale and Eckington areas. But I knew of them as I had friends who dated boys from P Street, R Street, and First Street. It's no coincidence that I had strong or weak ties to the young men in these cases: they all grew up in neighborhoods very similar to mine: working- to middle-class Black neighborhoods—either around or well above the citywide median household income, which was $31,449 in 1990. The median household income in the areas targeted by the raids ranged from $27,220 in Eckington to over $100,000 in Shepherd Park (all in 1990 dollars). In the 1990s, Shepherd Park and Mount Pleasant were integrated, and the other areas were over 90 percent Black. Operation Violent Gang Safe Streets used an inordinate amount of resources to arrest and prosecute a few dozen young Black men. The months of investigative work, hundreds of law enforcement agents, and extended jury trials are an example of carceral investment, that is, when the government uses its ample resources to control and punish people.

This chapter explains why Donnie Strothers was sentenced to life in prison for selling a couple of hundred dollars' worth of crack cocaine. By doing so, it also reveals three important findings: (1) the joint federal-local Operation Violent Gang Safe Streets Task Force engaged in large-scale efforts to take down crews that were not at the epicenter of drug-selling activity; (2) all these massive operations were in majority-Black working- to middle-class neighborhoods; and (3) the operations targeted these neighborhoods in part due to community complaints and community organizing. This all helps us see more clearly why, despite Black leadership and a majority-Black police force in a majority-Black city, the solutions proffered to handle the joint epidemics of gun violence and drug addiction had devastating consequences for the Black community.

THE KINGPIN CASES

DC's first cocaine kingpin was Cornell Jones. In the early 1980s, Jones and his associates took over Hanover Place, NW, located just across North Capitol Street from Eckington, and transformed it into the

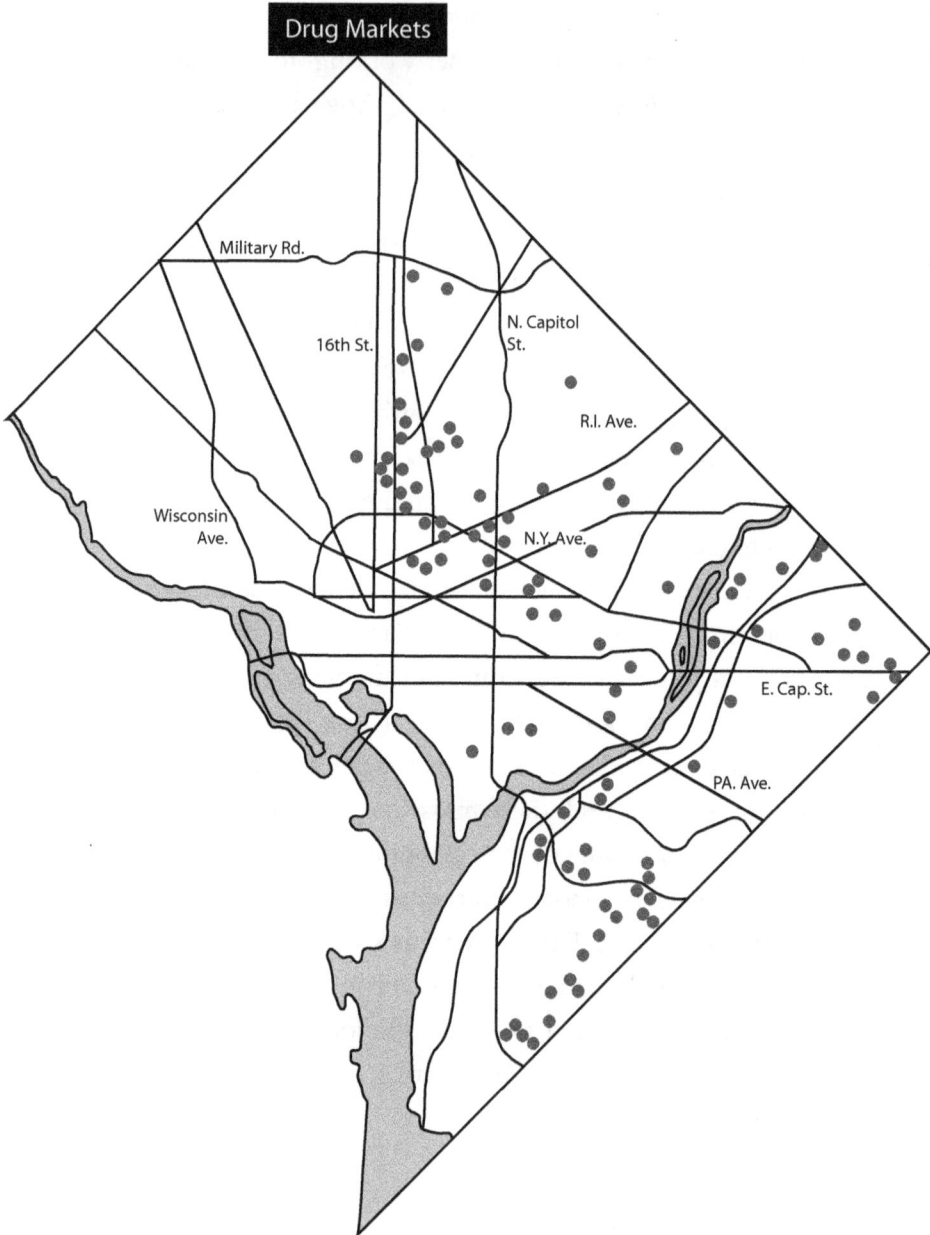

Map 3. (a) How drug markets compare with homicide locations in DC, 1988.

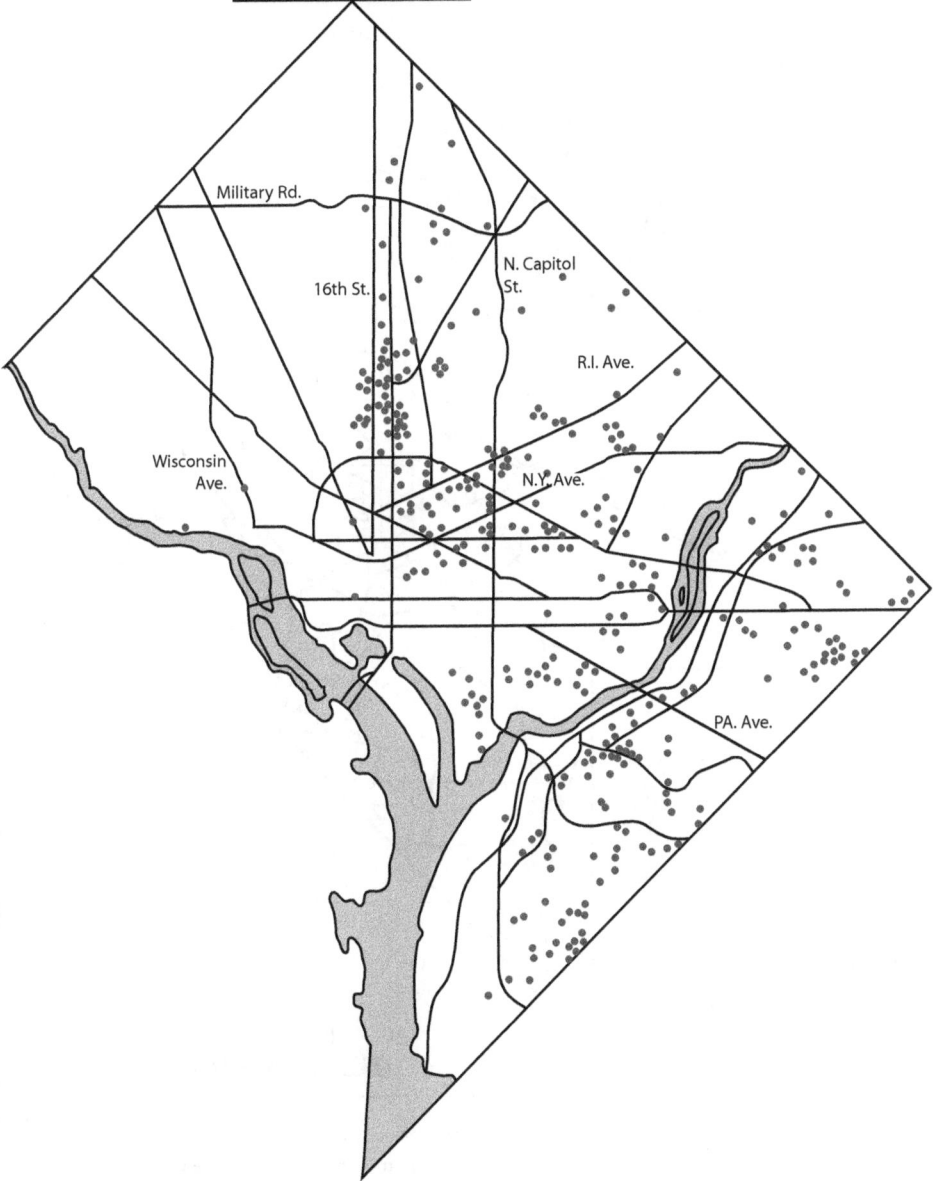

Homicide Locations

Military Rd.

16th St.

N. Capitol
St.

R.I. Ave.

Wisconsin
Ave.

N.Y. Ave.

PA. Ave.

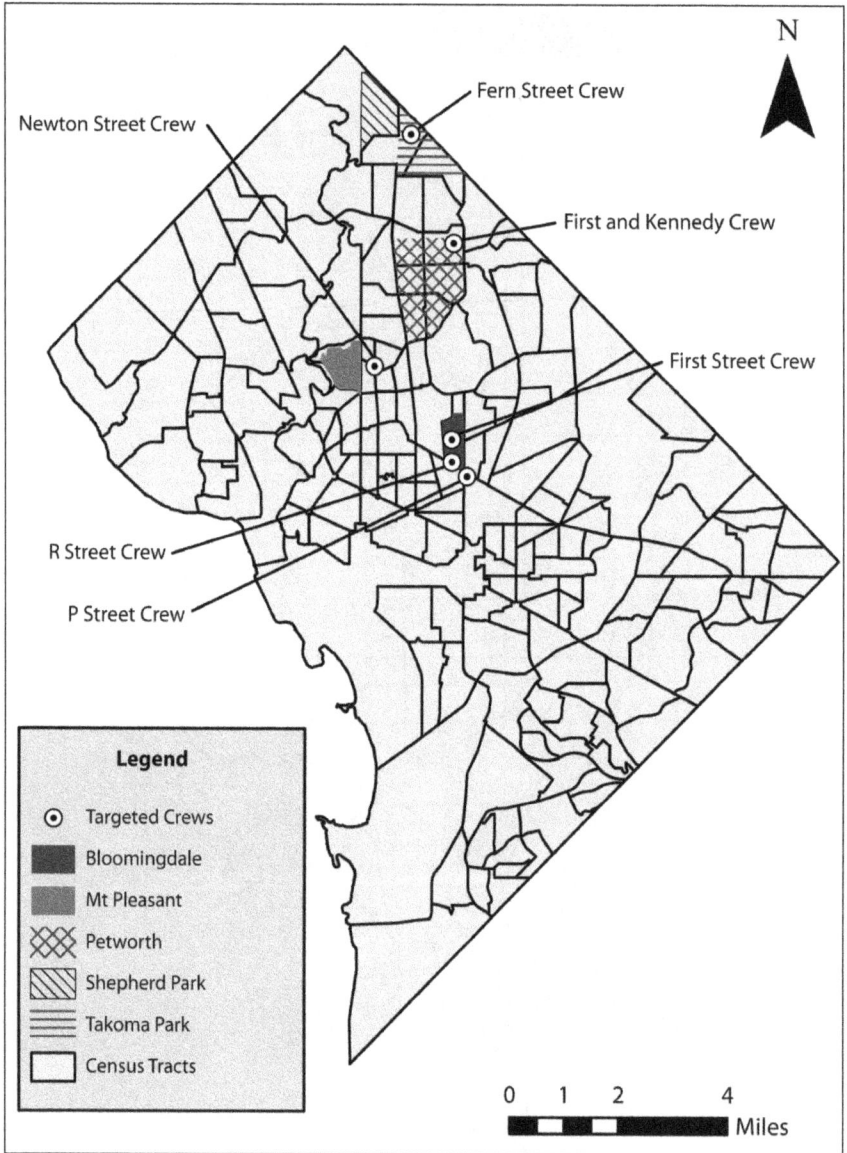

Map 3. (b) Locations of six targeted crews. The first two maps show the similarity in the patterns of where drugs are sold openly on the streets of DC and where most homicides occurred in 1988. The locations plotted are based on information from the DC police. Map 3a and b adapted from Brad Wye, "How Drug Markets Compare with Homicide Locations in D.C.," *Washington Post*, January 13, 1989.

largest open-air cocaine market in Washington, DC. It also was the scene of nightly shoot-outs. In 1985, the local police permanently installed a trailer in a vacant lot on Hanover Place and used it to patrol the eighteen-block radius. This strategy was dubbed Operation Avalanche and led to the arrest of thousands of people and the confiscation of tens of thousands of dollars in drugs, cash, and property.[5] This type of operation, as discussed in the previous chapter, was common across the city. Nevertheless, sweeps and mass arrests did not shut down drug markets because there was a steady supply of young men willing to sell drugs and earn cash. And when police set up trailers on one corner, drug dealers simply moved to the next corner. Law enforcement agents were, however, able to temporarily shut down the Hanover Place drug market with the arrest of Cornell Jones in October 1985.[6]

On January 8, 1986, Jones accepted a plea deal in which he pleaded guilty to conspiring to distribute and possession with intent to distribute cocaine. Jones was sentenced to nine to twenty-seven years in prison and fined $250,000. Officers seized $2.5 million from Jones in the form of cars, jewelry, and property.[7]

A couple of years after the arrest of Cornell Jones, a collaboration between the Metropolitan Police Department (MPD), the Federal Bureau of Investigation (FBI), and the Drug Enforcement Agency (DEA) led to the arrest of James Edwood Smith. On February 6, 1988, Smith was arrested after he sold 3 ounces of heroin to an undercover DEA agent. When Smith subsequently pleaded guilty to narcotics charges, he agreed to forfeit "five houses, a 20-acre farm, 38 automobiles, including three 1986 Mercedes, two Porsches and a BMW, more than $360,000 worth of gold jewelry and $118,277.65 in cash." Smith had been under investigation by DC police, the FBI, and the DEA since 1984.[8] Law enforcement considered Smith's arrest their most important takedown since the arrest of Cornell Jones because of the millions of dollars in cash, jewelry, property, and cars Smith owned that they were able to confiscate.[9]

Both Jones and Smith were prosecuted in federal court on conspiracy charges. Cornell Jones pleaded guilty to conspiring to distribute and possession with intent to distribute cocaine. James Smith pleaded guilty to heroin distribution, conspiracy, and tax evasion charges. Smith and Jones were both drug kingpins. Beginning in 1989, there was a shift in these prosecutions, and conspiracy charges were brought not only against alleged leaders of organizations but against their associates as well.

Jones's lieutenant, Tony Lewis, escaped prosecution in the Hanover Place sting operation. Lewis was an associate of Rayful Edmond III, who at the time had been selling cocaine for about a year, after his father had gifted him a kilo to get his business off the ground. With Jones out of the picture, Edmond and Lewis organized a highly structured crack-dealing system on a strip behind Seventh Street and Florida Avenue, NE—between Orleans Place and Morton Place—that was less than a mile from Hanover Place. Edmond was twenty-two in 1986 when his organization started bringing in enormous amounts of cash. He quickly climbed to the helm of the drug economy in Washington, DC.[10]

In 1987, Rayful Edmond, Tony Lewis, and several other members of their organization went to see a fight in Las Vegas. His glitzy entourage caught the eye of Melvin Butler, who was affiliated with the Crips in Los Angeles and had a direct connection to Colombian cocaine dealers. Butler was working with Mario Ernesto Villabona-Alvarado of the Cali Cartel and told Edmond they could get him as much cocaine as he wanted. With access to more cocaine than he could sell on his strip, Edmond began to sell cocaine wholesale across DC. At its peak in 1988, Rayful's organization had two hundred employees and moved somewhere between $10 million and $20 million worth of crack a month.[11]

Rayful Edmond's reign as the leader of the most profitable drug ring in Washington, DC, did not last long, as he soon found himself at the center of a major federal investigation. On April 15, 1989, the now twenty-four-year-old Rayful Edmond III was arrested in his girlfriend's house on the 900 block of Jefferson Street, NW, just a few blocks from my childhood home. Dozens of Edmond's associates were arrested in the following weeks.[12] This operation, which took over two years of investigatory work, relied on over one hundred agents from the DEA, FBI, and MPD. In this case, instead of targeting only the leaders, authorities charged twenty-nine defendants associated with Edmond with conspiracy to distribute more than 5 kilograms of cocaine.[13] The Rayful Edmond Organization allegedly controlled between 20 percent and 50 percent of the cocaine and crack markets in DC and was suspected of being involved in thirty homicides.[14]

Rayful Edmond III was charged with nine major felonies, including conducting a continuing criminal enterprise, three homicides, and engaging in a conspiracy ranging over a three-year period to possess and distribute massive amounts of cocaine. He received three life sentences for the charge of Continuing a Criminal Enterprise and conspiring to violate federal narcotics laws, along with other charges.[15] The Continuing Criminal Enterprise offense alone carries a mandatory minimum term of life imprisonment without parole. Tony Lewis was also sentenced to life in prison on drug charges. Lewis's son, Tony Lewis Jr., mounted a campaign for his release—on the grounds that three decades in prison is more than enough for a person convicted only of drug-related offenses.[16] As a result, on March 30, 2023, Tony Lewis Sr. was released, after serving thirty-four years in prison. Rayful Edmond remains behind bars, although in February 2021, he requested a sentence reduction based on his long-standing cooperation with federal prosecutors.[17]

Rayful Edmond III was only twenty-four when he was arrested, yet he was already a household name in Washington, DC. He was well known for his wealth, conspicuous consumption, and generosity. He chartered planes to take his associates on all-expenses-paid trips to the Super Bowl and Mike Tyson fights. He bought bottles of Dom Perignon champagne at nightclubs, drove luxury cars, rode in chauffeured limousines, and wore designer brands and gold jewelry worth thousands of dollars. When his associate Tony Lewis was arrested, police found clothing and shoes with $6,000 price tags, much of which had not been worn. Edmond paid his employees up to $5,000 a week, paid for lawyers for any of his associates who were arrested, and gave families thousands of dollars if anyone who worked for him was murdered. He was also known for handing out $100 bills to children.[18] The courtroom was packed for his arraignment. The *Washington Post* ran a dozen articles—some of them in-depth pieces—on this operation in the months following his arrest in 1989.

The takedown of Edmond, nevertheless, did not put a dent in the crack cocaine market in Washington, DC, and homicide rates continued to rise. Law enforcement doubled down on their tactics. In October 1991, local law enforcement worked with federal agents to create Operation Violent Gang Safe Streets, which included DC Police, the FBI, the Bureau of Alcohol, Tobacco, Firearms and Explosives (ATF), US Marshals, and other agencies. The Violent Gang Safe Streets Task Force became the vehicle through which local law enforcement could work directly with the FBI to tackle the problem of violent street gangs.[19] Dozens of FBI agents were assigned to work on local crime issues as they found themselves with less work chasing spies after the Cold War. One of their first tasks was to break up the R Street Organization.[20]

TARGETING BLOOMINGDALE AND ECKINGTON WITH RACKETEERING LAWS

When Congress signed the Organized Crime Control Act (OCCA) in 1970, it included the RICO statutes and the CCE, or Kingpin, Statutes. The purpose of the OCCA was to provide law enforcement with new legal tools to aid in the fight against organized crime. The primary focus at that time was dismantling the Mafia.[21] In the 1980s, the fear of the Mafia dissipated with its loss of power. Federal prosecutors turned their attention to urban street gangs and began to use RICO and CCE to prosecute them. RICO can be used against any criminal organization, whereas CCE deals specifically with the distribution of illegal drugs.[22] The OCCA broadened the ability of law enforcement to seize property, as well as the definition of conspiracy and what it means to engage in criminal enterprise.[23]

The R Street Case

The R Street case was the first attempt by the United States Attorney's Office (USAO) to use federal racketeering laws against a neighborhood drug organization in the District of Columbia. Whereas the USAO had used the Kingpin Statutes—justifiably, one could argue—against Rayful Edmond III and his multimillion-dollar operation, they decided to test the RICO laws in the R Street case. Authorities were again using DC as a test case in the War on Drugs by using two tactics: RICO laws and joint task forces. RICO laws have since been used in dozens of drug cases across the country; as of 2022, there were over 160 Safe Streets task forces.[24]

In an interview in *Washingtonian* magazine in 1996, the prosecutor Mike Volkov equated the R Street and other RICO cases with the kingpin cases, explaining that his office was dedicated to rooting out the "drug bosses." Linking these drug crews not only to the kingpins but also to the Mafia, Volkov continued, "We build cases using the drug-conspiracy [kingpin] laws and the racketeering, or RICO, statutes, which were originally passed in the Kennedy administration to target Mafia organizations. Eight years ago, our office was the first to apply the RICO laws to violent drug gangs."[25] Again, Volkov connects these RICO cases with Rayful Edmond's kingpin operation, describing how the USAO has "successfully prosecuted several significant drug organizations and their leaders—Rayful Edmond and his multimillion-dollar operation; Mark Hoyle and his violent Newton Street gang; Anthony

Nugent and the R Street organization; Antone White and the First Street Crew; Calvin Sumler and the Fern Street group; and recently the First and Kennedy Street gang."[26] Volkov used "organization," "group," "gang," and "crew" interchangeably to refer to these groups of young men, but the targets of his investigations would consider themselves members of a crew, not gang members. Federal authorities faced an uphill battle attempting to prove that these other drug-selling crews were large-scale criminal organizations like those in the kingpin cases.

To justify using RICO statutes, federal prosecutors claimed the R Street Crew brought in over $50 million over eight years and had cross-country connections to Los Angeles and New York.[27] Federal authorities charged twenty-four teenagers and young adults under RICO laws and with conspiracy to distribute narcotics, both of which carry life sentences. Four suspects, including the alleged leader, Kevin Williams-Davis, were also charged with Continuing a Criminal Enterprise, which also carries a life sentence.[28] It is worth noting that prosecutors were unable to confirm that these crews controlled large amounts of money or drugs. Thus federal and local authorities worked to arrest alleged members of drug crews on trumped-up charges and sentence them to life in prison.

The MPD and the FBI saw the trial of the R Street Crew as a testing ground for the use of conspiracy and racketeering charges against street gangs.[29] The case was split up into four separate cases because of the large number of defendants. The first case took five months to try and was watched closely by federal prosecutors around the country because it was one of a few attempts, and the first in DC, to use RICO charges against a suspected drug organization. A jury acquitted the four principal defendants of RICO charges, yet found them guilty of operating a Continuing Criminal (Kingpin) Enterprise, which carries a mandatory sentence of life without parole.[30]

In the second trial, five defendants—Andre P. Williams, 23; McKinley L. Board, 23; Gregory M. Thomas, 25; Derrin A. Perkins, 27; and

Donnell O. Williams, 21—were found guilty of conspiring to commit racketeering and conspiring to distribute crack cocaine. In both trials, jurors rejected RICO charges. Nevertheless, the defendants were convicted on other conspiracy charges that also carried life sentences.

Whereas prosecutors were able to establish that Cornell Jones, James Smith, and Rayful Edmond had access to large amounts of cash and valuables, they struggled to make the same case against the R Street Crew. In the R Street case, federal prosecutors sought the forfeiture of two houses, $60,000 in cash, and a dozen vehicles.[31] The jury decided that one of the houses, five cars, and $11,415 in cash were proceeds of an illegal drug operation and should be forfeited.[32] This forfeiture pales in comparison to the millions of dollars of cash and property seized and forfeited in the cases of Jones, Smith, and Edmond. The jury acquitted the alleged members of the R Street Crew on the RICO charges.

The P Street Case

The next target of the joint task force was the P Street Crew, whose headquarters were a few blocks from that of the R Street Crew. On January 31, 1992, more than 450 federal, state, and local law enforcement agents arrested eighteen alleged members of the P Street Crew—four times the number of agents used in the operation targeting Rayful Edmond. In an unusual move, Attorney General William Barr announced the arrests at a press conference. Normally, these arrests would have been announced by a local official. Yet in this case high-ranking officials came to the fore. US Attorney Richard Cullen, FBI Director William Sessions, and DEA chief Robert Bonner all praised the large-scale operation, pointing to the benefits of this new emphasis on charging drug organizations in federal court where defendants could receive sentences of life without parole.[33]

In the R Street case, federal prosecutors alleged the crew controlled $50 million. In the case against the P Street Crew, they alleged the crew had earned more than $100 million selling crack cocaine. They were unable to substantiate these claims. When the joint task force raided P Street, they confiscated nine buildings valued at $2 million, seven Mercedes Benzes, two Acuras, jewelry, watches, and two guns. But the buildings the government confiscated on P Street were not owned by the drug dealers but were rented from Audrey Thacker, owner of Thacker Caskets, one of the area's largest wholesale casket dealers. In an interview after the federal raid, a reporter asked law enforcement agents where the $100 million was. The official responded that the dealers must have spent it.[34] In summary, the federal government seized nine buildings that allegedly were the site of drug activity as well as cars and jewelry, but these seizures fell far short of the hundreds of millions of dollars authorities alleged they controlled, and the buildings did not even belong to the crew members.

Local and federal authorities had high hopes for the P Street case, yet they were not able to bring sufficient evidence to secure the sentences they were seeking. The P Street strip was one of dozens of open-air drug markets in the city in 1992. The organization was far from bringing in the kinds of profits federal authorities argued they were, or the amount that Rayful Edmond brought in, and this became evident in court.

The case was originally brought against the twenty-three defendants in a court in Virginia, where some of the drug activity had allegedly occurred, but a federal judge ordered that the case be tried in Washington, DC, as that is where the majority of the alleged crimes had taken place.[35] Prosecutors charged all the defendants with drug conspiracy and racketeering and charged the three alleged leaders with operating a continuing criminal enterprise. Fifteen of the twenty-three defendants pleaded guilty to lesser charges, and eight were released from the case entirely.[36] The lead defendant received eight and a half years in prison, and the other defendants were either released or received shorter sentences through plea bargains.[37] The trial ended on January 6, 1993, when the last defendant, Keith Robinson, pleaded guilty to carrying a firearm during a drug-trafficking crime, which carried a mandatory minimum sentence of five years. In return for this plea, prosecutors dropped all other charges, and this case, which started with much fanfare, ended without a trial.[38]

The First Street Case

The setbacks in the P Street case did not deter the task force. In 1993, federal authorities returned to target the First Street Crew, whose headquarters were very close to those of both P Street and R Street (see Map 3b). This time, federal authorities focused on the five alleged leaders and charged them on a twenty-six-count indictment, including conspiracy to distribute narcotics, RICO conspiracy, and Continuing a Criminal Enterprise.[39]

Two of the alleged leaders, Antone White and Eric Hicks, were also charged with murder. They pleaded not guilty and the case went to jury trial. The jury found Hicks and White guilty of the drug and drug conspiracy charges and not guilty on the weapons and murder charges. At their sentencing in 1994, Judge Harold Green decided that life sentences were warranted because "if witnesses can be intimidated, injured or killed, all the crime bills Congress may pass will be just illusions, limited in practical effect." Although Hicks and White were not found guilty of witness intimidation or murder, the judge took these allegations into account when deciding their sentences. Thus Antone White and Eric Hicks were sentenced to life in prison on a drug conspiracy count, to run concurrently with a life sentence on a RICO conspiracy count and with 240- and 480-month sentences on individual drug distribution and aiding and abetting counts.

The government dropped the RICO charges against Dan Hutchinson and Ronald Hughes in the First Street case. Ronald Hughes thus received a life sentence on the drug conspiracy count, to run concurrently with 240-month sentences on each of three drug distribution counts. And Dan Hutchinson was sentenced to 300 months in prison on the drug conspiracy count, to run concurrently with 300-month sentences on each of two drug distribution counts. The final defendant, Derrick Ballard, pleaded guilty to drug conspiracy and assault charges.

In October 2000, a judge reduced Hughes's sentence to 360 months. Thus, in May 2019, Hughes was released. In 2019, Antone White and Eric Hicks filed an appeal—seeking reductions in their sentences based on the First Step Act, a bipartisan bill passed in 2018 that is intended to help address racial disparities in mass incarceration. The act allows early release for nonviolent offenders who complete recidivism reduction programs, such as anger management, literacy, or other certification programs, and maintain good behavior; it also curbed mandatory sentences, especially for drug offenses. In August 2019, Chief US District Judge Beryl Howell denied their appeals and wrote in the opinion that there is "ample evidence" White and Hicks committed murder—while conceding that the jury did not find them guilty beyond a reasonable doubt.[40] Just over a year later, in December 2020, Judge Edwards of the US Court of Appeals for the District of Columbia Circuit overturned this finding and ruled that the court had to revisit their sentences based on the First Step Act.[41] On August 25, 2022, after serving nearly three decades behind bars, Antone White and Eric Hicks were released from prison.

After successfully prosecuting White and Hicks with RICO charges in the First Street case, the task force set their sights farther uptown.

TARGETING CREWS UPTOWN

The crews uptown included the Newton Street Crew in tree-lined Mount Pleasant, the Fern Street Crew in upscale Shepherd Park, and the First and Kennedy Crew in Petworth. These crews were all located in integrated or Black middle- to working-class areas.

The Newton Street Case

On July 29, 1992, four hundred DC police and federal agents arrested fifteen members of the Newton Street Crew.[42] Over the next few weeks, a total of twenty-six alleged crew members would be arrested and indicted on various drug-related charges. Alleged crew leaders Mark Hoyle, John W. McCullough, and Donald Price were charged with Continuing a Criminal Enterprise.[43]

Members of the Newton Street Crew had known each other since they were students at Bancroft and Holy Cross Elementary Schools in Mount Pleasant.[44] The crew members were raised in Mount Pleasant, a historic neighborhood adjacent to Rock Creek Park that at the time was one of the few racially integrated neighborhoods in the city. The mayor of Washington, DC, from 2007 to 2011, Adrian Fenty, also grew up in this neighborhood. A few houses down from him, Mark Hoyle was raised in a brick row house like the one Fenty's family owned. Whereas Fenty went on to Oberlin College and became mayor, Hoyle became a member of the Newton Street Crew, which controlled drug sales on a one-way street in neighboring Columbia Heights.

The Newton Street case resulted in a lengthy jury trial, in which the leaders as well as lower-level members were found guilty on conspiracy charges and sentenced to life without parole.[45] After their failed attempts with the R Street and P Street Crews, prosecutors were able to convince a jury to convict several members of the Newton Street Crew on conspiracy charges.

This case, nevertheless, was riddled with problems, and all the defendants were eventually released on various technicalities. The technicalities were not minor; the prosecutor, Paul Howes, was disbarred when it came to light that he had illegally disbursed tens of thousands of dollars in witness vouchers in this and other cases. Witness vouchers are cash payments given to witnesses when they show up in court. Howes, however, was giving out far more witness vouchers than there were witnesses, meaning he was either giving them out as payment to people who were not actually witnesses or he was giving witnesses more than their share of vouchers.[46] In other words, he was paying witnesses, which is illegal and may have influenced their testimonies.

The Fern Street Case

After Newton Street, prosecutors turned their attention all the way uptown to the integrated middle-class neighborhood of Shepherd Park. On July 15, 1995, two hundred law enforcement officers raided Fern Street and arrested thirteen alleged members of the Fern Street Crew.[47] In this case, the prosecutor claimed that the Fern Street Crew had sold more than $50 million in narcotics in the past seven years and was responsible for several murders.[48] The government brought fifty-four charges against the thirteen alleged crew members, including conspiracy to distribute narcotics, RICO conspiracy, armed robbery, kidnapping, and several acts of murder. During the raid, officers seized three homes but did not uncover hard evidence of millions of dollars in cash or drugs.[49] At the trial, Calvin Sumler denied the claim that he had become rich from drug sales, stating, "I would just like to say this is ridiculous. Running a $50 million enterprise today doesn't make sense. Here I was living in an apartment with bad credit? I supposedly made over $7 million a year and I have a court-appointed lawyer? It doesn't make any sense."[50] Nevertheless, Sumler, along with Michael Jefferson and Gerald Smith, was convicted of conspiracy, racketeering, and murder and sentenced to life in prison.[51]

In 2021, a few weeks before his fiftieth birthday and a couple of days after Kyle Rittenhouse was found not guilty of killing Black Lives Matters protesters, Gerald Smith texted me from a federal penitentiary to let me know that the judge overseeing his appeal from the Fern Street case is the same one overseeing the case involving the takeover of the

US Capitol on January 6, 2020. He noted that the takeover of the US Capitol was much more of an actual conspiracy than his involvement in selling drugs with a few friends from his neighborhood. Gerald pointed out that the courts seem very willing to convict Black people of conspiracy, but the laws are not applied equally across racial lines. As of this writing in January 2023, both Gerald Smith and Calvin Sumler are waiting for decisions on their appeals and thus to find out if they will ever again be free.

The First and Kennedy Case

The final target of the Safe Streets task force considered here is the First and Kennedy Crew. The decision to target this crew appears to be retaliation for the actions of one of its members. In 1994, Bennie Lee Lawson attacked the local police district headquarters and killed a police sergeant, two FBI agents, and himself.[52] The brazen attack shook both the FBI and the MPD. Their intensive investigation into the First and Kennedy Street Crew was part of their search to understand why Lawson attacked the police headquarters. They learned that Lawson believed he was going to be charged with a triple murder that he, along with two other members of the First and Kennedy Street Crew, allegedly committed. Officials believe the purpose of his attack on the police headquarters was twofold: he did not want to return to prison, and he did not want his associates to believe he was a snitch.[53]

On September 21, 1995, nine members of the First and Kennedy Street Crew were arrested in a joint effort by FBI agents, DC police officers, and officers of the US Marshals Service and the Department of Housing and Urban Development.[54] In all, fourteen crew members were charged on fifty-three counts, including racketeering, drug dealing, robbery, and kidnapping.[55] On October 17, 1996, Kobi Mowatt pleaded guilty to a count of RICO.[56] Both Kobi Mowatt and Jermaine

Graves were sentenced to thirty-five years in prison for their leadership roles in the crew.[57] They both remain behind bars.

These three raids—Newton Street, Fern Street, and First and Kennedy—were all in uptown Northwest neighborhoods. These neighborhoods were historically all-White but experienced an influx of Black residents beginning in the 1950s. Both Newton Street and Fern Street were integrated in the 1990s, whereas First and Kennedy was nearly all-Black.

TARGETING BLACK MIDDLE-CLASS NEIGHBORHOODS

The crews I discussed above were not at the epicenter of drug-dealing activity in the city. None of them had reached the levels of profitability that Rayful Edmond had. There were community-based efforts across the city to "clean up" neighborhoods with open-air drug markets and crack houses. Neighborhoods were in crisis, and community members banded together to demand that something be done.

In Washington, DC, in the 1980s and 1990s, residents from a variety of neighborhoods organized to root out drug dealers. Residents in the Fairlawn neighborhood in Southeast DC, as well as in Shaw, were highly organized in the fight against drug dealing.[58] Leroy Thorpe, who became an Advisory Neighborhood Commission (ANC) commissioner in Shaw in 1986 and remained in that position for twenty years, made "clean[ing] up the neighborhood" his mission. Thorpe created a community group in his neighborhood known informally as "red hats," similar to the "orange hats" prevalent in Shepherd Park, Petworth, Park View, Anacostia, and other areas of the city. Thorpe and his fellow red hats took pictures and videos of drug dealers and shared them with law enforcement. Thorpe told the author Shilpi Malinowski that he personally closed fifty-six crack houses.[59] Thorpe's activity was adjacent to the R Street, P Street, and First Street Crews, so it is possible his activism played a role in these cases. However, there were also active crews right in Thorpe's ANC area, such as the Fifth and O Crew, that were not targeted by the Violent Gang Safe Streets Task Force in the 1990s.

When residents of Black middle-class neighborhoods organized to demand action against drug activity, the government responded with a tremendous show of force. When trying to understand why the Violent Gang Safe Streets Task Force targeted these specific crews with these raids and RICO laws, the Fern Street case provides us with some answers. Fern Street is in Shepherd Park, which in the 1990s was an integrated but primarily Black upper-middle-class neighborhood. The Shepherd Park community has a long history of community activism. The organization founded by Marvin Caplan in 1958, Neighbors, Inc., had its headquarters in Shepherd Park and worked for decades to stabilize the neighborhood, improve the schools, and promote the neighborhood as a desirable and integrated middle-class community. In the 1970s, they also began to focus on closing liquor stores and other businesses members perceived to have a negative effect on their community. And in the late 1980s, they turned their organizational skills and networks to help the effort to stop illegal drug distribution.[60] Their sister organization, Concerned Neighbors, worked closely with the police and met regularly with District Attorney Eric Holder to convey their concerns. Community members took note of and recorded suspicious activity and reported all perceived drug sales to the police.[61] The residents of Fern Street had more resources than most people in the city and used these resources not only to organize their neighbors to fight crime but also to get legal help to do so. Two DC law firms donated their services to the community to ensure that local and federal prosecutors responded to the drug activity on Fern Street.[62] In this case, a concerted community effort to root out drug dealers led to the arrest and conviction of the leaders of this crew.

There is strong evidence that the conspiracy case against the Fern Street Crew was prompted by community organizing and activism. Law enforcement agents reported that the First and Kennedy Crew case was in response to Bennie Lee Lawson attacking the police headquarters. As for the other four cases, these communities also organized against drug dealers, but it is not clear that they organized more than other neighborhoods. All communities—both poor and wealthy—decry activities such as open-air drug markets that exacerbate violence and drug use in their neighborhood. A majority-Black police force and city leadership answered the calls of majority-Black working- and middle-class communities to do something about gun violence and drug selling by soliciting the help of federal agents to take down drug crews. These efforts led to young Black men like Donnie Strothers getting life sentences in prison.

CONCLUSION

The government's efforts to establish that the six crews discussed in this chapter were large-scale criminal organizations involved significant irregularities, which led to most of the life sentences eventually being overturned. In the Newton Street case, the federal prosecutor, Paul Howes, was disbarred for illegally giving out tens of thousands of dollars in witness vouchers—making him the first federal prosecutor to be disbarred for ethics violations in a criminal case in over a decade.[63] Although dozens of the Black men indicted in these six cases were sentenced to life without parole, only a handful remain behind bars today. All the defendants in these cases have appealed their convictions. Some have been successful and are back home. Others have not been successful and remain behind bars. As for Donnie Strothers, his life sentence was overturned in 1996 after his lawyers made the case that the judge had given coercive instructions to the jury. Nevertheless, Donnie served fourteen years for selling a couple of hundred dollars' worth of drugs to an undercover agent.

The targets of these raids were all young Black men from working- to middle-class neighborhoods in DC. They are just several dozen of the tens of thousands of young Black men arrested in Washington, DC, in the early 1990s. Nevertheless, it is worth raising the question as to why these particular men were targeted. The illegal labor market, just like the legal labor market, is gendered. Thus although women are involved in the drug trade, they are not usually at the center of operations. A combination of the fact that women were on the sidelines and that law enforcement's preconceived notions about who sells drugs created a situation where all the arrestees in these cases were men. Why were all the arrestees Black? Although DC was a majority-Black city, there were also non-Black people selling drugs there. Nevertheless, law enforcement's anti-Black biases led to using these coercive strategies in majority-Black neighborhoods and targeting Black men in those neighborhoods.

It can be helpful to think of these questions in terms of individual officers' and agents' biases, but it is also helpful to think in terms of systems. What role did systems of power play in creating a situation where these men were targeted? Patriarchy—a system in which men hold most of the power in the family, society, and government—helps us understand why men held most of the power and money in the illegal drug trade. Anti-Black racism—a system in which Black people are denied opportunities and disproportionately subjected to both coercive policies such as incarceration and premature death—helps us understand why Black people and Black neighborhoods were targeted.[64] An analysis of capitalism, more specifically, racial capitalism, helps us understand why local and federal officials chose to spend their resources on policing young Black men rather than investing in schools, community centers, and libraries.

Decades of disinvestment in Black neighborhoods as varied as Navy Yard and Eckington created a scenario where both crack using and selling became prevalent. When the state decided to respond to the proliferation of crack cocaine and the uptick in violence, it did not address the underlying causes of failing schools and a lack of services. Instead, the state squandered funds on policing and prisons.

Imagine for a moment if the city had chosen to reinvest in the youth of DC instead of choosing carceral investment. Imagine if the city and federal governments had spent the millions of dollars on youth services, health care, schools, and drug rehabilitation instead of on rounding up Black boys and men and investigating the crews. This not only would have created a healthier and more vibrant community; it also would have prevented gentrification, as gentrification is only possible in disinvested communities.

Each of the neighborhoods where these six drug-selling crews were headquartered experienced an intense wave of gentrification and racial turnover in the twenty-first century—a subject addressed in the next chapter.

PART THREE

REINVESTMENT

THE DISPOSSESSION OF BLACK MIDDLE-CLASS RESIDENTS made it possible and profitable for investors to purchase devalued houses, foreclosed homes, and forfeited properties to create new homes for new people. Disinvestment combined with low housing prices, record-low interest rates, and tax incentives made Petworth attractive to investors after decades of abandonment. Disinvestment made reinvestment profitable.

In 2016, a real estate company ranked Petworth first in the nation for the profits investors could make from flipping a home—with an average profit of over $300,000 per sale.

The Chinese carry-out where my best friend Nmadilaka and I used to get fried chicken wings with mumbo sauce is still there. Next to it, there's a restaurant whose specialty is raw hamachi with pomegranate sauce, preserved lemon, and za'atar. Each time I visit Petworth, there are more and more upscale restaurants and fewer and fewer Black people.

5

CHOCOLATE CITY NO MORE

Gentrification through White Reclamation

‖‖

I ATTENDED AN OUTDOOR NEIGHBORHOOD fund-raiser for Crispus Attucks Park in Bloomingdale on a bright sunny afternoon in October 2021. The park is not maintained by the city, and the residents hold fund-raisers to maintain and improve it. They had pizza, wine, and popsicles—and a band playing soft guitar music. Neighbors gathered in circles on colorful blankets and chatted with one another in what was once a majority-Black neighborhood. But in 2021, nearly all the attendees were White. Bloomingdale is just to the west of Eckington and just north of Hanover Place. This area of the city is a microcosm of the changes Washington, DC, has experienced in the twenty-first century.

In the 1980s, Hanover Place was one of the largest open-air cocaine markets in DC (Fig. 7). Tony Lewis and his associates were able to bring in large profits on this strip from the high volume of cocaine sales. In 1985, there were thirty small two-story brick homes on Hanover Place. Six were

Figure 7. Open-air drug market on Hanover Place, 1984. Photo by Linda Wheeler/*Washington Post*.

occupied by home owners. Ten were abandoned. The city had assessed them at about $25,000 apiece. With abandoned homes, an open-air drug market, accumulated piles of trash, and frequent shootings, Hanover Place had become a symbol of all that was wrong with the city. Police chief Isaac Fulwood vowed to change this and enacted Operation Avalanche in 1985, which involved stationing sixty police officers at Hanover Place. Fulwood told a *Washington Post* reporter, "Businesses will come if they know the police are going to be there."[1]

It would take more than just carceral investment, yet Hanover Place has indeed transformed. By 2021, the row houses and abandoned buildings on Hanover Place had been converted to condominiums—some priced at over three-quarters of a million dollars.[2] These homes are marketed as highly walkable, as residents can walk to Harris Teeter, Trader Joe's, a bevy of new restaurants, and the remodeled Union Market, which features a gourmet food hall, restaurants, and a movie theater.

Gentrification, the process of neighborhood change whereby high-income residents (the gentry) move into a neighborhood once dominated by low-income residents, is usually characterized by scholars as a process that happens exclusively in poor, disinvested neighborhoods with aging housing stock.[3] The transformation of Hanover Place from a blighted block into a block with upscale condominiums meets most definitions of gentrification. However, just a few blocks north of Hanover Place lie Bloomingdale and Eckington, which were home to Black working- and middle-class residents in the late twentieth century. The Black gentry—civil servants, doctors, lawyers, college professors, and teachers—lived in these neighborhoods alongside the Black working class—police officers, plumbers, janitors, and bus drivers. In Bloomingdale, many of the homes feature charming architectural details and are over 3,000 square feet. One such Bloomingdale home is located at 50 V Street, NW, adjacent to the Crispus Attucks Park where I attended the fund-raiser. It was built in 1909; it has five bedrooms and four baths and features a Victorian-style fireplace, exposed brick walls, and a Queen Anne roof. This historic row house sold for an astonishingly low $64,900 in 2002, as decades of disinvestment in Bloomingdale had devalued the housing stock. This in turn created an opportunity for profit-driven reinvestment. Ten years later, in February 2012, buyers paid $1 million for the house.

Bloomingdale has experienced racialized reinvestment as public and private investments in community well-being (as opposed to solely in policing and prisons) have accompanied the arrival of White residents. An analysis of Bloomingdale over the past seventy years makes it clear that the cycles of investment, disinvestment, and reinvestment are directly correlated with the arrival and departure of White residents. In Bloomingdale and across DC, neighborhoods where White people have moved in have experienced private reinvestment, as evidenced by rehabilitated houses as well as new coffee shops, bars, and eateries. They also have experienced public investment, as evidenced by public works, clean streets, and newly rebuilt schools and libraries.

The first two chapters of this book explain the extent to which neighborhoods originally built for White occupancy like Petworth,

Eckington, and Bloomingdale experienced disinvestment after White people left. The next two chapters describe how the city and federal government responded with carceral investments to the social issues created by disinvestment. This chapter explains how these neighborhoods came to experience reinvestment and how this reinvestment is racialized. To understand how these neighborhoods have experienced racialized reinvestment, it will be useful to first consider in more detail how gentrification played out in Washington, DC.

ONE HUNDRED THOUSAND NEW
HIGH-INCOME RESIDENTS

In Washington, DC, city officials promoted gentrification as a solution to its fiscal woes. At the end of the twentieth century, the city was embroiled in a series of crises that included high levels of violent crime, heavy policing of Black neighborhoods, disinvested schools, and a lack of public services that culminated in a congressional takeover of the city's budget. In 1995, Congress passed legislation that created the Control Board; it took responsibility for the city's budget away from elected officials. One upside of this takeover is it allowed members of Congress to see clearly that congressional mandates had created insurmountable deficits. Washington, DC, has the unique status of being a city that is not within a county or a state. It thus must operate a motor vehicle office and a prison system as a state would and a library system and a jail as a county would, in addition to all the other functions a city normally performs. Moreover, Congress had severely limited the city's revenue sources by banning a commuter tax and preventing the city from taxing any of the land owned by the federal government, embassies, and nonprofits. At the end of the twentieth century, these mandates meant that two-thirds of the income earned in DC was taxed in Virginia and Maryland and that the city was prevented from drawing property taxes from 42 percent of its land. Despite these fiscal constraints, the city had to provide services to commuters and non-taxpaying residents.[4]

To address the budgetary crisis caused by its mandates, Congress passed the National Capital Revitalization and Self-Government Improvement Act. This Revitalization Act was designed to reduce the city's deficit by having the federal government assume the city's pension obligation as well as control of many city services. This included the management of DC residents convicted of crimes. The local prison, Lorton Reformatory, was closed in 2001, and prisoners were dispersed to federal prisons around the country. This continues to be the case today: DC does not have its own prison system.[5]

The Revitalization Act provided a much-needed bailout to the city and eventually created a situation where the Control Board could be dismantled. However, Congress was not willing to return power to the city while Marion Barry held elected office. The creation of the Control Board had taken nearly all power from the city's elected mayor. With the stripping of Barry's power, along with a series of personal and political crises, the much-beloved "Mayor for Life" announced he was not running for office in 1998. This sudden announcement paved the way for the city's chief financial officer, Anthony Williams, to run for and win the mayoral election. Shortly after Williams took office, the Control Board returned much of its budgetary control to the mayor's office, making it clear that the board's qualms primarily had to do with Marion Barry. Three years after voters elected Anthony Williams, in 2001, the Control Board disbanded entirely and left the city with a balanced budget.

Although these reforms led to a balanced budget, the city was still constrained in its taxing authority and needed to find ways to address its revenue problems. Mayor Williams thus commissioned a study, which concluded that the city needed to attract new middle-class residents to increase revenue. In short, the city needed gentrifiers to move into the city to ensure enough tax revenue to provide services to its residents. The city did not need to go far to find potential residents; it simply needed to convince high earners already working in DC to live there rather than commute to the suburbs. Mayor Williams announced a ten-year plan to reverse five decades of population loss and attract one hundred thousand new high-income residents.[6]

Anthony Williams did not seek reelection in 2006. Adrian Fenty swept up 89 percent of the votes to become the city's next mayor. Fenty, like Williams, is African American. Whereas Williams styled himself as a quiet bureaucrat, Fenty positioned himself as a hip cosmopolitan ready to take the city in new directions. He appointed Michelle Rhee chancellor of the school system. Rhee's neoliberal reforms moved the schools further along a path toward privatization, alienating many DCPS teachers and parents in the process. Fenty also eliminated bureaucratic hurdles for developers, leading to a boom in high-end apartment and condominium construction as well as an array of upscale restaurants and bars. These new developments, like the changes to the school system, ignored the needs of long-term Black residents. Ultimately, Fenty's failure to pay attention to his Black constituents led to his loss in the 2011 mayoral election to Vincent Gray.[7]

Although many people mocked Williams when he announced his plans to attract 100,000 new residents to DC, the population increase exceeded even these lofty expectations, first during Williams's administration and then during Fenty's. The city's population reached nearly 700,000 in the 2020 US Census, up from 572,059 in 2000. At the same time, the city has become wealthier and Whiter. Some neighborhoods, however, have changed more than others. The area south of Hanover Place, closer to downtown, has been completely redeveloped. In the 1990s, this area was disinvested, with abandoned buildings, light industry, public housing, government buildings, parking lots, and cheap motels, where teenagers would hang out after going to the go-go. It has now experienced new-build gentrification: older buildings have been leveled and high-rises built in their place. The area has become completely unrecognizable to long-term residents. When I visit the area south of Hanover Place, I have no sense of familiarity with the place. In contrast, Bloomingdale and Eckington, where racially restrictive covenants and petitions kept Black residents out in the 1940s, have been gentrified through rehabilitation of older housing stock. When I walk through these neighborhoods, the streets and housing look similar to how they looked in the 1980s and I don't feel disoriented. Here the physical changes in the housing landscape have been more cosmetic, and the neighborhood retains its historic character.

BLACK DISPLACEMENTS

Gentrification requires city planners to designate areas for growth and private investors to decide to invest their funds in these areas. In 2002, the Office of Planning developed a strategic action plan for each neighborhood in the city.[8] These neighborhood-level plans were incorporated into the 2006 Comprehensive Plan and have since been carried out to different degrees. For example, the 2006 Comprehensive Plan indicated that "Kennedy Street should evolve into a more vibrant mixed use shopping area, with vacant storefronts reoccupied once again and new opportunities for local-serving businesses," but the Kennedy Street Corridor Revitalization Plan was not adopted until 2008, and the street continued to be under construction in 2023.[9] In some cases, the plans have gone nowhere. The 2006 Comprehensive Plan notes that the area around Capitol View was underserved by retail stores and services, including sit-down restaurants, banks, hardware stores, and drugstores, but this continues to be the case as commercial private investors have not yet been attracted to the area (although, notably, in 2021, this area had the highest percentage of investor-purchased homes in the city).[10] In other cases, the redevelopment plans have taken off.[11] The NoMa Vision Plan and Development Strategy was adopted in 2009, and as a result of the implementation of the NoMa Business Improvement District (BID) in 2007, that area has undergone a complete transformation. The BID is funded by a special tax assessment collected from property owners within a thirty-five-block area that lies just south of Eckington.[12]

Although early scholarship on gentrification highlighted what happens when high-income residents move into a low-income neighborhood, recent scholarship on Washington, DC, makes it clear that race is paramount. Gentrification in DC involves attempts to redefine and reshape Black spaces. For many Black long-term residents, DC has long been a "Chocolate City," a city where Black people held both the demographic and political majority and where Black people created their own spaces of belonging, pride, and self-reliance.[13] The equation of gentrification and Black displacement in DC is so salient that a recent study of gentrification in Bloomingdale focuses almost exclusively on race, practically ignoring class. The author, Allison Helmuth, argues that gentrification is not simply the "displacement of lower-income people," but "provides a context in which white residents effectively, efficiently, and powerfully claim space."[14] As Zawadi Rucks-Ahidiana astutely explains, gentrification occurs in places defined by both race and class and is always both racialized and focused on the accumulation of profit.[15] This relationship can be seen clearly in Bloomingdale: when White residents reclaim space, housing prices go up.

Recent work on gentrification in DC, including Derek Hyra's *Race, Class, and Politics in the Cappuccino City* and Brandi Thompson Summers's *Black in Place*, focus primarily on neighborhoods that became sites of concentrated poverty and racial isolation in the aftermath of the 1968 uprisings. Summers describes how Blackness came to be valued as a prized aesthetic at the same time that Black people were experiencing the heavy policing, predatory lending, and displacement that make possible and accompany the gentrification of Black neighborhoods.[16] Similarly, Hyra describes how the Shaw neighborhood—which transformed from 90 percent Black in 1970 to 30 percent Black by 2010—promotes its history as the cultural epicenter of the Black community with odes to

Marvin Gaye, Langston Hughes, and Duke Ellington in the names and artwork of new establishments that cater to White residents. Hyra also explains how new residents implement the changes they want even when these changes do not meet the needs of long-term residents.[17] Thus Black residents experience both political and cultural displacement as they have lost political and economic power. Hyra argues that the current wave of gentrification, which involves the wholesale demolition of public housing projects, is "the new urban renewal."[18] On the other hand, the anthropologist Gina Pérez describes a slower process of gentrification whereby disinvested neighborhoods experience reinvestment through housing rehabilitation designed to attract residents with higher incomes.[19] My analysis makes it clear that both kinds of gentrification are happening in DC and that both forms of reinvestment are racialized. A comparison across neighborhoods makes this clear.

WHITE FLIGHT TO WHITE RECLAMATION

In the 1940s, there were racially restrictive covenants on homes in neighborhoods across Washington, DC, from Chevy Chase to Shepherd Park to Petworth to Benning Road to Anacostia. These covenants existed primarily on blocks with single-family brick homes built for White occupancy. After the Supreme Court ruled in 1948 that the covenants were not legally enforceable, White people began to leave Bloomingdale, Eckington, and Petworth, which then quickly became over 90 percent Black. Mount Pleasant and Shepherd Park became majority Black by the 1980s, although significant numbers of White residents remained. Intense activism by interracial coalitions of residents helped prevent many White residents from fleeing to the suburbs. However, in the rest of the city racial turnover was quick and comprehensive, with many neighborhoods turning from 100 percent White to nearly 100 percent Black in less than a generation. Today these neighborhoods are rapidly losing Black residents.

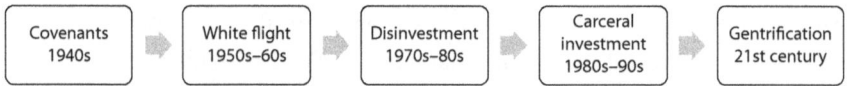

Figure 8. White reclamation trajectory.

I call this trajectory from racially restrictive covenants to White flight to disinvestment and carceral investment to gentrification *White reclamation*—the process whereby White people return to neighborhoods originally built for White occupancy (Fig. 8). I use *reclamation* to signal the fact that these areas were developed for White people. This historical trajectory is important and largely unexplored by previous researchers. Scholars who focus on White flight tend to highlight neighborhoods that became sites of concentrated poverty.[20] Few scholars have considered the direct linkages between the coercive policies of the War on Drugs and gentrification in working- to middle-class Black neighborhoods, although there is a growing literature on policing and gentrification.[21] This discussion of gentrification through White reclamation explains what happened when Black families bought homes in previously all-White neighborhoods and how disinvestment and then carceral investment laid the groundwork for gentrification and the return of White people to neighborhoods originally built for White occupancy.

Uptown neighborhoods like Mount Pleasant, Petworth, Bloomingdale, Eckington, and Shepherd Park experienced disinvestment beginning in the 1970s, although to different degrees. Even Shepherd Park, an elite area with expensive homes, a high median income, and a college-educated population, experienced public and private disinvestment in the 1980s. The local high school, Coolidge High, was physically deteriorating. Liquor stores, hair salons, corner stores, and fast-food places were the primary establishments in the area. If residents wanted a sit-down meal, they would have to travel to primarily White areas of the city or across the District line to Silver Spring, Maryland. The uptown areas were described by the local media as war zones, with lurid descriptions of violence and the drug trade. Operation Violent Gang Safe Streets targeted them with massive raids in the 1990s, followed by an exodus (in varying degrees) of the middle-class Black population. Had these working- to middle-class Black neighborhoods not experienced disinvestment followed by carceral investment, they would not be gentrifiable.

FROM DISINVESTMENT TO GENTRIFICATION IN ECKINGTON AND BRIGHTWOOD PARK

The White reclamation trajectory is clear in both Brightwood Park and Eckington, which transformed from all-White to nearly all-Black and back again between 1950 and the present. Brightwood Park went from 1 percent Black in 1950 to majority Black in 1960. By 1970, only 458 White residents remained in Brightwood Park, accounting for 8 percent of the population. By 1980, it was 96 percent Black. In the 1980s, this middle-class, primarily Black neighborhood suffered from a cascade of crises, including increased criminalization of Black youth, the devastating effects of HIV/AIDS, a severe recession that caused many businesses to shutter, and the migration of middle-class Black families to the suburbs.

Brightwood Park's population also declined from 6,612 to 4,631 residents between 1970 and 2000. The people who departed were most of the 445 White residents who lived there in 1970 but also over 1,000 Black residents. In the six-month span between September 16, 1990, and March 3, 1990, four men—Stanley Lee, Luis Robert King, Ruel McPherson, and Milford Rucker—were shot and killed in separate incidents in the unit block of Longfellow Street, NW. Brightwood Park was not poor but experienced the violence of disinvestment.

Similarly, Eckington had a median income around the citywide median but also very high homicide rates. The Eckington neighborhood transitioned from working- and middle-class White to working- and middle-class Black in the 1970s. Eckington's McKinley Tech continued to be an excellent high school after desegregation, but in the 1970s and 1980s, when the neighborhood became majority Black, the school experienced disinvestment and decline. In the early 1990s, there were several violent incidents on the campus of McKinley Tech. Four shootings occurred in the first two weeks of September 1991; and in 1994, a student stabbed another student after a basketball game. In 1997, McKinley Tech closed its doors after 180 graduates walked across the stage. The city cited reduced enrollment and lack of available funding for repairs as the reasons for the closure. The school remained closed until 2004.[22]

Decades of disinvestment in Eckington and Brightwood Park created a situation where the housing stock became devalued and gentrification became possible and profitable. Both Eckington and Brightwood Park had average household incomes around the citywide median during the second half of the twentieth century. These neighborhoods shifted from White to Black during this time, but most socioeconomic indicators remained the same—with the percentage of people with higher education and median household incomes close to the citywide median in 2000. These neighborhoods became gentrifiable not because of the presence of low-income residents but because of depressed housing values and disinvestment. At the end of the twentieth century, housing prices had barely budged from their 1980 values (after taking inflation into account).

Since 2000, these neighborhoods have experienced gentrification, as evidenced by higher housing values, higher numbers of college-educated residents, and increased home values (Figs. 9a and 9b). These changes have been accompanied by an increase in White residents and a decrease in Black residents.

The primary form of reinvestment visible in Eckington and Brightwood Park is the rehabbing of older housing stock.[23] This is an ongoing process, as both neighborhoods have some houses that are in visible

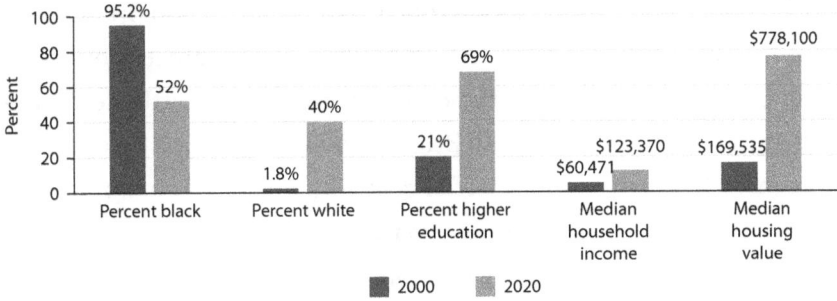

Figure 9a. Eckington (Census Tract 87.01) demographics, 2000 and 2020.

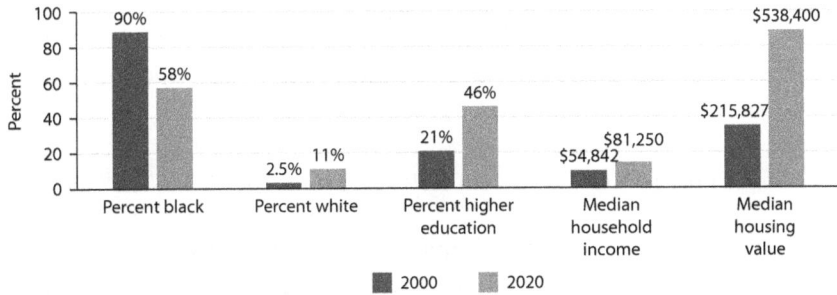

Figure 9b. Brightwood Park (Census Tract 21.02) demographics, 2000 and 2020.

need of repair. In 2020, Brightwood Park had eleven boarded-up houses. Eckington had just three. In both neighborhoods, most blocks had some houses with minor decay—meaning that the paint was peeling, or the roof showed some signs of the wood cracking, or something else along those lines. There were also some homes with major decay, such as large cracks in the roof or decaying wood in the windows. Our housing survey used the "time travel" feature in Google Street View to look at how the neighborhoods had changed since 2007, the earliest year available for most blocks. We were able to see that in both areas most blocks had at least some houses that had minor upgrades such as new landscaping or exterior paint. In Brightwood Park, only six, however, had major upgrades such as the addition of an entire floor. Eckington, in contrast, had twenty-four houses with major upgrades.

Although the city designated Kennedy Street (which is in Brightwood Park) as an area for commercial revitalization, this process has been slow. Our study shows that these neighborhoods had little new-build gentrification as of 2020. In both Brightwood Park and Eckington, there were just a few signs of commercial gentrification. In Brightwood Park, for example, there is the Library Tavern, a bar with a colorful patio and a wide beer selection; Jackie Lee's, a hipster dive bar; and La Coop Café, which offers a wide variety of coffee drinks in a tranquil setting. There were just three locales like this in Eckington in 2020: Qualia Café, which serves Ethiopian coffee; a Boba Tea Shop; and a social club. In Brightwood Park, there were three large-scale new developments. In Eckington, there was just one: the Gale Eckington apartment building.

FROM REDLINING TO GENTRIFICATION IN PETWORTH

The same pattern of White reclamation that occurred with a few thousand people in the two census tracts of Brightwood Park and Eckington occurred in the larger area of Petworth, which has a total population of about 25,000 residents and three commercial streets, Georgia Avenue, Kennedy Street, and Upshur Street—all of which the city has designated for redevelopment. Petworth has never been a poor neighborhood. The median household income remained around the citywide median until 2019, when it increased to about $10,000 above the citywide median. When I was growing up in Petworth in the 1980s, most homes were well maintained and landscaped. Many of my friends lived in intergenerational homes, often ones their grandparents had purchased. However, there were signs of economic disadvantage: a 9 percent unemployment rate and 22 percent of children living in poverty in 1990 (Table 4). In addition, the local schools were not serving students well and the crime rate was high. These structural disadvantages were an outcome of disinvestment in the neighborhood, making it ripe for gentrification.

TABLE 4
Petworth: Population and Socioeconomic Factors, 1970–2019

Race/Ethnicity						
	1970	1980	1990	2000	2010	2019
Total	30,662	26,849	24,553	22,957	23,078	25,499
White	1,687	716	696	1,012	3,057	6,463
Black	28,780	25,824	23,279	19,691	15,822	14,162
Asian (including PI)	n/a	64	98	127	319	480
Latinx (Hispanic/ Spanish)	n/a	336	926	2,519	4,933	5,243

Socioeconomic Indicators						
	1970	1980	1990	2000	2010	2019
% Unemployment	3.7	6.4	8.1	9.1	12.8	7.8
% Poverty	9.2	10.7	10.0	15.1	11.4	7.4
% Childhood poverty (under 18 years)	n/a	n/a	11.3	22.0	17.0	3.6
Median household income (adjusted in 2019 $)	n/a	58,007	62,333	58,081	61,724	95,528

Home Ownership						
	1970	1980	1990	2000	2010	2019
Black home owners	4,431	5,007	5,013	4,645	3,884	3,121

Home Value						
	1970	1980	1990	2000	2010	2019
Median home value (adjusted in 2019 $)	—	192,029	192,603	190,275	442,139	584,700

SOURCE: Manson et al., IPUMS National Historical Geographic Information System: Version 17.0 [dataset].

NOTES: Data are from Census Tracts 21.01, 21.02, 22.01, 22.02, 23.01, and 24.00. The population totals are different from the sum in each column due to missing data on racial identification as well as the fact that, starting in 1980, people could identify as both Hispanic and with a racial group.

Home values in Petworth remained stagnant between 1980 and 2000. At the turn of the twenty-first century, Petworth's good housing stock, stagnant home values, and record-low interest rates rendered it attractive to investors. Investors bought and flipped brick row houses in the neighborhood—turning a high profit in a short time that far exceeded the profits the long-term residents netted.

In 2016, Petworth was ranked *first in the nation* for the profits one could make from flipping a home, with online articles even specifying that "grandma's house" was most likely to have profit potential.[24] These opportunities for profit coincided with decreases in the number of Black residents but not in increases in wealth for those residents. For example, Dr. Hinton purchased a home in Petworth in 1953 for about $20,000. He was the first Black resident on his block. By 1970, his block had become nearly all-Black. In 1998, the Hintons sold their home for $230,000 to a Black family. In 2019, this family sold the home for $700,000 to investors. Six months later, the investors had flipped the home and sold it for $1.3 million, turning a greater profit in six months than the Hintons had on a property they owned for forty-five years. Once White people began to move into Petworth, property values soared, and real estate investors profited immensely. By 2019, just 55 percent of the residents of Petworth were Black (see Table 4).

Stagnant home prices between 1980 and 2000 meant that many long-term Petworth residents had little equity in their homes and thus were not in a position to take out home equity lines of credit to remodel their aging homes and flip them themselves. Moreover, it was difficult to secure home equity lines of credit in the late twentieth century because banks redlined Petworth and other majority-Black areas of the city. James Lloyd interviewed real estate professionals who worked in DC in the 1970s, 1980s, and 1990s and found evidence of continued redlining. One realtor explained to Lloyd that banks were often unwilling to grant loans in majority-Black areas. One woman owned a home in Mount Pleasant and wanted to take out a home equity line of credit in the 1970s, but the bank denied her request even though her home was fully paid for. A young lawyer wanted to purchase a home in Brookland (a majority-Black neighborhood similar to Petworth), but the bank denied the loan request, alleging the electrical wiring was faulty. The young lawyer had the resources and connections to contest this denial. However, most prospective buyers and home owners did not have these resources and had to resort to securing mortgages from mortgage bankers rather than savings and loans, which often had more favorable terms. Of course, paying higher interest and fees on mortgages also inhibits building home equity.[25]

Lloyd's study makes it clear that redlining and lending discrimination continued well into the 1990s, despite laws that had rendered both practices illegal. In one egregious example, a study found that only 3 percent of the mortgages made by the Chevy Chase Federal Savings Bank between 1976 and 1992 were in DC neighborhoods that were not White. Moreover, an employee admitted that they were explicitly told not to issue mortgages "south of Calvert Street NW or east of Connecticut Avenue, with exceptions only for Capitol Hill and Dupont Circle." Consequently, the Department of Justice ordered the Chevy Chase Federal Savings Bank to both open branches in Black neighborhoods and commit to making home loans in those areas.[26]

These legacies of anti-Black policies and practices mean that many Black families do not have enough wealth to purchase a home in Petworth. In 2019, the census reported a median home value of $584,700 in Petworth, but this does not fully reflect home prices. The city has subsidized a few affordable housing sites along Kennedy Street. Many of these are owner-occupied apartment condominiums that have replaced row houses. In November 2021, a two-bedroom apartment in one of these buildings was advertised for $209,000, available to families of four earning less than $100,000. In the nonsubsidized market in November 2021, there was one unrenovated row house for sale for $625,000 and one renovated row house for sale for $939,000.[27] It is difficult to become a home owner in Petworth unless you have intergenerational wealth.

"THEY CHANGE IT, THEY PUSH YOU OUT"

In 2017, the *Washington Post* reported that Upshur Street in Petworth was one of the best places to eat in the city. The journalist Holley Simmons wrote that before the arrival of hot new restaurants like Timber and Himitsu, Petworth had "little more than a Pizza Hut, a few takeout joints and Domku, a since-shuttered Scandinavian restaurant."[28] Of course, though Simmons was not aware of it, Petworth had also been home to Goins Restaurant, one of the most popular soul food restaurants in DC since 1963—until it closed in 2007. And in the 1960s, there were several eateries along both Kennedy Street and Georgia Avenue, the other two commercial streets in Petworth. Today these streets feature new businesses that cater to gentrifiers. Along these streets, many of the brick row houses and apartment buildings built in the 1930s and 1940s are being replaced by four- and five-story condominiums made of less sturdy material (Fig. 10). In July 2021, after a few days of rain, a building under construction on Eighth and Kennedy Streets in Petworth collapsed.

The day the building collapsed, my brother and I had decided to visit three of the new bars on Kennedy Street. We were incredulous that we could go bar hopping on Kennedy Street. Our first stop was Anxo, a cider brewery. From there, we went to the Library Tavern, which featured a comedy night that evening. Then we went to Jackie Lee's, a dimly lit bar that hosted Trivia Night on the second floor. Nearly all the patrons in these three establishments were White. Two of the patrons in Anxo were tourists who had found the cider brewery on Yelp and had come all the way up to Kennedy Street to check it out. There were few tourists in Petworth in the 1980s and 1990s because there were few destinations that catered to them. Instead Petworth was primarily a residential community with few sit-down restaurants. It did have bars and nightclubs that catered mostly to African Americans in their forties or older. There were also a couple of spots farther up Georgia Avenue that catered to a younger

Figure 10. Kennedy Street, June 2021. Two older row houses in center flanked by two new constructions that also used to be row houses. Photo by author.

crowd, such as the Ibex, which frequently had go-go bands and turntables, which had a DJ who played dancehall every weekend.

Many long-term Petworth residents view the changes favorably. It is nice to have sit-down restaurants in the neighborhood. It is great that the corner store sells sparkling water, oat milk, and Sauvignon Blanc from New Zealand. And it's hard to lament the closure of liquor stores that residents fought against being opened in the first place. The real question is: Why did these changes take so long?

Carl grew up in Petworth. He pointed out that when he was growing up there was a strip club and a pool hall on Georgia Avenue, just down the street from his house. Carl explained that these locales were also adjacent to the public school and public library:

> I remember there was a pool hall down the street on Georgia Avenue. It used to be a strip club down there. . . . [I]t's right across the street from a library. I didn't think about that back then. But now, of course, you don't want that element around your children. . . . Me being fifty years old, I can appreciate the direction that DC is going in. And I'm not saying I like it, but if I think about the long run, if I think about what type of city I would want my grandchildren to come up in, of course I can appreciate the direction it's going in.[29]

In addition to having more family-friendly locales such as an improved public library and restaurants where children are welcomed, interviewees reported that their neighborhoods are safer than they used to be, as Kwame—who also grew up in Petworth—emphasized in his interview: "Any time crime will go down, it's better. At one time, you couldn't really go anywhere unless you had a pistol with you. Now it's more comfortable, U Street and H Street, Adams Morgan, and even Georgia Avenue, the whole corridor . . . I like it."[30]

Darnell lives a couple of blocks from the Midlands Beer Garden in Park View, whose website describes a thoughtful draft and bottled beer selection, including twenty-six beers on tap. The website also notes that Midlands is dog-friendly. Park View is just south of Petworth. My brother and I went to check out Midlands in 2019. Nearly all the patrons were White. The twenty-six beers included a sour from Belgium and a local IPA, but the only beer I had heard of was Pabst Blue Ribbon. Midlands is located across the street from what is now a dental office but was once home to the Black Hole, a club that regularly hosted go-go bands in the 1980s and 1990s, including Rare Essence and Junkyard Band. When I used to go to see these bands, I never saw any other

White people. In those days it would have been surprising to see a White person at that intersection at any time of the day or night. As my brother and I sipped our beers in Midlands, a group of White young people dressed in bikini tops and shorts passed by the bar, carrying towels, headed to the neighborhood pool. Darnell opined:

> It's amazing to see people just running and jogging through the alley. White women walking around with short-shorts on, walking through the crowds of teenage Black guys. Seeing dog stores, little pet shops open up where it used to be liquor stores. Yoga, salsa dancing schools, all this is along the area where it used to be heroin strips, and where all the true, deep alcoholics used to hang out.[31]

Like Park View and Petworth, much of the city is changing. These changes involve not only the arrival of White people but also the transformation of the neighborhood into a site of profit. The White people who moved into Petworth in the 1990s were less well-off than its Black residents. In 2000 White residents had a per capita income (in 2019 dollars) of $23,835, as compared to Black residents' per capita income of $28,391. Latinx residents have consistently been the least well-off group in the neighborhood, with a per capita income of $17,903 in 2000. The arrival of low-income White and Latinx residents paved the way for higher-income White people, who began to arrive in the twenty-first century.

Kwame said that he doesn't have a problem with gentrification or racial changes, but the problem is "when you move in and push everybody else out."

> Nobody cares about living next door to White people. . . . You're automatically expecting that we're about to get pushed out because when they come in, that's their goal. Most White people don't really like to live around Black and Brown people, from what I experience. I think that's the problem with gentrification. I guess it wouldn't be called gentrification if

two White people move into a Black neighborhood, and it stays the same way. I think the gentrification comes in when they change it, they push you out. Twenty years later, it's no Blacks in this neighborhood.

You definitely see it has to have some racism involved because the rest of them wouldn't have come if these wasn't here obviously.[32]

As Kwame astutely pointed out, the arrival of a small number of White people makes the neighborhood more comfortable and appealing to other White people. In turn, those White residents start to make the neighborhood uncomfortable for long-term residents. Kwame explained, "So now the same people that used to live in the neighborhood could come into a place that you've been your whole life, and people are looking at you strange like you don't belong here. You feel uncomfortable."[33]

Some of the newer White residents make it clear to the long-term Black residents that they do not like Black people or Black culture. This creates tensions. Tyrell's family moved to Clifton Street when the neighborhood was experiencing White flight and not too long after the racially restrictive covenants were lifted. Clifton Street is just south of Park View. By the time Tyrell was in high school, all the White families except for one had left. Tyrell lived on this block for forty-seven years. He moved a few blocks north when he retired in 2012 but returns nearly every day to shoot the breeze with his buddies. He and his friends set up plastic chairs and hang out on the corner, as they have done for decades. My research assistant and I interviewed Tyrell on Clifton Street. Throughout the interview, Tyrell shouted out greetings to folks passing by and even invited a couple of folks to come over to share their perspectives. One of the people he invited over was a Black man in his eighties who had lived in the neighborhood for fifty years. He was one of twenty-three (of 289) long-term residents who was able to stay in his mixed-income building where market-rate two-bedroom apartments are renting for $4,000 a month.[34]

Some of the new White residents, however, take issue with their use of public space and call the police on them. Tyrell explained that the police know they are not doing anything wrong and leave them alone. Another new resident threatened to call the police on Tyrell because of where he parked his car. Whereas long-term residents are unlikely to use the police to settle these kinds of issues, some of the newer White residents are quick to call the police for anything they perceive as an inconvenience. Tyrell told me about the prejudice he experienced:

> There is a lot of prejudice. I really acknowledge people want to move from wherever they have been and where they are coming from to transition to something else. But you have to look at people that have been here all these years. You want to be the new neighbor in the neighborhood; rules and regulations are not going to change because of you.[35]

Tyrell thinks newcomers should adapt to their surroundings rather than try to force changes on the neighborhood.

The finding that many Black people feel that gentrifiers try to make them feel out of place in their own neighborhood is similar to the findings of other researchers in DC. Kathryn Howell describes similar racialized battles over public space in nearby Columbia Heights. Allison Helmuth also finds that White gentrifiers claim space in ways that can make Black people feel unwelcome. And Sidney Holt finds that White gentrifiers either call the police or threaten to call the police on Black people simply for congregating in their own neighborhood.[36] Our finding is confirmed by quantitative analyses: data from the Metropolitan Police Department reveal higher levels of policing of Black residents in historically Black neighborhoods that have recently experienced an influx of White residents.[37]

Both Carl and Darnell agreed that there are negative and positive sides to gentrification. Darnell said he sometimes feels "out of place" because of the changes, but some of the changes are positive. Carl explained:

> It changed drastically, drastically. Absolutely. Absolutely. I look at it as a good thing and somewhat negatively, just in, as far as people come in the

neighborhood, I get the feeling sometimes that they look at us like we don't belong, and that bothers me sometime. We've been born and raised here. . . . But you make it seem like we are visitors in our own city.[38]

Antwan summed up a lot of the responses to gentrification: "I like to see the new things. The city is clean. Crime is down. Prices are too high. It's good and bad."[39]

In a survey of one thousand residents of DC, 85 percent of White people agreed that gentrification was mainly a good thing, whereas only 42 percent of Black people agreed with that statement.[40] Our qualitative findings reveal that many people can see both the positive and negative effects. Long-term residents of Petworth and other uptown neighborhoods built for White occupancy were happy with many of the changes that gentrification has brought about. They like the reduction in crime and welcome the new businesses and cleaner streets. The downside, however, of White people moving in was twofold: some of the new White residents behave in exclusionary ways toward long-term Black residents; and the arrival of White residents has coincided with an increase in the cost of housing.

BLACK HOME OWNERSHIP AND INTERGENERATIONAL WEALTH

There was not a lot of variation in how our interviewees described gentrification—whether they were from uptown or downtown, from middle-class or poor neighborhoods. Nearly everyone defined gentrification as White people moving into the neighborhood and the changes that came along with that, particularly increases in the price of housing. These findings are similar to what the psychologist Sidney Holt found in her focus groups with eighty-three Black men in DC in 2013: the arrival of White people and the displacement of Black people are critical aspects of gentrification in DC.[41]

Although the home values in Petworth began to increase in the twenty-first century, this has not translated into prosperity for Petworth's Black families. Of the thirty-seven returning citizens we interviewed, thirty-three came from families where either their parents or grandparents had owned a home in DC. (In Washington, DC, activists and advocates refer to formerly incarcerated people as returning citizens.) Nineteen of the men we interviewed were from uptown, and either the parents or grandparents of these men owned homes. The grandparents were the generation most likely to have owned a home: in twenty-five of the thirty-seven cases, at least one of the grandparents had owned a home in DC. Home ownership, however, did not translate into intergenerational wealth for these men. A consideration of the structural factors sheds light on why this is.

The stagnation of home values along with labor market disparities have interfered with intergenerational wealth transmission. Home values were stagnant in majority-Black neighborhoods, which put a serious dent in Black people's ability to build wealth. The joblessness crisis of the 1980s meant that there are relatively few cases where Black men in DC were raised in homes with two working parents. This financial insecurity continues. In 2016, the unemployment rate for Black residents of DC was 17 percent, as compared to 3 percent for White residents. Contemporary labor market disparities are a result of decades of disinvestment and carceral investment: inadequate public schooling means that Black people in DC are less likely to have completed college than White people, and carceral investment means that Black people are more likely to have spent time in prison. Only 3 percent of people with bachelor's degrees or higher in DC are unemployed, whereas over two-thirds of DC's returning citizens who are in community supervision programs are unemployed.[42]

Despite the history of home ownership in their families, only four of the thirty-seven returning citizens we interviewed own homes—two in DC and two in Maryland. In one case, James owns a home in Shaw because he purchased it before his incarceration and his sister took care of it during the sixteen years he was behind bars. In another case, Carl shares ownership of his grandparents' home in Petworth. Carl's grandparents left the home to his mother, who in turn left the home to Carl and his sister. Carl would like to buy his sister out so he can move into the home, which they are currently renting out. He may eventually be able to do that as he is married and both he and his wife have steady employment. Edward and Dodson both own homes in Maryland that they were able to purchase after securing employment with the DC government. Dodson lost his job with the DC government and was working as an Uber driver when I interviewed him. He and his girlfriend were still able to make the mortgage payments.

Thirty-three of the thirty-seven men we interviewed came from families with a history of home ownership in DC. In twelve of these cases, the home was still in the family. In most cases, however, having a home in the family is unlikely to translate into home ownership for future generations, often because there are too many heirs. In an effort to keep the home in the family, Black home owners in DC often name one individual as the heir. For example, when Edward's grandmother died, she named his aunt as the sole heir of her home. Similarly, Darnell's grandmother named his aunt as the sole heir. When there is one person in the family who earns enough to maintain the home and who has earned the grandparent's trust, the grandparent often leaves the home to that person. This was not the case for any of our formerly incarcerated interviewees, but some of my childhood friends have become home owners by being designated as the sole heir. Black home owners in DC are tenacious about keeping the home in the family; naming one heir is often the best way to do this.

In some cases, there are several homes in a family, and this increases the chance that an heir will inherit one of them. For example, Troy's family bought several homes in DC and still owns some of them. Both sets of Troy's grandparents owned homes: one in Petworth and the other in Shepherd Park, two neighborhoods where many of the District's upper-middle-class Black families lived in the 1970s. Troy's mother went to university and became a journalist. She divorced his father, who fell into drug addiction, and remarried. Troy's stepfather was often out of work, so his mother was the primary breadwinner. Nevertheless, she was able to purchase a home in Shepherd Park in the 1970s.

Troy and his wife rent an apartment in the Maryland suburbs. Troy would like to own property uptown, as his grandparents and mother did. With several home owners in his family, Troy expects an inheritance at some point. In his case, this may translate into his ability to purchase a home because, like Carl, Troy is married, and he and his wife both have incomes. Troy and Carl are the only two interviewees who can see a path to home ownership uptown.

In nineteen of the cases with a history of home ownership in DC, the home is no longer in the family. In some cases, the interviewee's parents were home owners and decided to sell and move elsewhere when they retired. For example, Terrence's parents owned a home in Petworth. They both had stable jobs: his mother was a registered nurse, and his father was a bus driver. His parents retired and moved to Maryland. Other people's parents sold their homes and moved into retirement residences.

In other cases, the homes are no longer in the family and property ownership is out of reach for the whole family. For example, several interviewees recounted that their parents had inherited the grandparents' home but had lost it because of prolonged financial stresses. Kendall's grandparents owned a four-unit apartment building in the Trinidad neighborhood that they had purchased in 1977. They lost it as a result of overdue taxes in 2012. The building is now worth well over $1 million. Similarly, Malik's grandparents lost their home in Anacostia because of overdue taxes in 2016. It was sold in a tax sale for $60,000 in 2016. Five years later, the home was valued at half a million dollars.

Another reason home ownership did not translate into intergenerational wealth transmission is that parents or grandparents sold the home when it was not worth a great deal. Although they often had owned these homes for decades, the homes had not increased in value, and it would have been hard to predict that home values were going to increase any time soon.

Arthur's grandparents owned a home in Mount Pleasant. It may have seemed like a good deal when they sold their home for $200,000 in 2000. That home today, however, is worth over $1 million. Similarly, Clarence's mother, a nurse, owned a home in Trinidad, which she sold for $170,000 in 2010. That home today is worth around $750,000. Antwan's parents bought their home in Bloomingdale in 1981. They sold it twenty years later for $60,000. Today it is worth $750,000. Sean's family sold his grandmother's home in Trinidad when she died in 1994 for $36,000. Today it is worth nearly $700,000. Christopher's parents owned the three-bedroom home where he was raised. They sold the home in 2001 for $72,550. Its value today is about $450,000.

Few of the interviewees continue to live in the neighborhood where they were raised. Most live in other parts of the city or, more commonly, in the primarily Black Maryland suburbs. Arthur is an exception; he lives in the neighborhood where he was raised. He is renting an apartment at a below-market price and will be able to stay there if the building is not sold or renovated. Darnell lives in his great-grandmother's house in the neighborhood where he was raised. He will be able to live there so long as his aunt, who currently owns the home, allows him to do so. As Darnell, who lives in the home his great-grandmother purchased, explained, the changes in the neighborhood affect him both emotionally and financially: "[The neighborhood has] changed a great deal. I'm almost feeling like I'm out of place when I step out of the house. . . . I can't even afford to live there if I wanted to buy a house. It's becoming a place where I truly would not be able to afford to live."[43] Darnell captures the cognitive dissonance experienced by long-term residents. His neighborhood, once ravaged by violence, now features several hip bars and other businesses that cater primarily to monied White residents. Whereas it would have been rare to see White people on this part of Georgia Avenue in the 1980s and 1990s, today they are commonplace. The influx of White people has led to higher housing costs. If Darnell's aunt decides to sell her home or if she names an heir who does not want him to live there, Darnell will have to leave the neighborhood.

Maurice is from the Trinidad neighborhood. He captured a common sentiment: "I went away for twenty-five to twenty-six years. It's totally different. . . . It was few and far between that you would see a European or a person of another race walk down our street."[44] Clarence is from the same neighborhood. I asked him how the neighborhood has changed since the 1990s. "Well," he replied, "at one o'clock in the morning, you see somebody that's White walking their dog at night, and that would never happen back in the late eighties and early nineties like that. It would've never happened at midnight . . . it was everything Black only in our neighborhood, and now it's not."[45]

Many of the new buildings on Kennedy Street and Georgia Avenue in Petworth are part of DC's inclusionary zoning program, a system that makes homes available to purchase below market prices by low-income home buyers. These one- and two-bedroom condos are selling for around $200,000. At these prices, they are affordable for many of our interviewees and many other returning citizens who have secured stable employment. However, they are offered through a lottery program. As of 2015, about three hundred homes had been listed through the inclusionary zoning program, yet five thousand people had registered for the lottery.[46] Some of our interviewees had registered for the lottery program but none had heard back. Thus home ownership, even in the form of a small condo on Kennedy Street, remains elusive. As Clarence explained, "The Caucasians basically took over all the houses in Trinidad. It's like, once again, they pushing us out, because they know we can't afford no million-dollar, $700,000 houses right now."[47]

Most people we spoke with grew up in neighborhoods where it would be unusual to see White people in the 1980s. It was particularly jarring to see White people in neighborhoods that were 98 or 99 percent Black in the 1990s. The exceptions to this are those people who grew up in Takoma Park, Shepherd Park, and Mount Pleasant, where, Troy explained, "you had government workers, business owners, White, Black, Italian, Koreans; we had everything on that block."[48] Similarly, Elijah described Takoma Park as diverse when he was growing up: "Some of the cultural changes and diversity changes you see are not really new. It may be more prevalent or more in your face. But when I was a kid we went to school with Spanish people, White people, all types. That part of Northwest was just like that. I mean even with West Indians and South Americans."[49]

Nevertheless, nearly everyone we asked about gentrification in DC pointed to race. Marcus, from Bloomingdale, described the changes in a similar way:

> It's become more diverse. I've seen more people of different ethnicities and different backgrounds living in my neighborhood that normally wouldn't be living there. . . . Biggest shock of coming home was just how developed DC is and just . . . I don't know, I feel like a foreigner. I feel like an alien and I'm a native Washingtonian. It's been difficult to wrap my mind around.[50]

CONCLUSION

Decades of disinvestment in Black neighborhoods in DC meant that home values remained stagnant in Petworth, Bloomingdale, and Eckington between 1970 and 2000. This stagnation in home values created what the gentrification scholar Neil Smith calls a rent gap, that is, the difference between the land value and its potential price after the neighborhood is rehabilitated.[51] Stagnation in home values both created a rent gap that made neighborhoods like Petworth and Eckington attractive to investors and prevented many Black home owners from accumulating wealth through home ownership.

In the twenty-first century, these areas have become sites of potential profit because of the existing housing stock, the desire of monied White people to live in these places, and the devaluation of property values in the twentieth century. These neighborhoods were built for White occupancy, and White residents have returned to lay claim to them. White people are able to purchase these homes because of their access to intergenerational wealth and higher education.

Anti-Black racism has a significant effect on housing prices in a racial capitalist system. When White people leave a neighborhood, real estate prices fall, and when they move back in, prices increase. Anti-Black racism also shapes public investments. When Coolidge, Roosevelt, and McKinley Tech became majority Black, they experienced disinvestment. Thus they all had high dropout and low college-enrollment rates in the 1980s and 1990s. The primary investments these neighborhoods received were carceral. As these neighborhoods have experienced an influx of White residents, there have been increases in investments in the community's well-being. Reinvestment, accompanied by the arrival of White residents, has led to significant increases in home values, which in turn has made the neighborhoods unaffordable to many long-term residents—due in large part to the decades of disinvestment and carceral investment.

White families who moved to the suburbs in the mid-twentieth century found excellent schools. Their homes steadily increased in value. When White teenagers in Bethesda engaged in illegal activity, the likelihood that they would end up in prison was practically zero. These families, unlike many Black families who stayed in the city, have been able to build the wealth necessary to reclaim land in DC's now-coveted historic districts. The next chapter discusses in more detail neighborhoods that have been demolished and their different trajectory to gentrification.

6

RACIALIZED REINVESTMENT

HOPE VI, New Communities, and the
End of Public Housing

IF YOU VISITED KENNEDY STREET in the 1990s and returned today, you would notice that several row houses have been replaced by small condominium buildings. You would see a smattering of upscale bars and cafés. You might wonder what happened to the two dry cleaning shops, some of the carryout restaurants, the laundromat, and the arcade. You may note that the Black-owned Sewell Music Conservatory, which had been there since 1952, has been replaced by condominiums, and the welfare office has been replaced with a yoga studio. You may notice that one of the funeral homes now has signs in Spanish and that there is a small grocery store with a Spanish name. It would be hard to miss the presence of permanently stationed police cars and tall surveillance stations on Fifth, Seventh, and Ninth Streets. You would observe that although there are still groups of Black men and boys hanging out on the corner, there are far more White people milling about than there used to be. If you are from this area, you may wonder why the upscale restaurants, bars, and yoga studio only came along once White people moved in.

If you were to visit Navy Yard after being away for two decades, the changes on Kennedy Street would seem insignificant by comparison. Navy Yard has been completely transformed, and you would be unlikely to recognize any landmarks or even intersections. Reshena Johnson, who grew up in Navy Yard, explained:

> I'm born and raised in DC. I'm from Southeast. For me, where the stadium is, that's the part of Southeast where I grew up. I don't even recognize it anymore. It took me a long time to be able to ride through that area without crying because it was like my whole childhood was obliterated.[1]

To say Navy Yard has been gentrified is an understatement. It would be more accurate to say the neighborhood was demolished and built anew. Nearly everything in the neighborhood has been destroyed: single-family homes, apartment buildings, public housing, gas stations, warehouses, nightclubs, a boathouse, government buildings, a trash transfer station, fast-food restaurants, and vehicle depots. The buildings that were not demolished, such as the St. Vincent de Paul Catholic Church at 14 M Street, SE, and the Carroll Senior Apartments at 410 M Street, SE, are the exception rather than the rule in Navy Yard.

Unlike the working- and middle-class majority-Black neighborhoods analyzed in chapter 5 as examples of White reclamation in areas developed for White residents and therefore without public housing, this chapter focuses on three neighborhoods that were once dominated by public housing: Navy Yard (Census tract 72), Capitol View (Census tract 99.03), and Barry Farm (Census tract 74.01) (Map 4). This analysis makes clear that the trajectory leading to gentrification in these neighborhoods looks very different from the trajectories in areas originally developed for White occupancy.

In chapter 1, I explained that the FHA map characterized Barry Farm, Capitol View, and Navy Yard as areas that had "undesirable

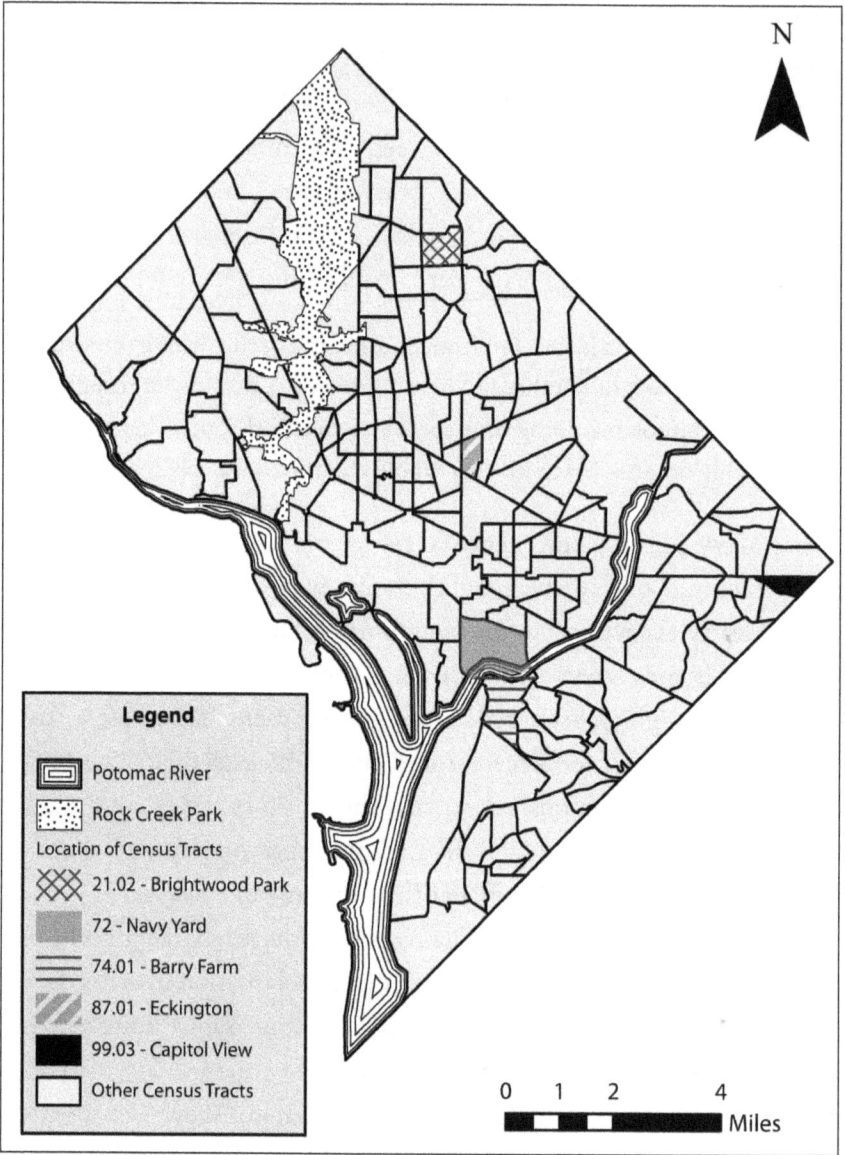

Map 4. Locations of census tracts.

| Slum clearance 1940s | Public housing 1950s–60s | Disinvestment 1970s–80s | Carceral investment 1980s–90s | Demolition 2000s | New-build gentrification 2010-present |

Figure 11. From slum clearance to gentrification.

populations" and were "risky investments," thereby making them prime candidates for slum clearance in the 1940s. The federal government then built public housing in each of these redlined areas, yet, as explained in chapter 2, failed to invest in community well-being, which led to violence and subsequently carceral investment, as explained in chapter 3. This chapter picks up the story by focusing on public housing demolition and subsequent patterns of racialized reinvestment (Fig. 11).

The patterns of reinvestment in Navy Yard, Capitol View, and Barry Farm make clear how racial capitalism intersects with anti-Black racism. In a capitalist system, investments are made in a neighborhood when there is a clear potential for profit. These decisions, however, are made in the context of anti-Black racism. The desire for profit combined with anti-Black racism creates a situation in which investments in Black communities tend to be carceral while those in White communities often enhance community well-being.

FROM DISINVESTMENT TO RACIALIZED REINVESTMENT IN CAPITOL VIEW, BARRY FARM, AND NAVY YARD

Capitol View, Barry Farm, and Navy Yard experienced the violence of disinvestment in the late twentieth century and the large-scale demolition of housing projects in the early twenty-first century. These areas, once dominated by public housing, have become the targets of Homeownership and Opportunity for People Everywhere VI (HOPE VI) or New Communities Initiative (NCI) redevelopment plans, what Derek Hyra calls new urban renewal, but this renewal has taken different forms according to the racial composition of the population.[2] In majority-Black Capitol View, public housing was replaced by mixed-income

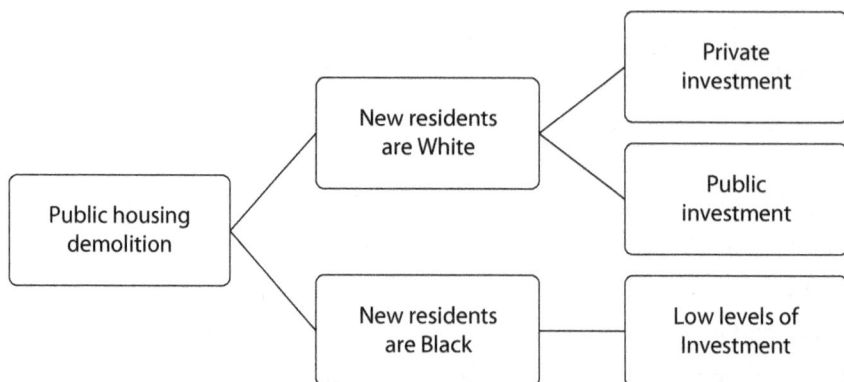

Figure 12. Racialized investments after new-build gentrification.

housing. Although Barry Farm Dwellings has been demolished, the planned new developments have yet to be built, and almost all the residents are Black and low-income, as has been the case for decades. Navy Yard has been built anew, and now nearly all the residents are White. These areas have experienced racialized reinvestment, meaning that the level of public and private investment in each of these neighborhoods is inversely correlated with the percentage of Black residents. The investment patterns subsequent to public housing demolition are clearly racialized. The pattern I delineate in this chapter is as follows: when the new residents are White, as they have been in Navy Yard, the area experiences a total transformation; when the new residents are primarily Black, the changes are minimal (Fig. 12).

The area around where Barry Farm Dwellings once stood experienced relatively little private reinvestment as of 2022, leaving a series of empty lots surrounded by shuttered businesses. This area has continued along its long trajectory of population decline. Our 2019 survey revealed there were fifty abandoned buildings, no structures with major upgrades, and no establishments that cater to gentrifiers.

In Capitol View, the new development has focused on residential housing. Here rows of new townhouses have replaced the two housing projects that once dominated the area. The rest of the neighborhood looks much as it has since the 1950s, with rows of small brick homes interspersed with redbrick apartment buildings. Capitol View has remained nearly all-Black, with a mix of Black home owners and public housing residents. In 2019, three-quarters of the homes in Capitol View were owner occupied, and 87 percent were single-unit houses.

In contrast, reinvestment and redevelopment have completely transformed Navy Yard. New high-rise buildings block the view of the freeway that defines the neighborhood's borders, separating it from Capitol Hill. Developers destroyed entire blocks of homes and small businesses to build Nationals Park, a massive baseball stadium. Two large housing projects were demolished and replaced with mixed-income communities. The city also built a modern river walk along the southern end of the neighborhood, transforming a riverbed with chain-link fences and overgrown weeds into a boardwalk with a white sculptural bridge and a water wall. According to analysts at the University of Minnesota, Navy Yard had the highest rate of gentrification in the country. In 2000, the neighborhood was 77 percent low income; by 2016, that number had plummeted to 21 percent. This is not the result of a sudden rise in income among the inhabitants but instead of large-scale displacement of low-income residents, facilitated by the demolition of the public housing projects.[3] At the same time, Navy Yard has become majority White.

NEW-BUILD GENTRIFICATION THROUGH PUBLIC HOUSING REDEVELOPMENT

The federal government introduced the HOPE VI program in 1992 to subsidize the replacement of traditional high-rise and barracks-style public housing with small-scale developments of mixed-income single-family homes and townhouses. HOPE VI was part of a series of government interventions designed to address the "destruction by neglect" that was rampant in public housing projects by the 1980s.[4] Policy makers developed HOPE VI based on social scientific research that showed the harmful effects of living in areas characterized by concentrated poverty and racial isolation.[5] The federal program invested billions of dollars to replace dilapidated public housing with mixed-income communities.

The DC Housing Authority applied for redevelopment grants from the HOPE VI program to demolish several of its housing projects, and since 1992, 4,000 of DC's 11,000 public housing units have been demolished, with plans to demolish even more.[6] When DC public housing residents are displaced, they either move to existing public housing or are given Housing Choice Vouchers, which allow them to rent homes in the private sector at discounted prices.[7] This is part of a national trend: as of 2011, only one million of the 4.5 million units of federally assisted housing in the United States were in traditional public housing. The remaining 3.5 million units consisted of privately owned units where either the tenants or the building owner received a subsidy to cover a portion of the rent.[8]

In 2005, Mayor Anthony Williams introduced a new program with goals similar to that of HOPE VI. This program, called the New Communities Initiative (NCI), has three key principles that distinguish it from HOPE VI: (1) one-for-one replacement of public housing units; (2) residents have a right to return; and (3) a build-first ethos meant to ensure new housing is built before demolition. NCI shares with HOPE VI the goal of building mixed-income communities. Navy Yard and Capitol View were redeveloped under HOPE VI grants, whereas Barry Farm is part of NCI, along with three other neighborhoods, Sursum Corda, Lincoln Heights, and Park Morton.[9] Although NCI started in 2005, it is far from complete. And although the promise to "build first" is a key part of NCI, this promise is often unfulfilled.

NAVY YARD: NEW-BUILD GENTRIFICATION AND BLACK DISPLACEMENT

When the Navy Yard Metro station opened in 1991, it was clear both to city officials and local developers that this waterfront area, just one mile south of the US Capitol, had profit potential. Real estate speculators purchased empty lots and warehouses in anticipation of a future real estate boom. These speculators also lobbied the DC Council to rezone large swaths of the area from industrial to mixed-use development.[10] Ten years later, the Capper/Carrollsburg Dwellings, the Southeast Federal Center, and the Navy Yard still occupied much of the acreage in Navy Yard. The demolition and repurposing of these three sites in the early twenty-first century was the first step in a dramatic transformation of this area.

It is conceivable that the massive changes in Navy Yard could have happened without the demolition of public housing, but they did not. In 2001, HUD issued a $34.9 million HOPE VI grant to demolish the Arthur Capper and Carrollsburg Dwellings and replace them with 707 public housing units, 525 affordable rental units, and 330 market-rate homes for purchase. When the residents of the public housing complexes heard that the DC Housing Authority (DCHA) planned to demolish their homes, they began to organize. Two-thirds of the residents signed a petition objecting to the proposal, stating concerns about the availability of substitute housing during the projected years between demolition and construction. They were right to be worried: many of them would have to wait over a decade to return to what had become an unrecognizable space, and most would not be able to return at all.[11]

DCHA decided to move forward with the plans anyway, although the residents' campaign did garner a promise of "one-for-one" replacement. In principle, this agreement meant at least one new unit of public housing would be built for each unit demolished. In practice, not all residents would be able to return. The 297 seniors in the senior building would be offered the opportunity to return to the 300 new units built for seniors. But while DCHA promised to rebuild 580 units to replace the 410 public housing units, most of these would be reserved for households earning between $27,000 and $73,000 a year—far higher than the average $8,000 annual income of the residents of the Arthur Capper and Carrollsburg Dwellings in 2001. Construction for the new housing development, called Capitol Quarter, began in 2004.[12]

Rose Oliphant is one of the few public housing residents who was able to return to Capitol Quarter, the affordable housing complex that replaced Arthur Capper Dwellings. It took years of planning and budgeting for her to do this. The DCHA and developers explained to Arthur Capper Dwellings residents that there would be units available for people who met the income and credit requirements. Ms. Oliphant participated in workshops, took on an additional part-time job, and worked to get her credit in order. Six years after she was displaced, she was able to return to a home that was in much better condition than the Arthur Capper Dwellings. In a short video made by the filmmaker Ellie Walton, Ms. Oliphant explains that she loves her new home; however, there are two caveats: when she walks outside, people look at her as if *she* doesn't belong in the neighborhood where she has lived for several decades, and she wishes more of her friends and neighbors from Capper were able to also enjoy the new homes in Capitol Quarter. The Capper/Carrollsburg Dwellings was a community, and that community was destroyed to make way for new developments.[13]

Nearly all the neighborhood's residents have been displaced. In 1950, over 6,000 Black people called Navy Yard home. This number declined steadily over the next seventy years. Jacqueline DuPree, a local documentarian, estimated there were fewer than 400 people in Census Tract 72 in 2005, after the demolition of the public housing and before the rebuild. The percentage of White residents has steadily increased since then, making up over two-thirds of the census tract's residents in 2020

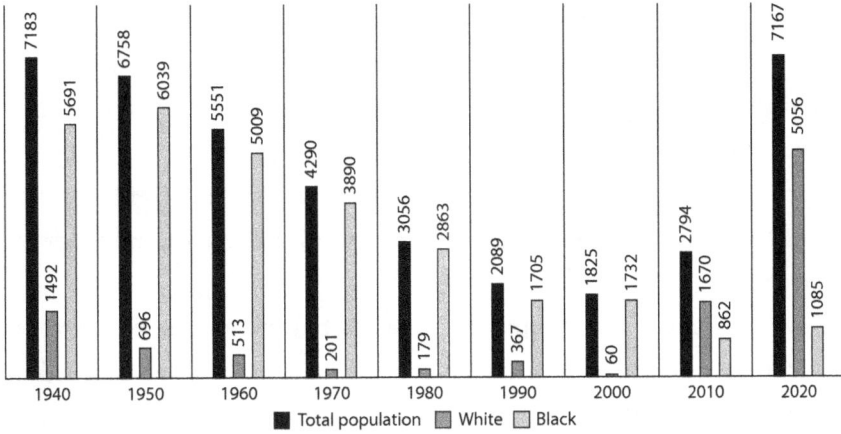

Figure 13. Navy Yard population by race, 1940–2020.

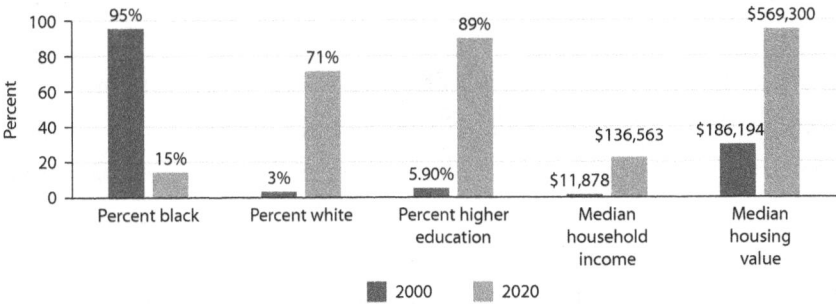

Figure 14. Navy Yard demographics, 2000 and 2020.

(Fig. 13). In addition to racial change, there were changes in class composition: between 2000 and 2020, the median household income in Navy Yard increased eleven-fold; the percentage of people with a college degree increased fifteen-fold; and the average home value increased threefold (Fig. 14).

By 2020, with a median income of $136,563, with 89 percent of adults having a college degree and with only 15 percent of the residents Black, Navy Yard was no longer an area of concentrated poverty or racial isolation (as this term is used to describe majority-Black spaces). This dramatic transformation, however, involved the displacement of nearly all the residents who were living there at the beginning of the twentieth century. The only people not displaced are the residents of a subsidized senior apartment building called Carroll Senior Apartments, which has forty-six one-bedroom apartments. The DCHA website indicates that Carroll Senior Apartments was built in 1964 and modernized in 1999.

In Navy Yard, redevelopment went far beyond the new HOPE VI housing development. A mixture of public and private funding led to significant developments, including the relocation there of Naval Sea Systems Command (NAVSEA), massive environmental cleanup of the Anacostia River, the redevelopment of Southeast Federal Center (SEFC), the creation of Nationals Park, and the development of Yards Park.

DC officials lobbied the navy to move NAVSEA to the Navy Yard because the arrival of thousands of workers was expected to bring revenue to the city and revitalization to a disinvested area. In January 2001, the site opened. Developers built three high-rise, mixed-use buildings adjacent to the site, with the expectation that the four thousand workers would want services such as restaurants, retail shops, and housing in the area. This development on the southeast corner of Navy Yard marked the beginning of its transformation. At the same time, a mix of nonprofit, public, and private entities came together to begin a much-needed cleanup of the Anacostia River, which would eventually transform it into a prime destination for kayaking.[14]

The navy had given the western portion of the Navy Yard land to the federal government's General Services Administration (GSA) in 1963. For decades, government officials debated what to do with the land and its buildings. In 2000, at the urging of DC's congressional representative, Eleanor Holmes Norton, Congress passed the Southeast Federal Center Public-Private Act of 2000, which allowed the GSA to enter into agreements with the private sector related to this fifty-five-acre parcel. In February 2002, the Department of Transportation agreed to be housed in a building at the northern edge of the site. GSA contracted with the JBG Development Corporation to build the new headquarters for the Department of Transportation, and the agency moved into the new building in 2007.[15]

In 2004, GSA contracted with Forest City developers to develop the remaining forty-four acres of the Southeast Federal Center. This project culminated in "The Yards," which includes loft apartments, a retail building, restaurants, a park, a grocery store, and a fitness center. The Yards, built by a developer, funded and owned by the DC government, and managed by the Capitol Riverfront Business Improvement District, was completed in 2013. In addition to commercial and residential real estate, the Yards includes a five-acre waterfront park with a promenade along the Anacostia River.[16]

In the 1990s, the southwestern area of Navy Yard featured an asphalt plant, a trash transfer station, car repair shops, warehouses, and nightclubs. In 2005, these businesses all received notice that they had to move. Property owners would be compensated, but the city needed the land for Nationals Park. After extended negotiations over the value of the land, the occupants had no choice but to sell to the city, and the baseball stadium broke ground in 2006.[17]

By 2018, the District of Columbia broke even on its $1.1 billion investment in Capitol Riverfront in the Navy Yard area.[18] The building of the stadium and the overall reinvestment also helped fulfill the city's goal of attracting high earners from the Maryland and Virginia suburbs to DC—both to spend money in the city and to make DC their home.[19] The area has experienced significant public and private investment, which has generated revenue for the city and profit for the private investors. This has not been the case (thus far) in Capitol View or Barry Farm; the major difference between these areas is that most of the new residents in Navy Yard are White.

Navy Yard is densely populated: it has 122 blocks with 445 structures, 343 of which are residential. Nearly all the historic single-family homes in Navy Yard have been destroyed. Thus the gentrification in Navy Yard is nearly all new-build. Unlike in the other neighborhoods where nearly all the buildings were old, in Navy Yard our housing survey revealed that over half the buildings were new. Only six buildings had major decay, and only five were boarded up. And there were over a dozen establishments that cater to gentrifiers, including trendy restaurants, cafés, bars, juice shops, and a Whole Foods. This was not the case in Capitol View.

CAPITOL VIEW: GENTRIFICATION WITHOUT BLACK DISPLACEMENT OR PRIVATE REINVESTMENT

The redevelopment project in Capitol View received a $30.8 million HOPE VI grant in 2000, the year before Navy Yard received its HOPE VI grant. As in Navy Yard, this grant was intended to demolish public housing and replace it with mixed-income housing and a retail center. The housing portion of the HOPE VI project was completed, yet the neighborhood has not experienced anywhere near the same level of development as Navy Yard.

Capitol View is a relatively isolated neighborhood on the far eastern edge of the city. The imposing Robert F. Kennedy Stadium and the Anacostia River separate it from the city's more central areas. Today it is mostly a quiet residential neighborhood with little foot traffic. It has a Metro station at each end, although you may have to walk up and down substantial hills to get to them, depending on how far you live from the main throughfare, East Capitol Street. If you were to pass through on a summer afternoon in 2021, you might see people sitting on their porches. Almost everyone you would see would be Black.

The two housing projects that once dominated Capitol View—East Capitol Dwellings and Capitol View Plaza—have been demolished. In 2003, after fifty years of neglect and disrepair, East Capitol Dwellings was razed, displacing 649 families. Of these, 428 families were given Section 8 vouchers to move to privately owned apartments, and 221 moved to other public housing projects. The white-and-beige siding on the townhouses that replaced East Capitol Dwellings strikes a contrast with the rows of redbrick houses and apartment buildings built in the 1950s.

Evelyn Brown moved to East Capitol Dwellings in 1969. She raised seven children there and led the tenants' council. In the 1990s, her daughter and two of her nephews were gunned down near her home. Still Ms. Brown, who was seventy years old in 2003 when the buildings came down, felt attached to the neighborhood. She used her Section 8 voucher to rent an apartment four blocks from her former home.[20]

Capitol View Plaza towers were built in 1971 and demolished in 2009. The new HOPE VI development, called the Capitol Gateway project, was designed to provide 761 mixed-income units, with 230 of the homes available for sale, in addition to a retail center. When Capitol Gateway Estates was completed in 2005, about one-third of the families from East Capitol Dwellings were able to return to the new development, which had 379 total units (151 senior housing units, 142 home owner units, and 86 rental units). In all, only seven East Capitol Dwellings families were able to return as home owners.[21]

The retail center never materialized. A 100,000-square-foot shopping center that was supposed to accompany the redevelopment was not built, in part because Walmart pulled out of the plan.[22] Thus residents continue to shop at a small and dilapidated strip mall and must travel several miles to access a grocery store. The neighborhood lacks grocery stores, cafés, and sit-down restaurants. The former site of Capitol View Plaza was home to a large urban farm in 2022.

The racial composition of Capitol View has barely changed since the 1990s. Although the neighborhood has technically gentrified, insofar as the median household income and the home value have increased and the poverty rate has decreased, little on the surface has changed.

The HOPE VI development has changed the demographics of the area. Between 2000 and 2020, the median household income in the cen-

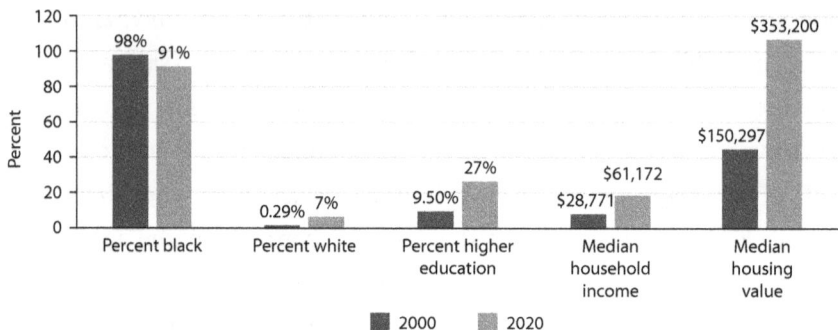

Figure 15. Capitol View (Census Tract 99.03) demographics, 2000 and 2020.

sus tract where this redevelopment project is located doubled, the percentage of people over the age of twenty-five with a college degree tripled, and the median home value more than doubled. The rise in average income, home value, and median educational attainment can be attributed to both the arrival of new home owners and the displacement of families living in public housing. The majority of new residents are Black, as was the case for long-term residents before development occurred, but they have higher incomes and higher levels of educational attainment than the residents they replaced. Nevertheless, the neighborhood's economic indicators remain below citywide averages. And housing prices have continued to rise, following national trends (Fig. 15).

Characterizing both Navy Yard and Capitol View as "gentrified" gives us little insight into the tremendous differences between these two neighborhoods. In 2019, my research team implemented a housing survey in Barry Farm, Navy Yard, and Capitol View to assess the level and forms of reinvestment in these neighborhoods. In Capitol View, the housing survey revealed moderate levels of both decay and rehabilitation, with 107 of 631 residential structures having minor upgrades and 149 having minor decay. Similarly, 26 nonresidental structures had major upgrades and 25 had major decay. What is remarkable about Capitol View is that despite demographic indicators of gentrification, there is a complete absence of commercial establishments associated with gentrification. As of 2022, there were no cafés, bars, or upscale eateries in Capitol View.

BARRY FARM: DEMOLITION OF PUBLIC HOUSING AND REDEVELOPMENT PLANS

In 2006, the city government announced its plans to demolish Barry Farm Dwellings' 441 housing units and create a mixed-income community. In response, residents of Barry Farm Dwellings formed the Barry Farm Tenants and Allies Association to appeal the redevelopment plans. They knew demolition would mean the end of the community they had lived in, some of them for decades, and fought against it. The disputes led the city to put the plans on hold until September 2020, when the city and activists came to a compromise and the city approved a new plan. This plan involved 380 replacement public housing units, 320 affordable housing units for rent, and 40 affordable housing units for sale, as well as 160 for-sale units at market rate. The new plan also included 40,000 square feet of retail. The timeline for this plan is eight to ten years.[23]

At the end of September 2022, the city broke ground on the Asberry, a building that will be completed in 2024 and is projected to have 108 units of affordable housing for seniors and 5,000 square feet of commercial space. The residents of Barry Farm had been relocated three years earlier, in 2019, with some of them moving into other public housing projects and others provided with housing vouchers.[24]

Paulette Matthews, born in 1959, is one of the displaced residents. Ms. Matthews's parents owned a large home in Northeast when she was a child, and she is the only member of her family to live in public housing. As a single mother of four children working in low-wage jobs, living in public housing allowed her to keep a roof over her family's head. For Ms. Matthews, the twenty years she lived in Barry Farm Dwellings brings both good and bad memories. On the one hand, she lamented being separated from the friends she had made there. On the other hand, she explained to Sabiyha Prince, who recorded her oral history, the DC Housing Authority was "the biggest slumlords that have been able to exist," as it allowed Barry Farm to fall into disrepair, with "rats, bedbugs, leaks," and other issues.[25]

This was a consistent refrain in the narratives from the Barry Farm Oral History Project: residents appreciated the large apartments and open spaces Barry Farm Dwellings offered, as well as the community feeling. They wondered why DCHA didn't fix the problems of leaks, decay, and rodent infestation and instead chose demolition. The DCHA claimed demolition was the best alternative, but residents found that hard to believe. Michelle Hamilton, for example, lived in Barry Farm Dwellings for twenty years. She wanted to stay because she liked her large apartment. However, after extended battles with bedbugs and rodents, she accepted an offer to move a short distance away to Sheridan Station, a new affordable housing development. Ms. Hamilton told Sabiyha Prince:

> I was living in horrible conditions. I didn't want to give up my three-bedroom so I sat living like that which I didn't have to. . . . I'm not fighting for Barry Farm no more, I gotta go 'cause I can't live like this, I wasn't raised like this and I'm not going to live like this no more. They gave me an apartment over the Sheridan I fell in love with it . . . I miss my friends . . . I don't miss the shootings and the killings.[26]

Another former resident, Nicole Odom, who was born and raised in Shepherd Park, had a five-bedroom apartment in Barry Farm where she, her husband, and their seven children lived. When she was given a housing voucher and told she had to leave Barry Farm Dwellings after living there for ten years, it was challenging to find a place large enough for her family. She eventually found a place in Park View that is close to the Metro stop as well as grocery stores and her children's schools. She can afford this home because of the Housing Voucher Program. When asked about her hopes for Barry Farm, Nicole reflected:

> I hope Barry Farm is redeveloped, but it doesn't turn into one of these typical new communities, mixed-income communities where . . . like over at Navy Yard or Arthur Capper where the lower-income people are discriminated against and just treated like crap and ignored and disrespected. And the people that move into the community just have no idea that that was a community before they moved in there.[27]

In Kalfani Nyerere Ture's 2017 dissertation on Barry Farm Dwellings, he describes several residents who were displaced from Arthur Capper Dwellings to Barry Farm Dwellings, only to be displaced once again when Barry Farm Dwellings was demolished. Ture also describes several other cases of repeated displacements, including a Black woman he calls Thelma Jenson, who was displaced from Shaw in the 1980s to Barry Farm Dwellings. Thirty years later, when the redevelopment plans for Barry Farm Dwellings were introduced, she fought hard not to be displaced from the community she had learned to call home. Thelma threw herself into community activism and eventually became president of the Barry Farm residents council. Nevertheless, DCHA moved her to Josiah's Terrace Apartments in 2012, where she lived until she passed away.[28]

The redevelopment plan in Barry Farm includes a one-for-one replacement of the 480 public housing units, although 100 of these units will be built off-site. Barry Farm was unusual in that it had large units, including six-bedroom apartments, and the redevelopment plan calls for three-, four-, five-, and six-bedroom units. The plan includes a total of 1,100 new residential units, and the remaining units will be for a mix of low- and moderate-income residents. In addition, the plan includes green spaces, grocery stores, restaurants, and business spaces.[29]

This plan is still in process, and the neighborhood has so far experienced little change apart from the displacement of the public housing residents. Census data tell us that the area around Barry Farm Dwellings has not gentrified. Median household income in the census tract declined from $21,166 to $14,859 (in 2020 dollars) between 2000 and 2020. In 2020, Census Tract 74.01 remained 89 percent Black, but that number is the smallest proportion of Black residents in this tract since 1970. The non-Black residents in 2020 were evenly divided between Asian, Latinx, and White. And although other gentrification indicators such as the percentage of people with a college degree and the average housing price have increased, they remain low. Between 2000 and 2020, the proportion of people over the age of twenty-five with a college degree increased from 2 to 14 percent, and the median home value increased from $214,775 to $272,500 (Fig. 16). It is worth noting, however, that the increase in housing prices during the COVID-19 pandemic has also affected this area. A three-bedroom home at 2529 High Street, SE, just half a mile from Barry Farm Dwellings, was sold for $290,000 to investors in August 2021; the investors remodeled it and listed it for $385,000 in October 2021. After three price reductions, it sold in January 2022 for $345,000. It remains to be seen if investors will be able to make profits in this neighborhood as in the sale mentioned above it appears that the investors barely broke even.

In Navy Yard, we witnessed a complete transformation of the neighborhood. Its physical landscape, economic indicators, and racial composition all underwent drastic changes. In Capitol View poverty has declined, but the neighborhood retains its feel as a community of Black home owners. In Barry Farm the changes are coming but have yet to materialize. So far, Barry Farm displays few signs of private investment.

Time will tell if Barry Farm will follow the path of Navy Yard or of Capitol View or if it will take a different path. Navy Yard's transition to a vibrant neighborhood involved the displacement of nearly all the Black residents. In Capitol View nearly all the residents are Black, as has been true historically, yet it has not transitioned to a vibrant neighborhood. This raises the question of whether the Barry Farm develop-

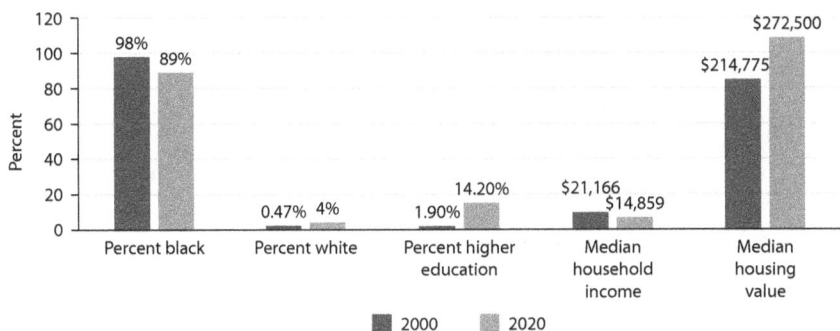

Figure 16. Barry Farm (Census Tract 74.01) demographics, 2000 and 2020.

ment will be able to remain a primarily Black community and experience the private and public investments its residents need to live comfortably and in community. In the rest of DC, both public and private investments have coincided with the arrival of White residents.

In 2007, the city approved the Capitol Riverfront BID in Navy Yard. In 2012, the city approved a BID in Anacostia, the neighborhood that abuts the land where the now-demolished Barry Farm Dwellings once stood. As of 2022, the Washington, DC, Economic Partnership described Anacostia as "bursting with potential" and Capitol Riverfront as "already thriving." Capitol View, in contrast, is only described as having "superior regional access" given its location abutting the District line.[30] The proximity of Navy Yard to the city center made the rent gap in this location potentially much bigger than in Capitol View. Nevertheless, the pattern whereby public and private investments in the neighborhood are correlated with the arrival of White residents is consistent across the city.

The Anacostia BID, one of eleven BIDs in DC, remained over 90 percent Black in 2019 and had a median household income that was less than half the citywide median. Although the BID has led to the development of a Starbucks, a Busboys and Poets, and a Capital One Café along Martin Luther King Jr. Avenue, the area continues to show more signs of disinvestment than of investment. Thus the BID has not led to high levels of investment in this majority-Black neighborhood, reinforcing the argument that investment is highly racialized.

RETURNING HOME TO A GENTRIFIED CITY

The Arthur Capper Dwellings occupied ten square blocks in Navy Yard. In addition to rows of brick townhouses, this area included ball fields and a recreation center. Some residents had lived there for decades. Ola Dixon, who worked in a mailroom at the Pentagon, is one of them. Ms. Dixon decorated her townhome with pride, putting in ceiling fans, new floors, fresh paint, and a cookout area in her backyard. Ms. Dixon's home was a central part of the community, where residents would gather to eat her famous fried chicken and enjoy a beer in her brick-lined backyard. She would grab items from the grocery store for her neighbors when she did her shopping, and they would return the favor. However, a series of hardships would cause Ms. Dixon's life to unravel. Her husband died in the mid-1980s; her elder son died of cancer in prison; and then her younger son, Keith McIlwain, was sent to prison in Winton, North Carolina, over two hundred miles away.[31]

The Revitalization Act stipulated that people convicted of crimes in DC would be held in a prison within a close radius of DC, but the Federal Bureau of Prisons has not complied. In 2010, a quarter of the 6,000 DC Code offenders in federal prisons were housed at facilities over five hundred miles away.[32] As of 2022, at least forty were in a federal penitentiary in Atwater, just ten miles from my workplace at the University of California, Merced.

In 2003, the DCHA told Ola Dixon she would have to move as the housing project was slated for demolition. She did everything she could to avoid leaving Arthur Capper Dwellings. She did not have a phone, and when the housing authority staff came to knock on her door she would not answer. Finally, in July 2004, they were able to convince her to move to Greenleaf Senior Home, a public housing high-rise in an adjacent neighborhood. Although Greenleaf Senior Home is just a few blocks from Arthur Capper Dwellings, sixty-five-year-old Ola Dixon felt stripped from her community. Her network of neighbors who used to help her with grocery shopping, car repairs, and yard work and were always willing to lend a friendly ear were gone. She worried whether her son would be able to find her when he was released from prison. Six months after she moved, ambulances were dispatched to her apartment; she had passed away a few days earlier from a stroke caused by hypertension. Had she stayed in Arthur Capper Dwellings, her neighbors would have noticed she was not doing well and may have been able to save her life. They certainly would have noticed if there was no movement in the apartment, and it is very unlikely so many days would have passed before her body was found. When her son, Keith McIlwain, was released from prison, he had no mother and no home to return to.[33]

Like Keith, many of our interviewees from poor neighborhoods struggled with affordable housing when they were released from prison. When their neighborhoods have gentrified, they can't afford to live there, and most of their family members have been displaced. When their neighborhoods have not gentrified, they often do not want to live there because the neighborhoods continue to be plagued by violence and poverty.

Most of the interviewees moved in with family members after their release. Sometimes this move was semipermanent. Sometimes it was temporary, until they could find a place of their own. Most returning citizens find it is extremely difficult to secure housing they can afford, even if they have full-time employment.

Malik grew up in a subsidized apartment building called Sursum Corda. His mother had grown up in a house her parents owned in Anacostia. However, she suffered from drug addiction and was not able to keep steady work, as her parents had done. Malik's father was incarcerated when he was young, further adding to the instability in his home life. Malik was locked up in 1997 for a murder he committed when he was sixteen. When Malik returned home from prison in 2020, Sursum Corda had been demolished under the New Communities Initiative and his grandparents' home had been lost because of overdue taxes. He was able to move in with his brother until he got back on his feet.

Malik did not have much trouble securing employment. A staff member from the prison where he was incarcerated took a liking to him and helped him find work with a transportation company upon his release. In addition, he got a part-time job counseling at-risk youth.

Malik did face other challenges, however. Having been incarcerated since he was eighteen years old, Malik had no credit history. Thus when he purchased a car to get to and from work, the interest rate was 22 percent. This contrasts sharply with the 1.9 percent interest rate I secured around the same time for my car loan. Whereas I would pay $31,766 over six years for my $30,000 car, Malik would pay $54,272.44 over six years for a car with the same price tag.

When Malik tried to find an apartment, landlords asked for references from previous places he had lived. He could only say that he lived with his brother and paid him $500 in cash for a room. His lack of formal rental history made finding an apartment challenging. Malik married a woman he had known since before his incarceration. Together they were able to find an apartment in Southeast. However, he does not like the neighborhood.

Malik told me he and his wife qualified for a mortgage for up to $250,000. They could purchase a home in the distant Prince George's County suburbs but not in DC for that amount, unless he was able to access the inclusionary zoning program, which requires winning a lottery. I asked Malik where he would like to live. He responded, "Somewhere there's no crime, where the crime rate is low, where there's peace and quiet."[34]

Edward has been home from prison for nearly a decade. In this time, he has established himself as a leader in the community of returning citizens. Despite his professional accomplishments, Edward can't afford to live in DC. He and his wife purchased a home in Prince George's County. Edward explained, "I love my city. I still do. I can't afford DC. I would love to live in my city but not at the price that it costs to live there."[35]

The few places in Washington, DC, that continue to be affordable to returning citizens are in communities like where Malik lives today—communities plagued by violence and with few local amenities. In the rest of the city, there is a sprinkling of affordable housing in expensive communities. Columbia Heights is an example of a neighborhood that has transformed from poor and working class to unaffordable. The area where Andre was raised had a median household income of nearly $100,000 in 2019, and the median value of owner-occupied housing was $659,000, with no owner-occupied homes valued at less than $300,000. It also was 45 percent White.

As Andre explained, today in Columbia Heights you have "million-dollar homes." The area also has lots of amenities, including a Metro stop, shopping, and eateries: "[You can now find] a Target, a Bed Bath & Beyond, a DWS, a Five and Below, Sports Authority, and then you have Giant, Starbucks, Chipotle, a lot of eateries around there. And the subway is there. It's a very convenient neighborhood to live in because you have access to so many things now."[36]

However, Andre can't afford to live there and benefit from these changes. As Christopher pointed out, "The only way you are going to be able to live in DC is if you're a doctor or a lawyer."[37]

The high price of housing was a key obstacle for formerly incarcerated people in DC. Another notable change was the arrival of White people in all parts of the city, as explained by Nigel: "My old neighborhood even changed. I mean, we saw two White girls walking with the little dog."[38] Nigel lives just across the District line from where he grew up in Southwest. His aunt had a house in Navy Yard, just across the river. When Nationals Park was built, his aunt was forced out. He explained that the stadium was built right where her house used to be. Nigel is thus hyperaware of the possibility that he could easily be pushed out, even if he were to buy a home. Nigel, like other interviewees, is not opposed to White people moving into his neighborhood. He just is aware of what happens when they do. Nigel explained that he expects to be pushed out of his neighborhood soon:

> I live right here by the harbor. They are putting all of these beautiful things up right here. All these new nice golf places. And every year our rent goes up, to the point where potentially we're going to have to move. They're still putting up new stuff and making it look pretty, and eventually, the Black folks are not going to be able to afford this no more, because the White people want to live closer to the harbor. And they're beginning to push us out.[39]

Although some neighborhoods have clearly changed more than others, there was not a lot of variation in people's responses to gentrification. There is a clear sense that the whole city, not just their neighborhoods, has changed. A couple of people pointed out that there are some areas that have changed less, like some parts of Southeast. But the sense that the whole city has changed takes on more importance in their minds.

CONCLUSION

This chapter makes clear the racialized patterns of investment subsequent to public housing demolition. I made the decision to analyze reinvestment patterns in Navy Yard, Barry Farm, and Capitol View based on census data. Based only on demographic data, Navy Yard was an ideal case of extreme gentrification, Barry Farm was an ideal case of a neighborhood that had not gentrified, and Capitol View was an ideal case of a neighborhood where the economic indicators had changed but the racial composition remained the same.

I had no idea about the major changes happening in Navy Yard or the lack of changes in Capitol View when I chose these cases. I visited the sites only after the case selection (which included Eckington and Brightwood Park, discussed in the previous chapter). Since that time, I have ridden a bike over most of DC. I find riding a bike preferable to windshield ethnography because it allows me to go more slowly and see things up close. It also allows me to cover more ground than walking. I also have ridden my bike to present and former public housing sites and along most of the city's new bike trails. In these trips, the pattern is consistent: When public housing demolition leads to an influx of White residents, private and public investment follows. When public housing is not demolished, there is little public or private investment, beyond continued carceral investment. And when public housing demolition leads to an influx of Black residents, there is little public or private investment. In neighborhood after neighborhood, high numbers of Black residents mean the neighborhood experiences carceral investment and high numbers of White residents mean the neighborhood experiences profit-driven private reinvestment.

My bike rides also allowed me to see that the city has funded the building of beautiful schools and libraries all over DC, in both poor and well-off neighborhoods. It is heartening to see architectural feats in some of the most impoverished areas. The Anacostia Library, the Capitol View Library, and the Francis A. Gregory Library are all beautiful, inside and out. The William O. Lockridge Library is in an area that is nearly all-Black and has a low median income and a high poverty rate, yet the library is gorgeous. The Lockridge and Gregory Libraries were designed by the renowned Ghanaian British architect David Adjaye, who also designed the Smithsonian National Museum of African American History and Culture.[40]

In an interview with the *Washington Post,* Adjaye told the reporter that public buildings "should offer places for people to see beautiful things, be inspired, just exist, engage or just do their own thing."

Adjaye was able to see something many other decision makers are perhaps willfully blind to: Black people can and should be able to enjoy and engage with beautiful spaces.[41] Navy Yard also has beautiful architectural features, but the buildings came only after nearly all the Black residents were displaced. Petworth has inviting wine bars and restaurants, also built only after the neighborhood was no longer majority Black. Park View has hip bars and upscale restaurants, built only after White people moved in. These racialized patterns of reinvestment are an unfortunate continuation of past harms.

CONCLUSION

Locked Up and Locked Out

WHEN I WAS FOURTEEN, I worked as a cashier at Mrs. Field's Cookies on Twelfth and F Streets, NW. After work, I would walk over to Metro Center to take the S bus home. There would often be a long line of Black people, mostly women, some with children, standing just south of my bus stop. They were waiting for the Lorton Bus, a chartered city bus that took visitors on the twenty-two-mile trip to Lorton Reformatory, where people from DC who were convicted of crimes were held. The proximity of the prison allowed DC residents to visit their loved ones on a regular basis.

The National Capital Revitalization and Self-Government Improvement Act, passed by Congress in 1997, was designed to reinvigorate the local economy by transferring some financial control to the federal government, including the management of DC residents convicted of crimes.[1] The local prison, Lorton Reformatory, was ordered fully closed by the end of 2001, and all adult male prisoners with felonies were sent to federal prisons around the country. This had long been the practice for women convicted of crimes in DC and now was extended to the much larger male incarcerated population.[2]

The closest federal prison is over 100 miles away, and there are no more daily buses for visitors. By 2010, a quarter of the 6,000 DC Code offenders in federal prisons were housed at facilities over 500 miles from the city.[3] Despite a 2010 congressional hearing and a promise from BOP to house DC Code offenders at closer facilities, between 2015 and 2018, 20 percent of people sentenced to prison for homicide were sent to prisons more than 500 miles from DC,[4] long drives or even plane rides away from their families.

In 2016, I received a text message that read, "This may come as a big surprise hearing from me (GERALD) if you can remember when we were young and you were living with NIKKI! I talked to MAN-MAN he told me he had an interview with you for your book. I'm interested in reading what you wrote."

I responded to Gerald's text message and asked him for the address where I should send him my books. To my surprise, the address he sent me was in Atwater, California, just a few miles from my workplace in Merced. I chose to move 2,800 miles from my hometown to teach sociology at the University of California, Merced. Gerald has no such choices as an inmate in the federal prison system and must go wherever the BOP sends him. Gerald, whose conviction was part of the Fern Street case discussed in chapter 4, has a sentence of life plus sixty years. The prison where Gerald is incarcerated, the United States Penitentiary (USP) Atwater, houses dozens of people from Washington, DC.

The closest airport to USP Atwater is Fresno Yosemite International Airport, seventy miles from the facility. There is no public transportation at the Fresno airport, nor are there any transit routes to USP Atwater. Thus a visitor would have to rent a car and stay a couple of nights in a hotel. The trip would cost a minimum of $1,200 and would take at least four days. A person without a driver's license and a credit card would find it nearly impossible to get from DC to Atwater. This is a far cry from the thirty-minute bus ride that took visitors from downtown DC to Lorton Reformatory before it closed.

In December 2019, I went to visit Gerald at USP Atwater. As I waited for Gerald to come into the visiting room, I overheard the conversation at the next table, where a White inmate covered in tattoos was explaining to his White girlfriend the importance of his Nordic roots as well as his plans for them to move to Oregon and form an all-White community when he was released.

I had never knowingly sat so close to a member of a White supremacist organization. When Gerald walked in, I turned my attention to him and tried to forget what I had just overheard. Although I didn't say anything, I couldn't stop thinking about the fact that Black men from Washington, DC, are incarcerated in places that are not only thousands of miles from their homes but also where White supremacist organizations are active.[5]

Sending DC Code offenders far away from their loved ones has severe consequences both while they are incarcerated and when they return home. Washington, DC, has the highest incarceration rate in the world.[6] And for many DC residents, the only way they can communicate with their incarcerated father, brother, uncle, cousin, sister, or mother is by phone, email, or text as travel to a facility hundreds of miles away is not feasible. These virtual connections are no substitute for in-person visits.[7]

The Universal Declaration of Human Rights clearly states that the right to have a family should be protected by society and the state.[8] When the BOP sends inmates hundreds or thousands of miles from their families, they are effectively denying them the possibility of seeing their parents, spouse, children, or other family members ever again. This is an additional punishment beyond their criminal sentence.

It is also punishing for their family members. For some family members, this distance means they may never see their loved one again. For others, it means they must take an onerous and expensive trip across the country to spend a couple of hours with their loved one in a prison visitation room.

These long distances also create significant hindrances upon release. In my interviews with returning citizens in Washington, DC, those that were placed far from DC had a long and complicated journey home. One of our interviewees, Calvin, recounted to me that he was transferred eighteen times during his twenty-three-year incarceration. He was sent to California, Arizona, Kentucky, Alabama, Atlanta, Florida, Pennsylvania, Indiana, Kansas, and other places he couldn't recall.

Calvin was released from USP Atwater and dropped off at a bus station in Modesto, California, with $50 and a bus ticket. He sat and waited to hear the call for a bus to Washington, DC. He hadn't realized he needed to take the bus to Fresno and then transfer a few more times before reaching his final destination. He waited two hours and after missing the bus, spoke to the gate agent who explained the route to him. He finally got on the bus to Fresno, and from there took a bus to Los Angeles, and then to Arizona and New Mexico—where he managed to miss the bus again. He was able to get back on the bus and go to Texas, then Tennessee, then Richmond, before finally making it to Union Station in Washington, DC, three long days after leaving USP Atwater.[9]

Calvin, Gerald, and the other Black men interviewed for this book were taken from their families and communities, first to DC Jail, then to Lorton Reformatory, and then all over the United States to federal penitentiaries. When I began this project, I set out to understand how this massive displacement of Black men from DC to carceral facilities had shaped the trajectory of the city. I also wondered how the significant transformations the city has undergone over the past twenty years would affect these men once they returned.

My conversations with returning citizens in Washington, DC, led to a widening and deepening of my analyses and led me to trace the history of Washington, DC, over the past century. Calvin, for example, told me that as a child he played on the steps of the US Capitol. His grandmother, who raised him, was a high-ranking government worker. She owned a home in Capitol Hill—one of the most expensive neighborhoods in the city. The family sold the home in 2003, while Calvin was incarcerated, for $500,000. Three years later, the house was resold for $1.5 million. Stories like Calvin's led me to ask how African Americans like his grandmother had purchased homes, why home ownership had not led to intergenerational wealth, and why middle-class status was not a protective factor for many Black youth in DC during the War on Drugs.

When I tell people from DC I am exploring the relationship between incarceration and gentrification, they nod their heads, as they can easily see the connections. Incarceration took Black people off the streets. Gentrification displaced Black people from their neighborhoods. This book has taken on the challenge of tying these threads together into an empirically based argument. To draw connections between slum clearance, redlining, White flight, disinvestment, Black suburbanization, mass incarceration, Black displacement, and gentrification, I relied on a conceptualization of racialized public and private investment that shows how investments are racialized. Black communities in DC experience disinvestment and carceral investment in ways White communities in DC have not.

I explained how high schools that had been excellent when they were all-White—McKinley Tech, Roosevelt, and Coolidge—became disinvested after Black students started attending them. I explored how these schools became sites of violence once the surrounding communities also experienced disinvestment. I described how the response to this violence was carceral investment. The connections between the War on Drugs and gentrification in Eckington—where McKinley Tech is located—are hard to deny: half of the six major joint local-federal task forces were set up in this neighborhood. And once the alleged kingpins were behind bars, real estate prices began to skyrocket.

When these neighborhoods were majority Black, the primary form of investment they received was carceral. As White people began to move in, this changed. When White people moved into areas originally built for White occupancy, so did public and private investments in community well-being. When public housing built for Black residents was demolished, the reinvestment that community sees is shaped by whether the new residents are White or Black.

Using racial capitalism as a theoretical framework allows us to see how anti-Blackness is imbricated in this history of dispossession, disinvestment, and displacement. Black neighborhoods across DC have experienced this trajectory of dispossession, disinvestment, carceral investment, and racialized reinvestment. These events happen in this order because each is a precondition for the next.

Although Gerald has been sentenced to life in prison, he hopes to be released one day. As of this writing in January 2023, his appeal is sitting on a judge's desk, as it has been for months. He occasionally asks me to send him books. Some of these requests are for history books for his edification, but most are related to business ventures he is considering. As a returning citizen and a modestly educated Black man, Gerald is well aware of the barriers he will face if he is released. He hopes to circumvent this discrimination by becoming an entrepreneur. The odds are stacked against him. However, there are some exceptions, and the existence of these exceptions gives hope to others.

Marcus Bullock, for example, was convicted of an armed carjacking when he was eighteen years old. He was released from prison after serving eight years in a Virginia state prison. When he was released in

2004, he found work with a painting company. He then set up a business and hired other returning citizens to do large-scale painting jobs. This first venture gave him the capital he needed to fund his own vision for a start-up—an app by which people can easily send a photo and a message to people behind bars. I downloaded the app and sent a photo to Gerald for 99 cents. As of January 2021, over half a million people had sent photos to loved ones using Marcus Bullock's creation, Flikshop.[10]

Halim Flowers, like many of the people introduced in this book, was raised in a two-parent household in the home his grandparents had owned in Washington, DC. When he was seventeen, he was sentenced to life in prison as an accomplice to felony murder. Flowers did not shoot anyone but was held accountable for the murder of fifty-one-year-old Elvern Cooper due to the accomplice liability provisions of the law. While incarcerated, Halim wrote and self-published eleven books. In 2019, Halim was released after twenty-two years in prison, when it was determined he qualified for the Incarceration Reduction Amendment Act (IRAA), which offers a resentencing option to anyone from DC convicted of crimes they committed before their eighteenth birthday. Today his paintings sell for over $10,000; his artwork is shown at galleries around the world; and in 2021, he sold about $1 million in artwork.[11] I was thrilled when Halim Flowers agreed to allow us to use his artwork for the cover of this book.

The success of returning citizens like Marcus Bullock and Halim Flowers is inspiring, but it's not the norm. It is hard for most returning citizens to find work that pays a living wage, in part because of the particularities of the DC labor market, where half of all new jobs require a bachelor's degree or more.[12] Many of the returning citizens introduced in this book were able to get a GED while incarcerated. A few even earned an associate degree. But none earned a four-year college degree. One reason is that in 1994 Congress passed a law that ended Pell Grant eligibility for incarcerated people. This made it much more difficult for incarcerated people to attend college. In 1991, before the bill's passage, nearly one of five people in federal prison had taken at least one college-level course. By 2014, only 2 percent of incarcerated people had completed an associate degree while incarcerated and only one percent had completed a bachelor's degree or higher.[13] In 2020, Congress reinstated Pell Grant eligibility for incarcerated people. This will take effect in 2023, and it remains to be seen how much of an impact this will have as programs that were dismantled due to lack of funding will have to be rebuilt.

Returning citizens face a variety of obstacles in the contemporary housing and labor markets. The District of Columbia has set up a wide variety of programs designed to facilitate their reintegration. These programs are limited in part because for the most part they begin after incarcerated people return home, instead of while they are behind bars. These programs are also limited because they are unable to address the underlying structural features that shape the lives of returning citizens: anti-Black racism and racial capitalism.

The persistence of racial capitalism and anti-Black racism in the United States means three things: (1) White people will continue to seek out communities where they are the majority; (2) as people of color move into neighborhoods, the value of the homes will decrease; and (3) private investors will perceive more market potential in White neighborhoods than in Black neighborhoods, and the former will have more amenities. Put simply, land and housing have been commodified within a racialized system that assigns differential value to property based on race. The higher the number of White people who live in a neighborhood, the higher the value of the homes there. Remarkably, Junia Howell and Elizabeth Korver-Glenn found that neighborhood racial composition had more of an influence on the value of homes in 2015 than it did in 1980.[14]

As the United States has moved away from public housing and left nearly all housing solutions to the private market, we have created a situation in which one of our most fundamental human rights—the right to shelter—has been left to market forces. At the same time, we have created a racialized economic system in which, to the extent that middle-class people have any wealth at all, that wealth lies in the value of their home. The monetary value of the home includes not just the bricks and mortar that constitute the structure but also the nearby public and private amenities.[15] When the public and private sectors choose not to invest in community well-being in Black neighborhoods, this leads to a devaluation of homes in Black neighborhoods. Moreover, the simple fact of a home and particularly a neighborhood being occupied by Black people decreases the value of that home. The barriers to wealth accumulation for Black people are not a bug in the system of racial capitalism but a feature.

There is one reason home values increase when White people move in: *racism*. There is one reason homes are assigned value at all: *capitalism*. The only real solution to these cycles of displacement and dispossession, then, is to dismantle both racism and capitalism. And given their interrelatedness and interconnectedness, this dismantling must be done simultaneously.

When I have shared this work with Black communities in DC, I am often asked: What is to be done? How can we change the racist and capitalist cycles that created Black displacement and dispossession? How can Black people build intergenerational wealth?

For one thing, we can support affordable housing developments and inclusionary zoning programs that allow people without intergenerational wealth to purchase homes. The expansion of these programs would surely benefit many returning citizens who struggle to afford housing. Many of the returning citizens we interviewed qualified for the inclusionary zoning program and were waiting for their turn to come up on the waiting list. Expanding this program would surely help many people.

At the same time, dismantling racism requires us to recognize that the ease with which Black people have been systematically and repeatedly displaced from DC—–through dispossession of their lands, foreclosure of their homes, and the carceral system—is rooted in anti-Blackness. In their edited volume, *Antiblackness,* Moon-Kie Jung and João H. Costa Vargas contend that the modern understanding of the social and the human excludes Black people and thus that our very understanding of what it means to be human and to be social must be upended to create a world without anti-Blackness. The more I think about the history and present day of housing in Washington, DC, I realize that insofar as anti-Blackness is rooted in the legacy of a capitalist logic that defined Black people as property for the purpose of extracting profit, we must reimagine this capitalist logic. Ending racism requires ending practices and ideologies that create racial inequality and anti-Blackness, and this does indeed require, as my colleagues Moon-Kie Jung, João Costa-Vargas, and Ruth Wilson Gilmore have put it, *changing everything.*[16]

Interviewees

Name	Minutes of interview	Year of interview	Year of birth	Childhood neighborhood	From poor neighborhood?	Grandparents own home?	Parents own home?	Years incarcerated	Current housing situation	Current occupation
Terrence	37	2016	1971	Petworth	No	Yes	Yes	23	Renting	Outreach coordinator
Earl	114	2016	1973	Parkview	Yes	Yes	No	18	Renting	Customer service
Derek	23	2016	1972	Mount Pleasant	No	No	Yes	14	Renting	Job coach
Travis	40	2016	1971	Mount Pleasant	No	Yes	No	18	Renting	Job coach
Milton	89	2016	1967	Mount Pleasant	No	Yes	No	23	Renting	Self-employed
Troy	115	2016	1971	Shepherd Park	No	Yes	Yes	9	Renting	Actuarial firm
Dodson	88	2017	1971	Shaw	Yes	Yes	No	8	Own home	Uber driver
James	64	2017	1970	Sursum Corda	Yes	No	Yes	21	Renting	Bus driver
Kwame	47	2017	1971	Petworth	No	No	Yes	23	Renting	Screenwriter
Darnell	145	2017	1970	Petworth	No	Yes	No	5	Lives with family	Bus driver
Arthur	55	2018	1971	Mount Pleasant	No	Yes	No	6	Renting	Cable wiring
Tyrell	59	2018	1965	U Street	Yes	No	Yes	13	Lives with family	Retired/Plumbing
Antwan	67	2018	1969	Eckington	No	No	Yes	23	Lives with family	Federal govt.
Calvin	150	2019	1965	Capitol Hill	No	Yes	No	26	Renting	Electrician
Marcus	78	2019	1976	Bloomingdale	No	Yes	No	23	Lives with family	Unemployed/Construction
George	82	2019	1968	SW	Yes	Yes	No	21	Homeless	Unemployed/Construction
Carl	34	2019	1969	Petworth	No	Yes	Yes	13	Owns home	Bus driver
Jamal	44	2019	1971	SE	Yes	No	No	28	Temporary housing	Restaurant janitor

Sean	97	2019	1968	Trinidad	Yes	Yes	Yes	35	Temporary housing	Parking attendant
Darius	90	2019	1976	NE	Yes	No	Yes	23	Lives with family	Roofing
Christopher	63	2020	1979	SE	Yes	No	Yes	26	Renting	Self-employed
Elijah	72	2020	1977	Takoma Park	No	Yes	No	17	Renting	Self-employed
Andre	116	2020	1978	Columbia Heights	No	Yes	No	17	Temporary housing	Outreach coordinator
Reginald	46	2020	1967	Shaw	Yes	No	Yes	17	Lives with family	Unemployed/ Construction
Edward	83	2020	1969	SE	Yes	Yes	No	22	Owns home	DC govt.
Kendall	95	2020	1969	Trinidad	Yes	Yes	Yes	4	Temporary housing	Unemployed/ Construction
Demetrius	109	2020	1974	SE	Yes	Yes	Yes	4	Renting	Nonprofit
Aaron	64	2020	1973	Susum Corda	Yes	No	No	19	Lives with family	DC govt.
Maurice	76	2020	1967	Trinidad	Yes	Yes	No	26	Lives with family	Nonprofit
Clarence	79	2020	1980	Trinidad	Yes	Yes	Yes	12	Renting	Nonprofit
Nigel	51	2020	1971	SW	Yes	No	No	4	Renting	DC govt.
Alonso	43	2021	1974	Deanwood	Yes	No	No	30	Renting	DC govt.
Malik	76	2021	1979	Sursum Corda	Yes	Yes	No	23	Renting	Nonprofit
Dion	43	2022	1978	Mount Pleasant	No	Yes	Yes	10	Renting	Nonprofit
Clinton	45	2022	1979	SE	Yes	No	No	22	Renting	Nonprofit
Andy	60	2022	1972	SE	Yes	Yes	No	22	Homeless	Unemployed/ Construction
DeAngelo	39	2022	1970	U Street	Yes	Yes	Yes	5	Temporary housing	Unemployed/ Landscaping

Oral Histories

Name	Interviewer	Source
Mariette Chrichlow	Sarah Shoenfeld	On file w/ author
Brinnie Whitehurst	Sarah Shoenfeld	On file w/ author
Angelyn Whitehurst	Sarah Shoenfeld	On file w/ author
Muriel Tillinghast	Sarah Shoenfeld	On file w/ author
Jean Urciolo	Sarah Shoenfeld	On file w/ author
John Urciolo	Sarah Shoenfeld	On file w/ author
Patricia Duncan Walker	Tanya Golash-Boza	On file w/ author
Charles Simmons	Tanya Golash-Boza	On file w/ author
Rene Copeland	Tanya Golash-Boza	On file w/ author
Coleman Hall	Sabiyha Prince	Barry Farm Oral History Project
Bobbie Jean Wills	Sabiyha Prince	Barry Farm Oral History Project
Detrice Belt	Sabiyha Prince	Barry Farm Oral History Project
Jewell Simms	Sabiyha Prince	Barry Farm Oral History Project
Michelle Hamilton	Sabiyha Prince	Barry Farm Oral History Project
Nicole Odom	Sabiyha Prince	Barry Farm Oral History Project
Deborah Campbell	Daniel Del Pielago	Barry Farm Oral History Project
Monica Canarte	Daniel Del Pielago	Barry Farm Oral History Project
Jane Souder	Sabiyha Prince	Barry Farm Oral History Project
Paulette Matthews	Sabiyha Prince	Barry Farm Oral History Project
Clinton Price	Jules Johnson	Voices of DC Fort Totten Storytellers Project
Fredrick Hollis	Stephanie Mills Trice	Voices of DC Fort Totten Storytellers Project
Marvin Kirby	Stephanie Mills Trice	Voices of DC Fort Totten Storytellers Project
Michael Stanley	Stephanie Mills Trice	Voices of DC Fort Totten Storytellers Project
Michael Swann	Stephanie Mills Trice	Voices of DC Fort Totten Storytellers Project
Patricia Smith Spencer Lee	Stephanie Mills Trice	Voices of DC Fort Totten Storytellers Project
Phillip Purvis	Stephanie Mills Trice	Voices of DC Fort Totten Storytellers Project
Reginald Rothwell	Jules Johnson	Voices of DC Fort Totten Storytellers Project
Vannie Kirby	Stephanie Mills Trice	Voices of DC Fort Totten Storytellers Project
Wendell Moore	Jules Johnson	Voices of DC Fort Totten Storytellers Project
Yolanda Lee	Stephanie Mills Trice	Voices of DC Fort Totten Storytellers Project
Arrington Dixon	Christopher Hacnik	Mapping Segregation in Washington, DC: School Integration in Ward 4
Diane Hinton Perry	Mara Cherkasky	Mapping Segregation in Washington, DC: School Integration in Ward 4

Audrey Hinton	Mara Cherkasky	Mapping Segregation in Washington, DC: School Integration in Ward 4
Carolivia Herron	Sarah Shoenfeld	Mapping Segregation in Washington, DC: School Integration in Ward 4
David Nicholson	Mara Cherkasky	Mapping Segregation in Washington, DC: School Integration in Ward 4
Francine Berkowitz	Mara Cherkasky and Sarah Shoenfeld	Mapping Segregation in Washington, DC: School Integration in Ward 4
Fannie Robinson	Sarah Shoenfeld	Mapping Segregation in Washington, DC: School Integration in Ward 4
Nadine Lockard	Sarah Shoenfeld	Mapping Segregation in Washington, DC: School Integration in Ward 4
Martha Saragovitz	Sarah Shoenfeld	Mapping Segregation in Washington, DC: School Integration in Ward 4
Barbara Saragovitz	Sarah Shoenfeld	Mapping Segregation in Washington, DC: School Integration in Ward 4
Phylicia Bowman	Mara Cherkasky	Mapping Segregation in Washington, DC: School Integration in Ward 4
Steve Nelson	Sarah Shoenfeld	Mapping Segregation in Washington, DC: School Integration in Ward 4
Lashonia Thompson-El	Kristin Adair	Women of the WIRE: Stories of DC's Formerly Incarcerated Women
Nicolette Williams	Kristin Adair	Women of the WIRE: Stories of DC's Formerly Incarcerated Women
Petrina Williams	Kristin Adair	Women of the WIRE: Stories of DC's Formerly Incarcerated Women
Saundra Sanders	Kristin Adair	Women of the WIRE: Stories of DC's Formerly Incarcerated Women
Tanisha Murden	Kristin Adair	Women of the WIRE: Stories of DC's Formerly Incarcerated Women

Notes

‖‖

INTRODUCTION

1. I use pseudonyms throughout the book to protect people's privacy. However, when given permission or when names are part of the public record, I use people's real names. Whether the names are real or pseudonymous, I have received permission to share each story I tell in this book. Mark's story is derived from conversations with him and his family members.

2. Board of Governors of the Federal Reserve System, *Disparities in Wealth by Race and Ethnicity in the 2019 Survey of Consumer Finances* (Federal Reserve, September 28, 2020), https:// www.federalreserve.gov/econres/notes/feds-notes/disparities-in-wealth-by-race-and-ethnicity-in-the-2019-survey-of-consumer-finances-20200928.htm.

3. National Association of Realtors, "America's Persistent Racial Homeownership Gaps," 2020, https://www.nar.realtor/sites/default /files/documents/policy-forum-2020-presentation-racial-home-ownership-gaps-02-06-2020.pdf.

4. Melvin Oliver and Thomas Shapiro, *Black Wealth, White Wealth: A New Perspective on Racial Inequality* (New York: Routledge, 2006).

5. Kilolo Kijakazi, Rachel Marie Brooks Atkins, Mark Paul, Anne E. Price, Darrick Hamilton, and William A. Darity Jr., "The Color of Wealth in the Nation's Capital," Urban Institute, 2016, https://www.urban.org/research /publication/color-wealth-nations-capital. Home ownership calculations based on US Census and American Community Survey data provided by the National Historical Geographic Information System (NHGIS).

6. Donald Braman, *Doing Time on the Outside: Incarceration and Family Life in Urban America* (Ann Arbor: University of Michigan Press, 2007); Andrea Leverentz, *Intersecting Lives: How Place Shapes Reentry* (Oakland: University of California Press, 2022); William Julius Wilson, *The Truly Disadvantaged: The Inner City, the Underclass, and Public Policy* (Chicago: University of Chicago Press, 2012).

7. Eric Lotke, "Hobbling a Generation: Young African American Men in Washington, DC's Criminal Justice System—Five Years Later," *Crime & Delinquency* 44, no. 3 (1998): 355–366.

8. Ruth Glass, *London, Aspects of Change* (London: Centre for Urban Studies, 1964); Neil Smith, *The New Urban Frontier: Gentrification and the Revanchist City* (New York: Routledge, 1996); Neil Smith, "Gentrification and the Rent Gap," *Annals of the Association of American Geographers* 77, no. 3 (September 1987): 462–465.

9. Ruth Wilson Gilmore, *Golden Gulag* (Berkeley: University of California Press, 2007); Nick Estes, Ruth Wilson Gilmore, and Christopher Loperena, "United in Struggle: As Racial Capitalism Rages, Movements for Indigenous Sovereignty and Abolition Offer Visions of Freedom on Stolen Land," *NACLA Report on the Americas* 53, no. 3 (2021): 255–267; Ruth Wilson Gilmore and Craig Gilmore, "Beyond Bratton," in *Policing the Planet: Why the Policing Crisis Led to Black Lives Matter,* ed. Jordan T. Camp and Christina Heatherton (London: Verso, 2016), 173–199; David Harvey, *The Limits to Capital* (New York: Verso, [1982] 2018).

10. Calculations based on US Census data from NHGIS.

11. Richard Rothstein, *The Color of Law: A Forgotten History of How Our Government Segregated America* (New York: Liveright Publishing, 2017); Beryl Satter, *Family Properties* (New York: Picador, 2007); Oliver and Shapiro, *Black Wealth, White Wealth.*

12. Oliver and Shapiro, *Black Wealth, White Wealth.*

13. Rothstein, *The Color of Law.*

14. The 1950 housing census for Washington, DC, reports 1,458 "contracts to purchase" alongside 96,915 traditional mortgages or deeds of trust. Later censuses do not separate these contracts from mortgages. The oral history interviews with Uptown residents do not indicate that the sort of predatory inclusion Taylor describes was prevalent in DC, although more research is needed. Keeanga-Yamahtta Taylor, *Race for Profit: How Banks and the Real Estate Industry Undermined Black Homeownership* (Chapel Hill: University of North Carolina Press, 2019). See also https://www2.census.gov/library/publications /decennial/1950/housing-volume-4/36965253v4p2ch8.pdf.

15. Lance Freeman, *A Haven and a Hell: The Ghetto in Black America* (New York: Columbia University Press, 2019); Wilson, *The Truly Disadvantaged*; Douglas Massey and Nancy A. Denton, *American Apartheid: Segregation and the Making of the Underclass* (Cambridge, MA: Harvard University Press, 1993); Mary Pattillo, *Black Picket Fences: Privilege and Peril among the Black Middle Class* (Chicago: University of Chicago Press, 2013).

16. Carolyn Gallagher, *The Politics of Staying Put: Condo Conversion and Tenant Right-to-Buy in Washington, DC* (Philadelphia: Temple University Press, 2016); Chris Myers Asch and George Derek Musgrove, *Chocolate City: A History of Race and Democracy in the Nation's Capital* (Chapel Hill: University of North Carolina Press, 2017).

17. James Forman Jr., *Locking Up Our Own: Crime and Punishment in Black America* (New York: Farrar, Straus and Giroux, 2017). See also Lawrence T. Brown, *The Black Butterfly: The Harmful Politics of Race and Space in America* (Baltimore: Johns Hopkins University Press, 2021), 136 and 157, for a discussion of White power and "operative Whiteness."

18. Michael Fauntroy, *Home Rule or House Rule: Congress and the Erosion of Local Governance in the District of Columbia* (Lanham, MD: University Press of America, 2003).

19. "District of Columbia Profile," Prison Policy Initiative, 2018, https:// www.prisonpolicy.org/profiles/DC.html.

20. Phil McCombs, "Where No Heat Is a Way of Life: For Project Residents, Lack of Heat Is Part of Life," *Washington Post,* November 26, 1978; Peter Earley, "Public Housing Tenants Still Shiver as Crews Battle Burst-Pipe Epidemic," *Washington Post,* December 29, 1980.

21. *Congressional Record*, 101st Cong., 1st sess., July 19, 1989.

22. Jordanna Matlon, "Racial Capitalism and the Crisis of Black Masculinity," *American Sociological Review* 81, no. 5 (2016): 1014–1038.

23. Gilmore, *Golden Gulag*; Tanya Golash-Boza, "A Critical and Comprehensive Sociological Theory of Race and Racism," *Sociology of Race and Ethnicity* 2, no. 2 (2016): 129–141.

24. Charisse Burden-Stelly, "Modern U.S. Racial Capitalism," *Monthly Review* 72, no. 3 (2020): 8–20, https://monthlyreview.org/2020/07/01/modern-u-s-racial-capitalism.

25. Junia Howell and Elizabeth Korver-Glenn, "The Increasing Effect of Neighborhood Racial Composition on Housing Values, 1980–2015," *Social Problems* 68, no. 4 (November 2021): 1051–1071, https://doi.org/10.1093/socpro/spaa033.

26. Prentiss A. Dantzler, "The Urban Process under Racial Capitalism: Race, Anti-Blackness, and Capital Accumulation," *Journal of Race, Ethnicity and the City* 2, no. 2 (2021): 113–134, https://doi.org/10.1080/26884674.2021.1934201.

27. Zawadi Rucks-Ahidiana, "Theorizing Gentrification as a Process of Racial Capitalism," *City & Community* 21, no. 3 (2021), https://doi.org/10.1177/15356841211054790.

28. Brandi Thompson Summers, *Black in Place: The Spatial Aesthetics of Race in a Post-Chocolate City* (Chapel Hill: University of North Carolina Press, 2019); Sabiyha Prince, *African Americans and Gentrification in Washington, DC: Race, Class and Social Justice in the Nation's Capital* (New York: Routledge, 2014); Derek S. Hyra, *Race, Class, and Politics in the Cappuccino City* (Chicago: University of Chicago Press, 2017); Michelle R. Boyd, *Jim Crow Nostalgia: Reconstructing Race in Bronzeville* (Minneapolis: University of Minnesota Press, 2008); Mary Pattillo, *Black on the Block* (Chicago: University of Chicago Press, 2010).

29. Pattillo, *Black Picket Fences.*

30. Kijakazi et al., "The Color of Wealth in the Nation's Capital."

31. "District of Columbia Profile," Prison Policy Initiative, 2018, https://www.prisonpolicy.org/profiles/DC.html.

32. For more on how sibling poverty shapes financial outcomes for adults, see Colleen Heflin and Mary Pattillo, "Kin Effects on Black-White Account and Home Ownership," *Sociological Inquiry* 72, no. 2 (2002): 220–239.

33. For more on go-go music, see Natalie Hopkinson, *Go-Go Live: The Musical Life and Death of a Chocolate City* (Durham, NC: Duke University Press, 2012).

34. The officially designated neighborhood names are Brightwood Park for my childhood home and Sixteenth Street Heights for the home where we moved when I was eleven. These names are not part of the popular parlance. I also draw from US Census data to see trends over time. When I do that, I consider Petworth the area encompassed by the following six 2010 census tracts: 21.01; 21.02; 22.01; 22.02; 23.01; 24. Brightwood Park is one of these tracts, 21.02.

CHAPTER 1. DISPOSSESSION AND DISPLACEMENT

1. "Elizabeth Proctor Thomas," National Park Service, 2019, https://www.nps.gov/articles/featured_stories_thomas.htm.

2. Katherine Grandine, "Brightwood: From Tollgate to Suburb," in *Washington at Home: An Illustrated History of Neighborhoods in the Nation's Capital,* 2nd ed., ed. K. Schneider Smith (Baltimore: Johns Hopkins University Press, 2010), 123–138.

3. "Native Peoples of Washington, DC," National Park Service, accessed February 11, 2021, https://www.nps.gov/articles/native-peoples-of-washington-dc.htm.

4. David Harvey, *A Brief History of Neoliberalism* (New York: Oxford University Press, 2007), 116.

5. Chris Myers Asch and George Derek Musgrove, *Chocolate City: A History of Race and Democracy in the Nation's Capital* (Chapel Hill: University of North Carolina Press, 2017).

6. Prologue DC, "The Displacement of Meridian Hill's African American Community," https://www.arcgis.com/apps/MapSeries/index.html?appid=825617c96aff4db59f2f216e83b9d713; Matthew Barak and Leigh Bianchi, "Fort Reno: Growth and Displacement," February 3, 2021, https://arcg.is/ojXinm; Neil Flanagan, "The Battle of Fort Reno," *Washington City Paper,* November 2, 2017, https://washingtoncitypaper.com/article/188488/the-battle-of-fort-reno; Sarah Shoenfeld, "The History and Evolution of Anacostia's Barry Farm," D.C. Policy Center, August 21, 2020, https://www.dcpolicycenter.org/publications/barry-farm-anacostia-history; Myers and Musgrove, *Chocolate City.* For an overview of multiple displacements of Black people in DC, also see Prologue DC's "Mapping Displacement: From Alley Clearance to Redevelopment," https://www.arcgis.com/apps/MapSeries/index.html?appid=ca5cad337d174bc18e01c40efcb91122.

7. The arguments in this chapter are based on a wide range of data sources, including oral histories, US Census and American Community Survey data, Department of Veterans Affairs data, Bureau of Labor Statistics data, congressional reports, government reports, Paul Wice's memoir, Marvin Caplan's memoir, Neighbors, Inc. Archive, community-based reports, newspaper articles, and archival data shared on the Mapping Segregation website. I coded the oral histories for emergent themes. I use descriptive statistics to describe trends. I searched congressional hearings for discussions of related themes. I searched the ProQuest historical newspapers database for articles related to segregation in Washington, DC. I read the memoirs to provide more context for the history of Brightwood Park, Manor Park, Takoma Park, and Shepherd Park. I read through the Neighbors, Inc., Archives and took photos of relevant documents to better understand and describe White flight from Brightwood Park, Manor Park, Takoma Park, and Shepherd Park.

8. Kate Masur, *An Example for All the Land: Emancipation and the Struggle over Equality in Washington, DC* (Chapel Hill: University of North Carolina Press, 2010); Shoenfeld, "The History and Evolution of Anacostia's Barry Farm."

9. Constance McLaughlin Green, *Secret City: A History of Race Relations in the Nation's Capital* (Princeton, NJ: Princeton University Press, [1967] 2015).

10. Robert D. Manning, "Multicultural Washington, DC: The Changing Social and Economic Landscape of a Post-Industrial Metropolis," *Ethnic and Racial Studies* 21, no. 2 (1998): 328–355.

11. Green, *Secret City*; Howard Gillette Jr., *Between Justice and Beauty: Race, Planning, and the Failure of Urban Policy in Washington* (Philadelphia: University of Pennsylvania Press, 2011).

12. Gillette, *Between Justice and Beauty*.

13. Edward J. Marolda, *The Washington Navy Yard: An Illustrated History* (Washington, DC: Naval Historical Center, 1999).

14. Prologue DC's Mapping Segregation project and website are an important source for much of the material in this book. I encountered Prologue DC's work in the early stages of its project and draw from many of the resources held at its website: https://www.mappingsegregationdc.org. This website contains the FHA map as well as a map of racially restrictive covenants in DC embedded in a visualization of census block data from 1940 to 1980. I referenced these and other materials multiple times while writing this book. The project's story

maps and associated resources are cited throughout, particularly, "How Racially Restricted Housing Shaped Ward 4." The principal historians at Prologue DC, Sarah Shoenfeld and Mara Cherkasky, also provided feedback on several chapter drafts and I am grateful to both of them for sharing their deep knowledge of DC history with me.

15. Federal Housing Administration, "Interim Report on Conditions in the Washington, DC, Housing Market as of June 1, 1940," 1940, http://mapping segregationdc.org/assets/negro-housing-rpt-1940_excerpt.pdf.

16. Brent McKee, "Carrollsburg Dwellings—Washington DC," Living New Deal, July 29, 2020, https://livingnewdeal.org/projects/carrollsburg-dwellings-washington-dc.

17. See Prologue DC, "Mapping Displacement: From Alley Clearance to Redevelopment," 2021, https://mappingsegregationdc.org/#story (see Mapping Displacement).

18. "Search the 1940 Census," National Archives and Records Administration, 1940, https://1940census.archives.gov/search/?search.census_year=1940.

19. Carl Hansen, *Danger in Washington: The Story of My Twenty Years in the Public Schools in the Nation's Capital* (West Nyack, NY: Parker, 1968); Asch and Musgrove, *Chocolate City*; Francesca Russello Ammon, "Commemoration amid Criticism: The Mixed Legacy of Urban Renewal in Southwest Washington, DC," *Journal of Planning History* 8, no. 3 (2009): 175–220.

20. Alcione Amos, *Barry Farm—Hillsdale in Anacostia: A Historic African American Community* (Charleston, SC: History Press, 2021).

21. Shoenfeld, "The History and Evolution of Anacostia's Barry Farm."

22. Shoenfeld, "The History and Evolution of Anacostia's Barry Farm."

23. "Housing Project Renews Beautification Campaign," *Washington Post*, April 5, 1959.

24. Rohit Acharya and Rhett Morris, "Reducing Poverty without Community Displacement," Brookings Metro, 2022, available online at https://www.brookings.edu/wp-content/uploads/2022/09/Indicators-of-inclusive-prosperity_final2.pdf.

25. Federal Housing Administration, "Interim Report on Conditions in the Washington, DC, Housing Market as of June 1, 1940."

26. One other exception was in 1954, when the FHA approved the development of a middle-class Black area in New Orleans. This case was reported in

Richard Rothstein, *The Color of Law: A Forgotten History of How Our Government Segregated America* (New York: Liveright Publishing, 2017).

27. Sandra R. Heard, "Making Slums and Suburbia in Black Washington during the Great Depression," *American Studies* 57, no. 4 (2019): 5–22.

28. "D.C. Building Soars in Week to $1,443,943: Permits Set New High for Year; Erection of 80 Homes Planned Year's Peak Set by D.C. Building," *Washington Post,* March 19, 1939, https://www.proquest.com/historical-newspapers /d-c-building-soars-week-1-443-943/docview/151220118/se-2.

29. "Harry Lucas, Presidential Porter, Buried," *Washington Post,* June 8, 1950,https://www.proquest.com/historical-newspapers/harry-lucas-presidential-porter-buried/docview/152237393/se-2.

30. "Amelia Lucas, Top Amateur Golfer, with FTC 35 Years," *Washington Post,* July 18, 1978, https://search.proquest.com/historical-newspapers/amelia-lucas-top-amateur-golfer-with-ftc-35-years/docview/146827870/se-2?.

31. "Amelia Lucas, Top Amateur Golfer."

32. "Capitol View Civic Association: Washington," Capitol View DC, accessed January 5, 2021, https://www.capitolviewdc.org.

33. Patricia E. Hallman, "Memories of Capitol View," Capitol View Civic Association, 2010, available at Office of Contracting and Procurement, https:// ocp.dc.gov/sites/default/files/dc/sites/op/publication/attachments/Capital%20 View%20Brochure.pdf?fbclid=IwAR0KPh3guZYsqCOOflYK7WIRtxbeyiJ7Qq 4bILZWg207kBn3Jqil4q20eaA; Dreck Spurlock Wilson, *African American Architects: A Biographical Dictionary, 1865–1945* (New York: Routledge, 2004).

34. Mike DeBonis, "End of an Error," *Washington City Paper,* February 22, 2008, https://washingtoncitypaper.com/article/235941/end-of-an-error.

35. "Washington Firm Is Awarded Contract to Build 391 Low-Rent Housing Units," *Washington Post,* May 20, 1953, https://search.proquest.com /historical-newspapers/washington-firm-is-awarded-contract-build-391-low /docview/152576437/se-2.

36. Flanagan, "The Battle of Fort Reno."

37. Elsie Carper, "Reno School Closing Nears as Student Body Dips to Six," *Washington Post,* October 3, 1950, https://www.proquest.com/historical-newspapers/reno-school-closing-nears-as-student-body-dips/docview/152223873 /se-2.

38. "Fort Reno Raze Victims Seek Homes," *Washington Post,* April 1, 1951.

39. Barak and Bianchi, "Fort Reno: Growth and Displacement."

40. Prologue DC, "How Racially Restricted Housing Shaped Ward 4," ArcGIS story map, 2017, http://www.mappingsegregationdc.org/#story.

41. Housing Market Analysis, Washington, DC, July 1937, Federal Housing Administration, Division of Economics and Statistics, August 5, 1937, pp. 19–26, Research and Statistics Division, Records Relating to Housing Market Analyses, 1935–42, Box 17, RG 31, National Archives, online at http://mappingsegregationdc.org/assets/residential-sub-areas-for-website-rev.pdf.

42. "Bloomingdale Acts to Reserve Section as Home of Whites: Overflow Meetings Effects Organization to Combat Entrance of Negroes. Churches Unite with Citizen Associations. $1,000 Raised to Further Aims of Meeting Said to Be 'in Defense of Homes,'" Washington Post, October 25, 1924, https://search.proquest.com/docview/149390286.

43. Prologue DC, "How Racially Restricted Housing Shaped Ward 4"; Sarah Jane Shoenfeld and Mara Cherkasky, "'A Strictly White Residential Section': The Rise and Demise of Racially Restrictive Covenants in Bloomingdale," Washington History 29, no. 1 (2017): 24–41, http://www.jstor.org/stable/90007372; Asch and Musgrove, Chocolate City.

44. For a map showing where the racial covenants were in Washington, DC, see MappingSegregationDC.com.

45. Shoenfeld and Cherkasky, "'A Strictly White Residential Section.'"

46. Oral history interview with Diane Hinton Perry and Audrey Hinton, by Mara Cherkasky, DC Public Library, Mapping Segregation in Washington, DC: School Integration in Ward 4, online at https://digdc.dclibrary.org/islandora/object/dcplislandora%3A282552; Prologue DC, "How Racially Restricted Housing Shaped Ward 4."

47. Mapping Segregation in Washington DC, https://mappingsegregationdc.org/.

48. Marvin Caplan and Ralph Blessing, "Shepherd Park: Creating an Integrated Community," in Schneider Smith, Washington at Home, 449–463; "Race and Real Estate in Mid-Century DC: The Neighbors, Inc. Records," http://www.mappingsegregationdc.org/neighbors-inc.html.

49. Paul Wice, "Safe Haven: A Memoir of Playground Basketball and Segregation," Washington History (Fall–Winter 1997): 55–71.

50. Wice, "Safe Haven."

51. Marvin Harold Caplan, *Farther Along: A Civil Rights Memoir* (Baton Rouge: Louisiana State University Press, 1999); Sarah Shoenfeld, "Teachable Moment: 'Blockbusting' and Racial Turnover in Mid-Century D.C." *Washington History* 30, no. 2 (Fall 2018): 50–54; Neighbors, Inc., files, available at http://www.mapping segregationdc.org/neighbors-inc.html.

52. Paige Glotzer, *How the Suburbs Were Segregated: Developers and the Business of Exclusionary Housing, 1890–1960* (New York: Columbia University Press, 2020); Manning, "Multicultural Washington, DC."

53. Clare Lise Kelly, *Montgomery Modern: Modern Architecture in Montgomery County, Maryland, 1930–1979* (Silver Spring: Maryland–National Capital Park and Planning Co., 2015); John Kimble, "Insuring Inequality: The Role of the Federal Housing Administration in the Urban Ghettoization of African Americans," *Law & Social Inquiry* 32, no. 2 (2007): 399–434; Kenneth T. Jackson, "Federal Subsidy and the Suburban Dream: The First Quarter-Century of Government Intervention in the Housing Market," *Records of the Columbia Historical Society, Washington, DC* 50 (1980): 421–451.

54. Kenneth Jackson, "Race, Ethnicity, and Real Estate Appraisal: The Home Owners Loan Corporation and the Federal Housing Administration," *Journal of Urban History* 6, no. 4 (1980): 419–452.

55. Gary Orfield and Jongyeon Ee, *Our Segregated Capital: An Increasingly Diverse City with Racially Polarized Schools* (Los Angeles: Civil Rights Project, 2017),https://www.civilrightsproject.ucla.edu/research/k-12-education/integration-and-diversity/our-segregated-capital-an-increasingly-diverse-city-with-racially-polarized-schools.

56. "Historical Statistics of the United States, Colonial Times to 1957," https://www2.census.gov/library/publications/1960/compendia/hist_stats_colonial-1957/hist_stats_colonial-1957-chN.pdf.

57. Orfield and Ee, *Our Segregated Capital.*

58. Adam Gordon, "The Creation of Homeownership: How New Deal Changes in Banking Regulation Simultaneously Made Homeownership Accessible to Whites and Out of Reach for Blacks," *Yale Law Journal* 115 (2005): 186; Lawrence T. Brown, *The Black Butterfly: The Harmful Politics of Race and Space in America* (Baltimore: Johns Hopkins University Press, 2021).

59. "Social and Economic Status of the Black Population in the United States, 1971," US Census Bureau, https://www2.census.gov/library/publications /1972/demographics/p23-042.pdf.

60. Beryl Satter, *Family Properties* (New York: Picador, 2007), 349.

61. Rothstein, *The Color of Law*; Ira Katznelson, *When Affirmative Action Was White: An Untold History of Racial Inequality in Twentieth-Century America* (New York: Norton, 2005).

62. Data on VA home loans provided by the Veteran's Administration through a FOIA request. Data archived by author.

63. Thomas Hanchett, "The Other 'Subsidized Housing': Federal Aid to Suburbanization, 1940s–1960s," in *From Tenements to the Taylor Homes: In Search of an Urban Housing Policy in Twentieth-Century America,* ed. John F. Bauman, Roger Biles, and Kristin M. Szylvian (University Park: Pennsylvania State University Press, 2000), 163–179.

64. Residential Finance Survey of the 1960 US Census, p. 402, table 2.

65. Data on VA home loans provided by the Veteran's Administration through a FOIA request. Data archived by author.

66. Calculations based on US Census and American Community Survey data provided by NHGIS.

CHAPTER 2. THE VIOLENCE OF DISINVESTMENT

1. The arguments in this chapter are based on a wide range of data sources, including oral histories, interviews, Department of Education statistics, crime statistics, congressional hearings, government reports, court cases, newspaper articles, and the vertical files at the Washingtoniana archive of the DC Public Library. I coded the oral histories and interviews for emergent themes. I use descriptive statistics to describe trends. I searched congressional hearings for discussions of related themes. I read court cases to understand historical events. I searched the Proquest historical newspapers database for articles related to schooling, public housing, and gun violence in Washington, DC. I read through the vertical files at the Washingtoniana archive on Roosevelt High School to describe the school's trajectory. I also had informal conversations with three people about Petworth and DC Public Schools more generally

in the late twentieth century: Delabian Rice-Thurston, Mary Levy, and Phylicia Bowman.

2. Nikki Jones, *The Chosen Ones: Black Men and the Politics of Redemption* (Berkeley: University of California Press, 2018).

3. Joseph Drew, "Recurring Themes of Educational Finance in the History of Washington, D.C., 1804–1982," Studies in D.C. History and Public Policy Paper No. 3, University of the District of Columbia, 1982; Steven J. Diner, "Crisis of Confidence: Public Confidence in the Schools of the Nation's Capital in the Twentieth Century," *Urban Education* 25, no. 2 (1990): 112–137.

4. Sterling Tucker, *Beyond the Burning: Life and Death of the Ghetto* (New York: Association Press, 1958); "Civil Rights Tour: Education—Browne Junior High, the Fight for School Desegregation—850 26th Street NE," DC Historic Sites, DC Historic Preservation Office, accessed January 5, 2021, https://historicsites .dcpreservation.org/items/show/918.

5. Paul Cooke, "Present Status of Integration in the Public Schools of the District of Columbia," *Journal of Negro Education* 24, no. 3 (1955): 205–218.

6. Drew, "Recurring Themes of Educational Finance in the History of Washington, D.C., 1804–1982."

7. Gary Orfield and Jongyeon Ee, *Our Segregated Capital: An Increasingly Diverse City with Racially Polarized Schools* (Los Angeles: Civil Rights Project, 2017), https://www.civilrightsproject.ucla.edu/research/k-12-education/integration- and-diversity/our-segregated-capital-an-increasingly-diverse-city-with-racially- polarized-schools.

8. Drew, "Recurring Themes of Educational Finance in the History of Washington, D.C., 1804–1982."

9. Diner, "Crisis of Confidence."

10. Hansen, *Danger in Washington*.

11. "Investigations of the Schools and Poverty in the District of Columbia," Hearings before the Task Force on Antipoverty in the District of Columbia of the Committee on Education and Labor House of Representatives, 89th Cong., Washington, DC, October 7, 8, 12, 26, 27, 1965; and January 13, 1966.

12. Green, *Secret City*.

13. Lawrence Feinberg, "99 Pct. of District Negroes Attend Schools Having Black Majorities: Resegregation Up in District Schools," *Washington Post*, Janu-

ary 4, 1970, https://www.proquest.com/historical-newspapers/99-pct-district-negroes-attend-schools-having/docview/147743362/se-2.

14. Hansen, *Danger in Washington.*

15. Hobson v. Hansen, 327 F. Supp. 844, 852 (U.S. Dist. 1971), LEXIS 13130.

16. Chris Myers Asch and George Derek Musgrove, *Chocolate City: A History of Race and Democracy in the Nation's Capital* (Chapel Hill: University of North Carolina Press, 2017).

17. Diner, "Crisis of Confidence."

18. Conrad P. Smith, "Ending the 'Benign Neglect' of D.C. Public Schools," *Washington Post,* May 8, 1978, https://www.proquest.com/historical-newspapers/ending-benign-neglect-d-c-public-schools/docview/146967556/se-2.

19. "Private Help for Public Schools," *Washington Post,* October 14, 1980, A18.

20. Edward D. Sargent, "Many D.C. Pupils Called Shortchanged: Below-Average Students Get Big Share of Funds, Group Notes More D.C. School Funds Sought," *Washington Post,* December 10, 1985, https://search.proquest.com/historical-newspapers/many-d-c-pupils-called-shortchanged/docview/138416564/se-2.

21. In 1991, the official dropout rate in the District of Columbia was 19.1%, as compared to 5.5% in Montgomery County, 5.3% in Fairfax County, VA, and 1.2% in Falls Church, VA. In Prince George's County, it was 9.3%. "Dropout Rates in the United States: 1991," US Department of Education, National Center for Education Statistics, https://nces.ed.gov/pubs92/92129.pdf.

22. David Plotz, "Schoolhouse Rock," *Washington City Paper,* November 11, 1994, https://washingtoncitypaper.com/article/290530/schoolhouse-rock.

23. Julius W. Hobson, individually and on behalf of Jean Marie Hobson and Julius W. Hobson, Jr., et al., Plaintiffs, v. Carl F. Hansen, Superintendent of Schools of the District of Columbia, the Board of Education of the District of Columbia et al., Defendants Civ. A, No. 82-66, US District Court for the District of Columbia 269 F. Supp. 401 (U.S. Dist. 1967), LEXIS 10662, June 19, 1967.

24. Interview 2019.

25. Interview 2019.

26. "In the Line of Fire: Victims of Homicide," *Washington Post,* December 29, 1991, https://www.proquest.com/newspapers/line-fire-victims-homicide-series-number-occ/docview/307457404/se-2.

27. "Body of D.C. Man Identified," *Washington Post*, Metro, May 5, 2002.

28. Interview 2020.

29. Nikki Jones, "Working 'the Code': On Girls, Gender, and Inner-City Violence," *Australian & New Zealand Journal of Criminology* 41, no. 1 (2008): 63–83.

30. Oral history with Nicolette Williams, Women of the WIRE, interview by Kristin Adair, May 5, 2018, https://digdc.dclibrary.org/islandora/object /dcplislandora%3A267287.

31. Oral history with Nicolette Williams, Women of the WIRE, May 5, 2018.

32. Eva Rosen, *The Voucher Promise* (Princeton, NJ: Princeton University Press, 2020).

33. David Farber, *Crack: Rock Cocaine, Street Capitalism, and the Decade of Greed* (New York: Cambridge University Press, 2019).

34. Joan Aldous, "Cuts in Selected Welfare Programs: The Effects on US Families," *Journal of Family Issues* 7, no. 2 (1986): 161–177.

35. Interview 2022.

36. William Brill Associates Inc., "Comprehensive Security Planning: A Program for Arthur Capper Dwellings, Washington, D.C., Final Draft," July 1977, available at HathiTrust, https://hdl.handle.net/2027/pur1.32754081250338.

37. William H. Jones, "Safeway to Expand Here," *Washington Post*, June 20, 1978, https://www.washingtonpost.com/archive/business/1978/06/20/safeway-to-expand-here/c2261c78-e8a9-4a2a-89f8-0a309aeb10f4.

38. William Brill Associates Inc., "Comprehensive Security Planning."

39. Brett Williams, "Beyond Gentrification: Investment and Abandonment on the Waterfront," in *Capital Dilemma: Growth and Inequality in Washington, DC,* ed. Derek Hyra and Sabihya Prince (New York: Routledge, 2015).

40. "Near Southeast Violent Deaths, 1987–2004," JDLand, accessed January 7, 2021, https://www.jdland.com/dc/cw-map.cfm.

41. John Mintz, "Photo IDs to Help Fight Drugs in Public Housing," *Washington Post*, June 15, 1989, https://www.washingtonpost.com/archive/local/1989/06/15/photo-ids-to-help-fight-drugs-in-public-housing/16ef1d07-47ad-4b67-8ffb-27742f8b58ce.

42. Natalie Hopkinson, "House of Blues; Marvin Gaye's Boyhood Home Awaits the Wrecking Ball or a Second Act," *Washington Post*, May 19, 2003, https://search.proquest.com/newspapers/house-blues-marvin-gayes-boyhood-home-awaits/docview/409466206/se-2.

43. Morton Mintz, "NCHA Told Construction Shows Faults," *Washington Post,* July 8, 1959, https://search.proquest.com/historical-newspapers/ncha-told-construction-shows-faults/docview/149118111/se-2; "East Capitol Dwellings Need $250,000 Repairs," *Washington Post,* May 8, 1959, https://search.proquest.com/historical-newspapers/east-capitol-dwellings-need-250-000-repairs/docview/149120338/se-2.

44. "NCHA Acts to Warm Chilly Housing," *Washington Post,* February 5, 1961, https://search.proquest.com/historical-newspapers/ncha-acts-warm-chilly-housing/docview/141331601/se-2.

45. Vincent Paka, "City Neglect Blamed in Community's Fall," *Washington Post,* May 16, 1970, https://search.proquest.com/historical-newspapers/city-neglect-blamed-communitys-fall/docview/1032789140/se-2.

46. Sam Smith, *Captive Capital: Colonial Life in Modern Washington* (Bloomington: Indiana University Press, 1974).

47. Phil McCombs, "Where No Heat Is a Way of Life: For Project Residents, Lack of Heat Is Part of Life," *Washington Post,* November 26, 1978, https://search.proquest.com/historical-newspapers/where-no-heat-is-way-life/docview/146938094/se-2; Peter Earley, "Public Housing Tenants Still Shiver as Crews Battle Burst-Pipe Epidemic," *Washington Post,* December 29, 1980, https://search.proquest.com/historical-newspapers/public-housing-tenants-still-shiver-as-crews/docview/147046504/se-2.

48. Sanford J. Ungar, "Community Changes Its Mind about Police: Center to Open Monday," *Washington Post,* May 20, 1970, https://search.proquest.com/historical-newspapers/community-changes-mind-about-police/docview/148010952/se-2?.

49. Edward D. Sargent, "Shielding Tender Targets: Parents Wage Heartfelt War against Drugs," *Washington Post,* October 16, 1980, https://search.proquest.com/historical-newspapers/shielding-tender-targets/docview/147164233/se-2?.

50. "A Very Open Drug Market," *Washington Post,* January 13, 1980, https://search.proquest.com/historical-newspapers/very-open-drug-market/docview/147296054/se-2.

51. Edward D. Sargent, "Dealing Dope among the Forgotten: East Capitol Projects Resist Drug Invasion," *Washington Post,* July 24, 1980, https://search.proquest.com/historical-newspapers/dealing-dope-among-forgotten/docview/147170260/se-2?.

52. Paul M. Barrett, "Elite Federal-Local Task Force Is Attempting to Combat Violent Crime in the 'Murder Capital': Stopping Crime," *Wall Street Journal*, November 25, 1994, https://www.proquest.com/historical-newspapers/elite-federal-local-task-force-is-attempting/docview/904968570/se-2.

53. "'Angels' from Barry Farms War on Public Housing Unit," *Washington Post*, February 27, 1966, https://search.proquest.com/historical-newspapers/angels-barry-farms-war-on-public-housing-unit/docview/142932003/se-2.

54. Edward D. Sargent, "Running Barry Farms: The Toughest Jobs in Town," *Washington Post*, June 25, 1981, https://search.proquest.com/historical-newspapers/running-barry-farms/docview/147338652/se-2.

55. Michael York and Maggie S. Tucker, "Taking Fear, Violence to Task; Cleanup Team at Barry Farms in SE Aims to Send Message of Hope," *Washington Post*, June 27, 1993, https://search.proquest.com/newspapers/taking-fear-violence-task-cleanup-team-at-barry/docview/307641149/se-2?accountid=14515.

56. Keith A. Harriston and Rene Sanchez, "Tracing D.C.'s River of Young Blood," *Washington Post*, June 26, 1993, https://www.washingtonpost.com/archive/politics/1993/06/26/tracing-dcs-river-of-young-blood/6f046f76-a8cc-4027-9683-f3cb3e7178d1.

57. Monte Reel, "D.C. Prosperity Bypasses Barry Farm," *Washington Post*, May 25, 2003, https://search.proquest.com/newspapers/d-c-prosperity-bypasses-barry-farm/docview/409479723/se-2.

58. DC Oral History Collaborative—Barry Farm Oral History Project, Narrator: Detrice Belt, Interviewer: Sabiyha Prince, July 31, 2019, https://dcplislandora.wrlc.org/islandora/object/dcplislandora%3A291802/datastream/PDF/view.

59. In 2019, the historian Sarah Shoenfeld of Prologue DC filed a landmark nomination for Barry Farm Dwellings on behalf of the Barry Farm Tenants and Allies Association to ensure that this site is not once again erased from history. The nomination highlighted the historic role of this community in the Civil Rights movement as well as the uniqueness of the layout of the streets and the large garden apartments. The landmark nomination was successful, although the Historic Preservation Review only approved preservation of part of the site. Sarah Jane Shoenfeld. "Opinion: Barry Farm's

Historic Landmark Designation Was Pitted against Affordable Housing," *Washington Post*, February 21, 2020, https://www.washingtonpost.com /opinions/local-opinions/barry-farms-historic-landmark-designation-was-pitted-against-affordable-housing/2020/02/20/8af206be-4c26-11ea-9b5c-eac5b16dafaa_story.html.

60. Erwin Knoll, "School Making Integration Progress," *Washington Post*, June 8, 1958.

61. Oral history interview with Diane Hinton Perry and Audrey Hinton, by Mara Cherkasky, DC Public Library, Mapping Segregation in Washington, DC: School Integration in Ward 4, https://digdc.dclibrary.org/islandora /object/dcplislandora%3A282552.

62. Carol J. De Vita, Carlos A. Manjarrez, and Eric C. Twombly, "Poverty in the District of Columbia—Then and Now," report prepared for the United Planning Organization, Urban Institute, Washington, DC, 2000, https://www .urban.org/sites/default/files/publication/62496/409454-Poverty-in-the-District-of-Columbia-Then-and-Now.PDF.

63. Oral history interview with Dr. Bowman, by Mara Cherkasky, DC Public Library, Mapping Segregation in Washington, DC: School Integration in Ward 4, https://digdc.dclibrary.org/islandora/object/dcplislandora%3A282542 /datastream/PDF/view.

64. Martin Austermuhle, "Listen: Diane Rehm and Isabel Wilkerson Remember Roosevelt High over the Years," WAMU (WAMU 88.5—American University Radio), August 22, 2016, https://wamu.org/story/16/08/22/listen_diane_rehm_and_isabel_wilkerson_remember_roosevelt_high_over_the_years.

65. Interview 2019.

66. Aaron Wiener, "Rough Ride," *Washington City Paper*, January 31, 2014, https://washingtoncitypaper.com/article/205682/rough-ride-roosevelt-high-school.

67. Peter Hong, "New Year's Violence Kills Six," *Washington Post*, January 2, 1994, https://www.washingtonpost.com/archive/local/1994/01/02/new-years-violence-kills-six/d7257eef-b5f7-4d87-a373-8ac8f9a352ca.

68. William H. Jones, "Big Newsweek Contract Goes to D.C. Printer," *Washington Post*, October 10, 1978, https://search.proquest.com/historical-newspapers/big-newsweek-contract-goes-d-c-printer/docview/146885966/se-2;

"Judd & Detweiler, Inc.," accessed October 3, 2022, https://www.doaks.org/research/library-archives/dumbarton-oaks-archives/collections/ephemera/names/judd-detweiler-inc.

69. "D.C. School Totals," *Washington Post and Times Herald,* November 1, 1958, https://search.proquest.com/historical-newspapers/d-c-school-totals/docview/149042600/se-2.

70. Robert Meyers, "For Half of McKinley's Seniors College Is a Way to Their Dreams," *Washington Post,* March 11, 1976, https://search.proquest.com/historical-newspapers/half-mckinleys-seniors-college-is-way-their/docview/146504509/se-2.

71. Bill Peterson and Staff Writer, "Seniors Living with Traditions, Looking to the Future," *Washington Post,* September 25, 1975, https://search.proquest.com/historical-newspapers/seniors-living-with-traditions-looking-future/docview/146274437/se-2.

72. Lynda Richardson, "Man Enters D.C. School, Strikes Teen," *Washington Post,* September 10, 1991, https://www.proquest.com/historical-newspapers/man-enters-d-c-school-strikes-teen/docview/140473746.

73. Lynda Richardson, "Many D.C. Students Balk at Banning Off-Campus Lunches," *Washington Post,* September 16, 1991, https://www.proquest.com/historical-newspapers/many-d-c-students-balk-at-banning-off-campus/docview/140470867.

74. Linda Wheeler, "D.C. Teen Charged in Stabbing," *Washington Post,* February 19, 1994, https://www.proquest.com/historical-newspapers/d-c-teen-charged-stabbing/docview/751076488.

75. Susan Ostroff, "Maps on My Past: Race, Space, and Place in the Life Stories of Washington D.C. Area Teenagers," *Oral History Review* 22, no. 2 (1995): 33–53, http://www.jstor.org/stable/3675423.

76. Interview 2018.

77. Interview 2019.

78. DC Open Data; 1980 US Census data.

79. Rene Sanchez and Sari Horwitz, "4 Wounded in Gunfire at Wilson High," *Washington Post,* January 27, 1989, https://www.washingtonpost.com/archive/politics/1989/01/27/4-wounded-in-gunfire-at-wilson-high/fe7606be-6f21-4644-84b8-b7b403acbcf2.

CHAPTER 3. CRACKING DOWN

1. Interview 2016.

2. Interview 2016.

3. "Champagne Wishes and Caviar Dreams," theme song sung by Dionne Warwick for Robin Leach's TV series, *Lifestyles of the Rich and Famous,* original release, March 31, 1984–September 2, 1995.

4. The data in this chapter come from several sources, including 37 interviews with formerly incarcerated men, 47 oral histories on file at the DC Public Library, Bureau of Justice Statistics data, Bureau of Labor Statistics data, congressional hearings on appropriations, newspaper articles in the *Washington Post,* and online writing by Mustafa S. F. Zulu, as well as a letter from him to me that describes his life story.

5. Tony Whitehead, "The Formation of the U.S. Racialized Urban Ghetto," CuSAG Special Problems Working Paper Series in Urban Anthropology, University of Maryland, College Park, September 15, 2000.

6. Sam Smith, *Captive Capital: Colonial Life in Modern Washington* (Bloomington: Indiana University Press, 1974).

7. Elliot Liebow, *Tally's Corner: A Study of Negro Streetcorner Men* (New York: Little, Brown, 1967).

8. William Julius Wilson, *When Work Disappears: The World of the New Urban Poor* (New York: Random House, 1997).

9. Lance Freeman, *A Haven and a Hell: The Ghetto in Black America* (New York: Columbia University Press, 2019).

10. Robert D. Manning, "Multicultural Washington, DC: The Changing Social and Economic Landscape of a Post-Industrial Metropolis," *Ethnic and Racial Studies* 21, no. 2 (1998): 328–355; "The Movement of Federal Facilities to the Suburbs," report by the District of Columbia Committee of the US Commission on Civil Rights, July 1971.

11. Michael A. Stoll, "Spatial Mismatch, Discrimination, and Male Youth Employment in the Washington, DC Area: Implications for Residential Mobility Policies," *Journal of Policy Analysis and Management* 18, no. 1 (1999): 77–98.

12. Julia Isaacs, "Economic Mobility of Black and White Families," Brookings Institution, 2007, https://www.brookings.edu/research/economic-mobility-of-black-and-white-families.

13. This became clear both in the oral histories I conducted and those conducted by the Mapping Segregation team and the Fort Totten Storytellers team, which focused on this generation. See appendix B for a list of oral histories.

14. Interview 2016.

15. James Forman Jr., *Locking Up Our Own: Crime and Punishment in Black America* (New York: Farrar, Straus and Giroux, 2017).

16. Tony Payan, *A War That Can't Be Won* (Tucson: University of Arizona Press, 2013).

17. Dan Baum, "Legalize It All," *Harper's Magazine*, March 31, 2016, https://harpers.org/archive/2016/04/legalize-it-all.

18. Elizabeth Hinton, *From the War on Poverty to the War on Crime* (Cambridge, MA: Harvard University Press, 2017).

19. Hinton, *From the War on Poverty to the War on Crime.*

20. Forman, *Locking Up Our Own.*

21. Peter Reuter, John Haaga, Patrick Murphy, and Amy Praskac, "Drug Use and Drug Programs in the Washington Metropolitan Area," report prepared for the Greater Washington Research Center, RAND Corporation, Santa Monica, 1988; District of Columbia Appropriations for 1988: Government Direction and Support, US Congress, House, Committee on Appropriations, Subcommittee on District of Columbia Appropriations.

22. David Farber, *Crack: Rock Cocaine, Street Capitalism, and the Decade of Greed* (New York: Cambridge University Press, 2019); Gary Webb, *Dark Alliance: The CIA, the Contras, and the Cocaine Explosion* (New York: Seven Stories Press, 2011).

23. Doris Provine, *Unequal under Law: Race in the War on Drugs* (Chicago: University of Chicago Press, 2007).

24. District of Columbia Appropriations for Fiscal Year 1990, Hearings before a Subcommittee of the Committee on Appropriations of the US Senate, 101st Cong., 1st sess., 1989; Barry's remarks, p. 216.

25. Christian Parenti, *Lockdown America: Police and Prisons in the Age of Crisis,* 2nd ed. (New York: Verso, 2012).

26. Farber, *Crack: Rock Cocaine, Street Capitalism, and the Decade of Greed.*

27. Hinton, *From the War on Poverty to the War on Crime,* Biden quote, 310; "Federal Prison System Cost per Inmate," Department of Justice, https://www.justice.gov/archive/jmd/1975_2002/2002/html/page117-119.htm.

28. District of Columbia Appropriations for Fiscal Year 1990, Hearings before a Subcommittee of the Committee on Appropriations of the US Senate, 101st Cong., 1st sess., 1989.

29. Forman, *Locking Up Our Own*.

30. Julius Hobson, "The Employment and Utilization of Negro Manpower in the District of Columbia's Government and Private Enterprise," in *Civil Rights in the Nation's Capital: A Report on a Decade of Progress,* ed. Ben Segal, William Korey, and Charles Manson (New York: National Association of Intergroup Relations, 1959), 19–33.

31. In a study of 108 Black mayors and 167 elections, Daniel Hopkins and Katherine T. McCabe find that the election of a Black mayor does not lead to policies that are substantially different from cities that elected a White mayor. The one exception is that cities with Black mayors hire more Black police officers. This also was the case in DC, where the police force became majority Black after Marion Barry was elected to office. Daniel Hopkins and Katherine T. McCabe, "After It's Too Late: Estimating the Policy Impacts of Black Mayoralties in U.S. Cities," *American Politics Research* 40, no. 4 (July 2012): 665–700, https://doi.org/10.1177/1532673X11432469.

32. Chris Myers Asch and George Derek Musgrove, *Chocolate City: A History of Race and Democracy in the Nation's Capital* (Chapel Hill: University of North Carolina Press, 2017).

33. Forman, *Locking Up Our Own*.

34. Linda Wheeler, "Operation Clean Sweep's Future Uncertain," *Washington Post,* January 26, 1988.

35. Dan Werb, Greg Rowell, Gordon Guyatt, Thomas Kerr, Julio Montaner, and Evan Wood, "Effect of Drug Law Enforcement on Drug Market Violence: A Systematic Review," *International Journal of Drug Policy* 22, no. 2 (2011): 87–94.

36. Parenti, *Lockdown America,* 59.

37. Keith A. Harriston and Mary Pat Flaherty, "D.C. Police Paying for Hiring Binge," *Washington Post,* August 28, 1994, https://www.washingtonpost.com/wp-srv/local/longterm/library/dc/dcpolice/94series/trainingday1.htm.

38. "The District's Troubled Police," *Washington Post,* August 28, 1994, https://www.washingtonpost.com/archive/politics/1994/08/28/the-districts-troubled-police/e99c70a1-b1ee-4aee-b324-83ac60eb2408.

39. Harriston and Flaherty, "D.C. Police Paying for Hiring Binge."

40. William J. Chambliss, *Power, Politics, and Crime* (Boulder, CO: Westview Press, 2001).

41. Forman, *Locking Up Our Own*, 172.

42. Interview 2020.

43. Forman, *Locking Up Our Own*, 171.

44. Allison Klein, "D.C. Police to Check Drivers in Violence-Plagued Trinidad," *Washington Post*, June 5, 2008, http://www.washingtonpost.com/wp-dyn/content/article/2008/06/04/AR2008060402205_pf.html.

45. Steven Alvarado, "The Complexities of Race and Place: Childhood Neighborhood Disadvantage and Adult Incarceration for Whites, Blacks, and Latinos," *Socius* (January 2020), https://doi.org/10.1177/2378023120927154.

46. Randol Contreras, *The Stickup Kids: Race, Drugs, Violence, and the American Dream* (Berkeley: University of California Press, 2013); Philippe Bourgois, *In Search of Respect: Selling Crack in El Barrio* (New York: Cambridge University Press, 2003).

47. Bourgois, *In Search of Respect*.

48. Interview 2017.

49. Interview 2017.

50. Interview 2019.

51. Interview 2017.

52. Interview 2020.

53. As indicated in note 4 above, Mustafa S. F. Zulu's story comes from his online writing as well as a letter he sent to me from prison describing his life story.

54. Interview 2017.

55. Interview 2019.

56. Interview 2017.

57. Interview 2018.

58. Oral history with Lashonia Thompson-El, Women of the WIRE, Interview by Kristin Adair, May 5, 2018, https://digdc.dclibrary.org/islandora/object/dcplislandora%3A267287.

59. Mary Pattillo, in *Black Picket Fences*, makes a similar point about how teens sometimes sold drugs as a way to alleviate boredom.

60. Judith A. Ryder and Regina E. Brisgone, "Cracked Perspectives: Reflections of Women and Girls in the Aftermath of the Crack Cocaine Era," *Feminist Criminology* 8, no. 1 (2013): 40–62.

61. Interview 2021.

62. Ryder and Brisgone, "Cracked Perspectives."

63. Forman, *Locking Up Our Own*.

64. Eric Lotke, "Hobbling a Generation: Young African American Men in Washington, DC's Criminal Justice System—Five Years Later," *Crime & Delinquency* 44, no. 3 (1998): 355–366.

65. "District of Columbia Profile," Prison Policy Initiative, 2018, https://www.prisonpolicy.org/profiles/DC.html.

CHAPTER 4. BRINGING IN THE FEDS

1. United States v. Strothers, Crim. No. 92-285.

2. William Gildea, "At Championship Game, Basketball a Certain Winner," *Washington Post,* March 9, 1992, https://advance.lexis.com/api/document?collection=news&id=urn:contentItem:3S8H-5040-000F-G3KH-00000-00&context=1516831.

3. United States v. Strothers, Crim. No. 92-285.

4. My research assistant, Eva Hernandez, and I did a search using LexisNexis to determine which street crews were charged with conspiracy-related charges between 1985 and 1995. Using the key words Washington DC, RICO, racketeering, continuing criminal enterprise, and street crews, we found all cases in the District of Columbia that included racketeering or conspiracy charges. The search revealed that six street crews were charged with racketeering or narcotics conspiracy charges between 1985 and 1995, all in high-profile cases. We found six RICO cases in DC between 1991 and 1995 that involved the distribution of crack cocaine (with no RICO cases before 1991). We then searched newspaper articles with these street crew names to find the media coverage in order to fill out the details of the crews' operations and the federal government's targeting.

5. Linda Wheeler, "NW Block Goes Cold Turkey and Savors It; D.C. Police Wrested Hanover Place from Drug Dealers and Made It Stick," *Washington Post,* April 23, 1988.

6. Nancy Lewis, "Defendant Ordered to Speak on Drugs," *Washington Post,* March 8, 1986.

7. Nancy Lewis, "Alleged Heroin Kingpin Arrested after Long Probe," *Washington Post,* February 20, 1998.

8. Nancy Lewis, "Md. Man Pleads Guilty in Heroin Case; Defendant Called One of Area's Biggest Dealers Forfeits 6 Houses," *Washington Post,* March 17, 1998.

9. Lewis, "Alleged Heroin Kingpin Arrested after Long Probe."

10. Henry S. Jaffe and Tom Sherwood, *Dream City: Race, Power, and the Decline of the City,* 2nd ed. (New York: Simon and Schuster, 2014).

11. Jaffe and Sherwood, *Dream City.*

12. Nancy Lewis and Sari Horwitz, "Area Sweep Nabs Alleged Drug Leaders; Federal, D.C. Forces Conduct Joint Raids," *Washington Post,* April 16, 1989.

13. United States of America v. Rayful Edmond, III, et al. Criminal No. 89-0162 (CRR), US District Court for the District of Columbia 730 F. Supp. 1144 (U.S. Dist. 1990), LEXIS 139.

14. Sari Horwitz, "Sweep Broke Drug Ring, Officials Say; 20–50% of Cocaine in D.C. Tied to Group," *Washington Post,* April 18, 1989.

15. Nancy Lewis, "Like Son, Like Father; Edmond Gets 18 Years," *Washington Post,* December 18, 1991.

16. Theresa Vargas, "How 'Free Tony Lewis' Became Both a Son's Plea and a Call on Biden to Create a National Clemency Program," *Washington Post,* April 10, 2021.

17. Keith L. Alexander, "After 30 Years behind Bars, '80s D.C. Drug Kingpin Rayful Edmond III Returns to Court in Hopes of Early Release; Prosecutors Say Edmond, Who Is Serving a Life Sentence, Helped Put Other Drug Dealers in Prison," *Washington Post Blogs,* October 15, 2019, https://advance.lexis.com/api/document?collection=news&id=urn:contentItem:5X8P-M501-DXKP-J0TH-00000-00&context=1516831; Martin Austermuhle, "Federal Judge Grants Sentence Reduction to D.C. Drug Kingpin Rayful Edmond," NPR, February 24, 2021, https://www.npr.org/local/305/2021/02/24/970530127/federal-judge-grants-sentence-reduction-to-d-c-drug-kingpin-rayful-edmond.

18. Elsa Walsh, "Addicted to the Dollar; Flashy D.C. Drug Lord's Generosity Lured Large Pool of Loyal Employees, Police Say," *Washington Post,* April 23, 1989.

19. "Violent Gang Task Forces," FBI, retrieved April 12, 2022, https://www.fbi.gov/investigate/violent-crime/gangs/violent-gang-task-forces.

20. Ruben Castaneda, "Federal Agents Are Now an 'Integral Part' of D.C. Law Enforcement," *Washington Post,* September 14, 1994.

21. Lesley Suzanne Bonney, "Prosecution of Sophisticated Urban Street Gangs: A Proper Application of RICO," *Catholic University Law Review* 42 (1992): 579; Lee Coppola and Nicholas DeMarco, "Civil RICO: How Ambiguity Allowed the Racketeer Influenced and Corrupt Organizations Act to Expand beyond Its Intended Purpose," *New England Journal on Criminal and Civil Confinement* 38 (2012): 241.

22. Susan Brenner, "RICO, CCE, and Other Complex Crimes: The Transformation of American Criminal Law," *William & Mary Bill of Rights Journal* 2, no. 2 (1993): 239.

23. William J. Chambliss, *Power, Politics and Crime* (Boulder, CO: Westview Press, 2001).

24. "Violent Gang Task Forces," FBI.

25. Interview by Ken Adelman, "Mean Streets; Prosecuting Drug Gangs Makes Mike Volkov Work with 'the Lowest of the Lows' but also with Some Courageous People," *Washingtonian*, November 1996, https://advance.lexis.com/api/document?collection=news&id=urn:contentItem:3SJ4-DTB0-0009-V1RD-00000-00&context=1516831.

26. Interview by Ken Adelman, "Mean Streets."

27. "Jury Selection to Begin Next Week in R Street Crew Racketeering Case," *Washington Post*, February 6, 1992.

28. Gabriel Escobar and Sari Horwitz, "24 Indicted as Members of Violent D.C. Drug Ring," *Washington Post*, September 26, 1991.

29. Michael York, "R Street Crew Trial Enters Fourth Week; Prosecutors in D.C. Case Plan to Trace Development of Drug Trade," *Washington Post*, March 9, 1992.

30. Michael York, "5 Convicted in R Street Drug Trial; Racketeering Law Used to Prosecute D.C. Gang Leaders," *Washington Post*, July 22, 1992.

31. Michael York, "R Street Crew Leaders Were Big Spenders, Prosecutors Say; Expensive Cars, $2,000 Pairs of Shoes Offered to Show Scope of Alleged Drug Operation," *Washington Post*, April 23, 1992.

32. Michael York and Linda Wheeler, "Fear Said to Affect R St. Jury: Concerns Revealed as Panel Ends Work," *Washington Post*, July 24, 1992.

33. Michael York, "Police Charge 18 in Drug Sweep; Arrests Said to Focus on P Street NE Group," *Washington Post*, February 1, 1992.

34. Courtland Milloy, "The Drug Raid That Went Thud," *Washington Post,* February 2, 1992; York, "Police Charge 18 in Drug Sweep."

35. "P Street Crew Drug Trial to Be Moved Back to D.C.," *Washington Post,* March 7, 1992.

36. Michael York, "All but One Defendant in P Street Drug Case Plea-Bargain," *Washington Post,* January 5, 1993.

37. "Drug Defendant Gets Eight Years," *Washington Post,* March 12, 1993, Metro, B7.

38. Michael York, "P Street Crew Case Ends without Trial; Last of 15 Defendants Accepts Plea Deal," *Washington Post,* January 7, 1993.

39. United States of America v. Antone R. White (#1), Eric A. Hicks (#2), Dan R. Hutchinson (#3), Ronald R. Hughes (#4), Derrick J. Ballard (#5), 1993, https://www.govinfo.gov/app/details/USCOURTS-dcd-1_93-cr-00097/summary, accessed February 1, 2023.

40. United States v. White (U.S. Dist. 2019), LEXIS 131687, 2019 WL 3719006 (US District Court for the District of Columbia, August 6, 2019, Filed), retrieved from https://advance.lexis.com/api/document?collection=cases&id=urn:cont entItem:5WRX-4DY1-F27X-6374-00000-00&context=1516831

41. United States v. White and United States v. Hicks [19-3058, 19-3059], December 29, 2020, Opinion [1877530] filed for the Court by Judge Edwards, https://www.govinfo.gov/app/details/USCOURTS-caDC-19-03058/context.

42. Michael York, "Group Accused of Violent Enterprise; 15 Arrested in Investigation of Newton Street Crew in NW," *Washington Post,* July 30, 1992.

43. Toni Locy, "Four Guilty of Murder in Newton Street Case; Drug Crew Members Face Life; 5th Man Cleared," *Washington Post,* October 14, 1994.

44. York, "Group Accused of Violent Enterprise."

45. Ruben Castaneda, "Agent's Killer Linked to Newton Street Crew," *Washington Post,* June 1, 1995; "2 Guilty in Newton Street Crew Case," *Washington Post,* May 20, 1993; "Alleged D.C. Gang Member Convicted," *Washington Post,* June 8, 1993; "D.C. Man Gets Life Term for His Role in Drug Gang," *Washington Post,* August 26, 1993.

46. In re Howes, 39 A.3d 1, 2012 D.C. App. LEXIS 87, 2012 WL 739420 (District of Columbia Court of Appeals March 8, 2012, Decided). Retrieved from https://advance.lexis.com/api/document?collection=cases&id=urn:contentItem: 554H-6261-F04C-F06D-00000-00&context=1516831.

47. Bill Miller and Hamil R. Harris, "13 Arrested in Raids on Gang in Northwest; More Than 200 Local, Federal Officers Involved," *Washington Post*, July 12, 1995.

48. Bill Miller, "NW Neighbors Gang Up to Roust Drug Dealers," *Washington Post*, August 7, 1995.

49. Miller and Harris, "13 Arrested in Raids on Gang in Northwest."

50. Bill Miller, "Leader of Fern Street Crew Gets Life Sentence," *Washington Post*, November 19, 1996, B03.

51. Toni Locy, "4 Convicted of Running Crack Ring; D.C. Residents' Patrol Helped Bring in Gang," *Washington Post*, August 9, 1996, https://www.washingtonpost.com/archive/local/1996/08/09/4-convicted-of-running-crack-ring/b6166a39-ef8f-4b3b-a8e2-9be6c21f044a.

52. Toni Locy and Nancy Lewis, "Clues in Deadly Attack on Police Sought after Crackdown on Gang," *Washington Post*, September 22, 1995; United States of America v. Kobi L. Mowatt, Defendant, 2010.

53. Toni Locy, "D.C. Crew Members Plead Guilty to Racketeering; Defendants' Gang Included Man Who Killed 3 at Police Headquarters," *Washington Post*, October 18, 1996.

54. Locy and Lewis, "Clues in Deadly Attack on Police Sought after Crackdown on Gang"; United States of America v. Kobi L. Mowatt, Defendant, 2010.

55. Toni Locy, "D.C. Crew Suspect Is Extradited; Man Linked to Gunman at Police Headquarters," *Washington Post*, March 7, 1996.

56. United States of America v. Kobi L. Mowatt, Defendant, 2010.

57. Locy, "D.C. Crew Members Plead Guilty to Racketeering."

58. Tucker Carlson, "Smoking Them Out; How to Close Down a Crack House in Your Neighborhood," *Police Review*, January 1, 1995, retrieved March 11, 2022, https://www.thefreelibrary.com/Smoking+them+out%3b+how+to+close+down+a+crack+house+in+your . . . -a016053747.

59. Shilpi Malinowski, *Shaw, LeDroit Park and Bloomingdale in Washington, DC: An Oral History* (Charleston, SC: History Press, 2021).

60. Tony Giancalo, "Concerned Neighbors March against Drugs," *Neighbors Ink* 31, no. 10, File Folder 13, January–September 1989, Box 34, Collection 110, Neighbors, Inc., Archive, Washingtoniana Collection, DCPL.

61. Miller and Harris, "13 Arrested in Raids on Gang in Northwest."

62. Miller, "NW Neighbors Gang Up to Roust Drug Dealers."

63. Derek Gilna, "DC Court Disbars Former Federal Prosecutor for Misconduct," *Prison Legal News*, March 15, 2013, retrieved October 2, 2022, https://www.prisonlegalnews.org/news/2013/mar/15/dc-court-disbars-former-federal-prosecutor-for-misconduct.

64. Gilmore, *Golden Gulag*.

CHAPTER 5. CHOCOLATE CITY NO MORE

1. Linda Wheeler, "From Drug Mart to Great Neighborhood? The Police Plan to Use Free-Market Capitalism to Start Hanover Place Boom," *Washington Post*, December 22, 1985, http://www.washingtonpost.com/archive/opinions/1985/12/22/from-drug-mart-to-great-neighborhoodthe-police-plan-to-use-free-market-capitalism-to-start-hanover-place-boom/bae402c2-f1fe-40fd-b2e6-3d263b721c6c/?tid=ss_tw.

2. Michele Lerner, "A Onetime Home for Horses in Northwest Washington Will Have 114 Condos in Place of Stalls," *Washington Post*, April 3, 2018, https://www.washingtonpost.com/realestate/a-onetime-home-for-horses-will-have-114-condos-in-place-of-stalls/2018/04/02/3fceod90-31cf-11e8-8abc-22a366b72f2d_story.html.

3. Ruth Glass, *London, Aspects of Change* (London: Centre for Urban Studies, 1964); Neil Smith, *The New Urban Frontier: Gentrification and the Revanchist City* (New York: Routledge, 1996); Neil Smith, "Gentrification and the Rent Gap," *Annals of the Association of American Geographers* 77, no. 3 (September 1987): 462–465.

4. Asch and Musgrove, *Chocolate City*; Natwar Gandhi, James Spaulding, and Gordon McDonald, "Budget Growth, Spending, and Inequality in DC, 2002–2013," in Hyra and Prince, *Capital Dilemma*, 177–197.

5. "Department of Corrections Closes Final Prison and Accomplishes Major Milestone," DC.gov, November 19, 2001, https://doc.dc.gov/release/department-corrections-closes-final-prison-and-accomplishes-major-milestone; Yesim Sayin Taylor, "Twenty Years after the Revitalization Act, the District of Columbia Is a Different City," D.C. Policy Center, December 19, 2017, https://www.dcpolicycenter.org/publications/twenty-years-revitalization-act-district-columbia-different-city.

6. Asch and Musgrove, *Chocolate City*.

7. Asch and Musgrove, *Chocolate City*.

8. District of Columbia, Office of Planning, *District of Columbia Strategic Neighborhood Action Plan: Neighborhood Cluster 17* (Washington, DC: Government of the District of Columbia, 2002).

9. District of Columbia, Office of Planning, Comprehensive Plan, 2006, https://planning.dc.gov/page/2006-comprehensive-plan.

10. Kevin Schaul and Jonathan O'Connell, "Investors Bought a Record Share of Homes in 2021. See Where," *Washington Post*, February 16, 2022, https://www.washingtonpost.com/business/interactive/2022/housing-market-investors.

11. Council of the District of Columbia, "The Comprehensive Plan for the National Capital: District Elements," DC Office of Documents and Administrative Issuances, 2006, quote from 22–26.

12. NOMA BID, accessed February 25, 2022, https://www.nomabid.org.

13. Sabiyha Prince, *African Americans and Gentrification in Washington, DC: Race, Class and Social Justice in the Nation's Capital* (New York: Routledge, 2014); Ashanté M. Reese, *Black Food Geographies: Race, Self-Reliance, and Food Access in Washington, DC* (Chapel Hill: University of North Carolina Press, 2019); Rebecca Summer, "Writing Out Black History in Washington, DC: How Historical Narratives Support a Performance of Progressiveness in Gentrifying Urban Spaces," *Urban Geography* (March 22, 2021): 1–20, https://doi.org/10.1080/0272363 8.2021.1902141.

14. Allison Suppan Helmuth, "'Chocolate City, Rest in Peace': White Space-Claiming and the Exclusion of Black People in Washington, DC," *City & Community* 18, no. 3 (2019): 746–769.

15. Zawadi Rucks-Ahidiana, "Theorizing Gentrification as a Process of Racial Capitalism," *City & Community* 21, no. 3 (2021), https://doi.org/10.1177 /15356841211054790.

16. Summers, *Black in Place*.

17. Hyra, *Race, Class, and Politics in the Cappuccino City*.

18. Derek S. Hyra, "Conceptualizing the New Urban Renewal: Comparing the Past to the Present," *Urban Affairs Review* 48, no. 4 (July 2012): 498–527, https://doi.org/10.1177/1078087411434905.

19. Gina Pérez, *The Near Northwest Side Story: Migration, Displacement, and Puerto Rican Families* (Berkeley: University of California Press, 2004).

20. Heather Ann Thompson, "Rethinking the Politics of White Flight in the Postwar City: Detroit, 1945–1980," *Journal of Urban History* 25, no. 2 (1999): 163–198.

21. Brenden Beck, "Policing Gentrification: Stops and Low-Level Arrests during Demographic Change and Real Estate Reinvestment," *City & Community* 19, no. 1 (2020): 245–272; Charles R. Collins, Forrest Stuart, and Patrick Janulis, "Policing Gentrification or Policing Displacement? Testing the Relationship between Order Maintenance Policing and Neighbourhood Change in Los Angeles," *Urban Studies* 59, no. 2 (2022): 414–433; Ayobami Laniyonu, "Coffee Shops and Street Stops: Policing Practices in Gentrifying Neighborhoods," *Urban Affairs Review* 54, no. 5 (2018): 898–930; Tanya Golash-Boza, Hyunsu Oh, and Carmen Salazar, "Broken Windows and Order-Maintenance Policing in Gentrifying Washington, DC," *Policing and Society* (2022). https://doi.org/10.1080/10439463.2022.2085268.

22. Valencia Mohammed, "Legendary McKinley Tech Re-Opens," *Afro-American Red Star*, August 21, 2004, A1, https://www.proquest.com/docview /369570087.

23. My research team implemented a housing survey in Eckington and Brightwood Park to assess the level and forms of reinvestment in these neighborhoods. Inspired by Jackelyn Hwang's Google Street View Observations survey, we adapted her survey and created a version suitable for Washington, DC. Most of the data collection took place in 2020. Graduate and undergraduate student researchers walked down every block in Eckington and Brightwood Park and assessed the level of public and private investment and disinvestment. This included a total of 62 block faces in Eckington and 154 in Brightwood Park. Each block face has at least one structure. The maximum number of structures on a block was 29. There were 1,452 structures in Brightwood Park and 721 in Eckington. The full results are reported on our website, MappingGentrification.com.

24. Michelle Goldchain "Petworth Is the Hottest Neighborhood in the Nation for Home Flipping," *DC Curbed,* March 18, 2016, https://dc.curbed .com/2016/3/18/11261440/home-flipping-washington-dc-petworth.

25. James Lloyd, "Community Development, Research, and Reinvestment: The Struggle against Redlining in Washington, DC, 1970–1995" (MA thesis, Ohio University, 2012).

26. Lloyd, "Community Development, Research, and Reinvestment."

27. Although the price of homes plummeted in the suburbs of DC during the Great Recession (2007–2009), particularly in majority-Black Prince George's County, home values in DC remained fairly steady.

28. Holley Simmons, "Why Upshur Street Has Evolved into the Best Place to Eat in DC Right Now," *Washington Post,* September 6, 2017, https://www .washingtonpost.com/goingoutguide/why-upshur-street-is-the-best-place-to-eat -in-dc-right-now/2017/09/06/20fa0532-8da5-11e7-8df5-c2e5cf46c1e2_story.html.

29. Interview 2019.

30. Interview 2017.

31. Interview 2017.

32. Interview 2017.

33. Interview 2017.

34. Manny Fernandez, "Longtime Residents Welcome Clifton Terrace Transformation," *Washington Post,* June 30, 2004, www.washingtonpost.com /wp-dyn/articles/A16029-2004Jun29.html.

35. Interview 2018.

36. Kathryn L. Howell, "'For the kids': Children, Safety, and the Depoliticization of Displacement in Washington, DC," *Journal of Urban Affairs* 40, no. 5 (2018): 721–739, https://doi.org/10.1080/07352166.2017.1360742; Kathryn L. Howell, "'It's complicated . . .': Long-Term Residents and Their Relationships to Gentrification in Washington, DC," in Hyra and Prince, *Capital Dilemma,* 255–278; Helmuth, "'Chocolate City, Rest in Peace"; Sidney L. Holt, Ana María del Río-González, Jenné S. Massie, and Lisa Bowleg, "'I Live in This Neighborhood Too, Though': The Psychosocial Effects of Gentrification on Low-Income Black Men Living in Washington, DC," *Journal of Racial and Ethnic Health Disparities* (2020): 1–14.

37. Golash-Boza, Oh, and Salazar, "Broken Windows and Order-Maintenance Policing in Gentrifying Washington, DC"; Tanya Golash-Boza, Hyunsu Oh, and Robert Kane, "Gentrification, White Encroachment, and the Policing of Black Residents in Washington, DC," *Critical Criminology,* https://doi.org/10 .1007/s10612-022-09670-9.

38. Interview 2019.

39. Interview 2018.

40. Carley M. Shinault and Richard Seltzer, "Whose Turf, Whose Town? Race, Status, and Attitudes of Washington DC Residents toward Gentrification," *Journal of African American Studies* 23, no. 1 (2019): 72–91.

41. Holt et al., "'I Live in This Neighborhood Too, Though.'"

42. Bruce Ormond Grant, "Reducing Barriers for Job Seekers," D.C. Policy Center, May 23, 2018, https://www.dcpolicycenter.org/publications/reducing-barriers-for-job-seekers-in-d-c-and-the-metro-region.

43. Interview 2017.

44. Interview 2020.

45. Interview 2020.

46. Kathryn Howell, *Affordable Housing Preservation in Washington, DC: A Framework for Local Funding, Collaborative Governance and Community Organizing for Change* (New York: Routledge, 2021); Brian Johnson, "Here's How DC's Inclusionary Zoning Program Works," *Greater Greater Washington,* September 1, 2015, accessed December 18, 2021, https://ggwash.org/view/39157/heres-how-dcs-inclusionary-zoning-program-works.

47. Interview 2020.

48. Interview 2020.

49. Interview 2020.

50. Interview 2019.

51. Neil Smith, "Toward a Theory of Gentrification: A Back to the City Movement by Capital, not People," *Journal of the American Planning Association* 45 (1979): 538–548.

CHAPTER 6. RACIALIZED REINVESTMENT

1. "The Navy Yard Reshena Knew," interview by Johanna Bockman, Arthur Capper website, accessed November 4, 2021, https://arthurcapper.omeka.net /items/show/44.

2. Hyra, "Conceptualizing the New Urban Renewal."

3. Institute on Metropolitan Opportunity, University of Minnesota Law School, "American Neighborhood Change in the 21st Century," April 2019, https://www.law.umn.edu/sites/law.umn.edu/files/metro-files/american_ neighborhood_change_in_the_21st_century_-_full_report_-_4-1-2019.pdf_ the_21st_century—full report—4-1-2019.pdf.

4. Johanna Bockman, "Removing the Public from Public Housing: Public-Private Redevelopment of the Ellen Wilson Dwellings in Washington, DC," *Journal of Urban Affairs* (2018): 3, https://doi.org/10.1080/07352166.2018.1457406.

5. Edward G. Goetz, "Obsolescence and the Transformation of Public Housing Communities in the US," *International Journal of Housing Policy* 12, no. 3 (2012): 331–345, https://doi.org/10.1080/14616718.2012.709671.

6. Nena Perry-Brown, "How Greenleaf Gardens' Redevelopment Is Wedded to the DC Housing Authority's Own Evolution," *Greater Greater Washington,* March 27, 2020, https://ggwash.org/view/76828/dcha-and-green leaf-gardens.

7. Meagan Cahill, "Using the Weighted Displacement Quotient to Explore Crime Displacement from Public Housing Redevelopment Sites," *Cityscape* 13, no. 3 (2011): 103–134.

8. Lawrence J. Vale and Yonah Freemark, "From Public Housing to Public-Private Housing," *Journal of the American Planning Association* 78, no. 4 (2012): 379–402.

9. Christopher A. Hart, "Old Solutions for New Communities: The Failed Promise of DC's New Communities Initiative" (thesis, George Washington University, 2020), https://www.proquest.com/dissertations-theses/old-solutions-new-communities-failed-promise-dc-s/docview/2408524393/se-2.

10. Christine Spolar, "Hopes Ride on Metro; Navy Yard Neighbors Look for Changes," *Washington Post,* December 25, 1991, https://www.proquest.com/newspapers/hopes-ride-on-metro-navy-yard-neighbors-look/docview/307459590/se-2.

11. Laura Lang and David Morton, "Hood Winked," *City Paper,* September 27, 2022, https://www.washingtoncitypaper.com/news/article/13025044/hood-winked; Peter A. Tatian, G. Thomas Kingsley, Margery Austin Turner, Jennifer Comey, and Randy Rosso, "State of Washington, DC's Neighborhoods," Urban Institute, September 30, 2008, https://www.researchgate.net/profile/Peter_Tatian/publication/238764250_State_of_Washington_DC's_Neighborhoods/links/54ae8de00cf2b48e8ed3ff41/State-of-Washington-DCs-Neighborhoods.pdf.

12. Lang and Morton, "Hood Winked"; Ellie Walton and Sam Wild, "Chocolate City," independent film, https://www.youtube.com/watch?v=P1NkfATQvj4.

13. Ellie Walton, "Struggling to Get Back," video, https://vimeo.com/6929949.

14. "The Yards," accessed October 3, 2022, http://jdland.com/dc/yards.cfm; Timothy D. MacKinnon, "Capitol Navy Yard: A 21st Century Transition" (PhD diss., Rutgers University, 2017).

15. "The Yards"; MacKinnon, "Capitol Navy Yard."

16. "The Yards"; MacKinnon, "Capitol Navy Yard."

17. David Nakamura, "Long before the World Series, This Ragtag Group of D.C. Property Owners Was Evicted to Make Way for Baseball," *Washington Post,* October 24, 2019, https://www.washingtonpost.com/local/long-before-the-world-series-this-ragtag-group-of-dc-property-owners-was-evicted-to-make-way-for-baseball/2019/10/24/50a945c8-f4d6-11e9-8cf0-4cc99f74d127_story.html.

18. "DC Will Break Even on Capitol Riverfront Investments This Year," WTOP News, February 14, 2008, https://wtop.com/business-finance/2018/02/dc-will-break-even-on-capitol-riverfront-investments.

19. Marc Fisher, "The Promise: Nationals Park Would Transform the City. Did It?," *Washington Post,* July 14, 2018, https://www.washingtonpost.com/classic-apps/the-promise-nationals-park-would-transform-the-city-did-it/2018/07/14/233c968e-7e0e-11e8-b660-4d0f9f0351f1_story.html.

20. Paul Schwartzman, "The End of the Dwellings: Prospects Uncertain for Those Who Leave East Capitol Complex," *Washington Post,* July 27, 2003, https://search.proquest.com/docview/2267670917; Natalie Hopkinson, "House of Blues; Marvin Gaye's Boyhood Home Awaits the Wrecking Ball or a Second Act," *Washington Post,* May 19, 2003, https://search.proquest.com/docview/409466206.

21. Debbi Wilgoren, "New Housing for Seniors Opens Doors at E. Capitol," *Washington Post,* May 20, 2005, https://www.proquest.com/newspapers/new-housing-seniors-opens-doors-at-e-capitol/docview/409904356/se-2; Donna Comrie, "Linking Public Housing to Education: A Comparative Case Study of HOPE VI," *Housing Policy Debate* 28, no. 4 (2018): 534–552, https://doi.org/10.1080/10511482.2017.1397725.

22. Comrie "Linking Public Housing to Education."

23. Nena Perry-Brown, "Barry Farm Redevelopment Illustrates How Far DCHA Still Has to Go," *Greater Greater Washington,* April 7, 2021, https://ggwash.org/view/80939/barry-farm-redevelopment-illustrates-how-far-dcha-still-has-to-go.

24. "Mayor Bowser Breaks Ground on The Asberry, the First On Site Building Delivered under the New Communities Initiative at Barry Farm," September 26, 2022, https://mayor.dc.gov/release/mayor-bowser-breaks-ground-asberry-first-site-building-delivered-under-new-communities; Shannen

Hill, "Barry Farm Residents Being Forced Out," *Afro-American Red Star,* February 2015, https://www.proquest.com/newspapers/barry-farm-residents-being-forced-out/docview/1663907178/se-2.

25. DC Oral History Collaborative, Barry Farm Oral History Project, Narrator: Paulette Matthews, Interviewer: Sabiyha Prince, June 21, 2019.

26. DC Oral History Collaborative, Barry Farm Oral History Project, Narrator: Michelle Hamilton, Interviewer: Sabiyha Prince, June 28, 2019, https://digdc.dclibrary.org/islandora/object/dcplislandora%3A291831.

27. DC Oral History Collaborative, Barry Farm Oral History Project, Narrator: Nicole Odom, Interviewer: Sabiyha Prince, August 2, 2019, https://digdc.dclibrary.org/islandora/object/dcplislandora%3A291810.

28. Kalfani Nyerere Ture, "Fighting the Farms: Structural Violence, Race, and Resistance in Washington, D.C." (PhD diss., American University, 2017), https://www.proquest.com/dissertations-theses/fighting-farms-structural-violence-race/docview/1881550137/se-2?accountid=14515.

29. Barry Farm Redevelopment Plan, accessed November 1, 2021, https://barryfarmredevelopment.org/about_the_redevelopment-2.

30. Washington DC Economic Partnership, "DC Neighborhood Profiles, 2021 Edition," https://issuu.com/wdcep/docs/2021-wdcep-nhoodprofiles-7-web-2.

31. Jason Cherkis, "The Cost of Leaving," *Washington City Paper,* May 20, 2005, accessed May 25, 2022, http://www.washingtoncitypaper.com/articles/30614/the-cost-of-leaving.

32. "Housing D.C. Felons Far Away from Home: Effects on Crime, Recidivism and Reentry," US Government Printing Office, May 5, 2010, https://www.govinfo.gov/content/pkg/CHRG-111hhrg58348/html/CHRG-111hhrg58348.htm.

33. Cherkis, "The Cost of Leaving."

34. Interview 2021.

35. Interview 2020.

36. Interview 2020.

37. Interview 2020.

38. Interview 2020.

39. Interview 2020.

40. "Francis A. Gregory Library," Adjaye Associates, retrieved October 3, 2022, https://www.adjaye.com/work/francis-a-gregory-library.

41. Philip Kennicott, "District's New Pair of Libraries Are Exuberant Additions to Distressed Areas," *Washington Post,* June 25, 2012, https://www.washingtonpost.com/entertainment/districts-new-pair-of-libraries-are-exuberant-additions-to-distressed-areas/2012/06/25/gJQAJ9Ej2V_story.html.

CONCLUSION

1. Yesim Sayin Taylor, "Twenty Years after the Revitalization Act, the District of Columbia Is a Different City," D.C. Policy Center, December 19, 2017, https://www.dcpolicycenter.org/publications/twenty-years-revitalization-act-district-columbia-different-city.

2. "Department of Corrections Closes Final Prison and Accomplishes Major Milestone," DC.gov, November 19, 2001, https://doc.dc.gov/release/department-corrections-closes-final-prison-and-accomplishes-major-milestone.

3. "Housing D.C. Felons Far Away from Home: Effects on Crime, Recidivism and Reentry," US Government Printing Office, May 5, 2010, https://www.govinfo.gov/content/pkg/CHRG-111hhrg58348/html/CHRG-111hhrg58348.htm.

4. "Housing D.C. Felons Far Away from Home," US Government Printing Office; Bailey Thamar, "Where Are DC Convicts Being Held?," DCwitness.org, November 14, 2018, http://dcwitness.org/where-are-dc-convicts-being-held.

5. Although White supremacist organizations are active in many state prisons, they were not active in Lorton, where nearly all imprisoned people were Black.

6. "District of Columbia Profile," District of Columbia profile, Prison Policy Initiative, 2018, https://www.prisonpolicy.org/profiles/DC.html.

7. Travis J. Meyers, Kevin A. Wright, Jacob T. N. Young, and Melinda Tasca, "Social Support from Outside the Walls: Examining the Role of Relationship Dynamics among Inmates and Visitors," *Journal of Criminal Justice* 52 (2017): 57–67, https://doi.org/10.1016/j.jcrimjus.2017.07.012; Grant Duwe and Valerie Clark, "Blessed Be the Social Tie That Binds: The Effects of Prison Visitation on Offender Recidivism," *Criminal Justice Policy Review* 24, no. 3 (2011): 271–296, https://doi.org/10.1177/0887403411429724; Logan M. Lee, "Far from Home and All Alone: The Impact of Prison Visitation on Recidivism," *American Law and Economics Review* 21, no. 2 (Fall 2019): 431–481, https://doi.org/10.1093/aler

/ahz011; Susan McNeeley and Grant Duwe, "Keep Your Friends Close and Your Enemies Closer: Prison Visitation, Spatial Distance, and Concentrated Disadvantage of Visitor Neighborhoods, and Offender Recidivism," *Justice Quarterly* 37, no. 4 (2020): 571–589, https://doi.org/10.1080/07418825.2019.1568521.

8. "Universal Declaration of Human Rights," United Nations, December 10, 1948, https://www.un.org/en/universal-declaration-human-rights.

9. Interview 2019.

10. Trung T. Phan, "The Hustle. He Was Facing Life in Prison. Now, He's the CEO of the 'Instagram for the Incarcerated,'" *The Hustle*, January 30, 2021, accessed December 16, 2021, https://thehustle.co/he-was-facing-life-in-prison-now-hes-the-ceo-of-the-instagram-for-the-incarcerated.

11. Elliot C. Williams, "Halim Flowers Was Given Two Life Sentences at 17. Now, His Art Is Shown Worldwide," NPR, December 3, 2021, accessed December 16, 2021, https://www.npr.org/local/305/2021/12/03/1061183998/halim-flowers-was-given-two-life-sentences-at-17-now-his-art-is-shown-worldwide.

12. Maurice Jackson, "An Analysis: African American Employment, Population, and Housing Trends in Washington, DC," submitted to the Commission on African American Affairs, District of Columbia Government, 2017.

13. Wendy Sawyer, "Since You Asked: How Did the 1994 Crime Bill Affect Prison College Programs?," Prison Policy Initiative, August 22, 2019, accessed April 4, 2022, https://www.prisonpolicy.org/blog/2019/08/22/college-in-prison.

14. Junia Howell and Elizabeth Korver-Glenn, "The Increasing Effect of Neighborhood Racial Composition on Housing Values, 1980–2015," *Social Problems* 68, no. 4 (November 2021): 1051–1071, https://doi.org/10.1093/socpro/spaa033.

15. Mary Pattillo, "Housing: Commodity versus Right," *Annual Review of Sociology* 39 (2013): 509–531.

16. Ruth Wilson Gilmore, *Change Everything: Racial Capitalism and the Case for Abolition* (New York: Haymarket, 2022); Moon-Kie Jung and João H. Costa Vargas, eds., *Antiblackness* (Durham, NC: Duke University Press, 2021).

References

Acker, C. "How Crack Found a Niche in the American Ghetto: The Historical Epidemiology of Drug-Related Harm." *BioSocieties* 5 (2010): 70–88. https://doi.org/10.1057/biosoc.2009.1.

Aldous, Joan. "Cuts in Selected Welfare Programs: The Effects on US Families." *Journal of Family Issues* 7, no. 2 (1986): 161–177.

Alvarado, Steven. "The Complexities of Race and Place: Childhood Neighborhood Disadvantage and Adult Incarceration for Whites, Blacks, and Latinos." *Socius* (January 2020). https://doi.org/10.1177/2378023120927154.

Amos, Alcione M. *Barry Farm—Hillsdale in Anacostia: A Historic African American Community.* Charleston, SC: History Press, 2021.

Asch, Chris Myers, and George Derek Musgrove. *Chocolate City: A History of Race and Democracy in the Nation's Capital.* Chapel Hill: University of North Carolina Press, 2017.

Baumer, Eric. "Poverty, Crack, and Crime: A Cross-City Analysis." *Journal of Research in Crime and Delinquency* 31, no. 3 (1994): 311–327.

Beck, Brenden. "Policing Gentrification: Stops and Low–Level Arrests during Demographic Change and Real Estate Reinvestment." *City & Community* 19, no. 1 (2020): 245–272.

Betancur, John J. "The Politics of Gentrification: The Case of West Town in Chicago." *Urban Affairs Review* 37, no. 6 (July 2002): 780–814. https://doi.org/10.1177/107874037006002.

Blumstein, Alfred. "Homicide and Crack Connection." *Criminology* 15, no. 4 (1999): 379–406.

———. "Youth, Guns, and Violent Crime." *The Future of Children* 12, no. 2 (Summer–Fall 2002): 38–53. https://doi.org/10.2307/1602737.

Bockman, Johanna. "Removing the Public from Public Housing: Public-Private Redevelopment of the Ellen Wilson Dwellings in Washington, DC." *Journal of Urban Affairs* (2018). https://doi.org/10.1080/07352166.2018.1457406.

Bonney, Lesley Suzanne. "Prosecution of Sophisticated Urban Street Gangs: A Proper Application of RICO." *Catholic University Law Review* 42 (1992): 579–613.

Boston, Amanda T. "Manufacturing Distress: Race, Redevelopment, and the EB-5 Program in Central Brooklyn." *Critical Sociology* 47, no. 6 (2021): 961–976.

Bourgois, Philippe. *In Search of Respect: Selling Crack in El Barrio.* New York: Cambridge University Press, 2003.

Bowling, Benjamin. "The Rise and Fall of New York Murder: Zero Tolerance or Crack's Decline?" *British Journal of Criminology* 39, no. 4 (1999): 531–554.

Boyd, Michelle R. *Jim Crow Nostalgia: Reconstructing Race in Bronzeville.* Minneapolis: University of Minnesota Press, 2008.

Braman, Donald. *Doing Time on the Outside: Incarceration and Family Life in Urban America.* Ann Arbor: University of Michigan Press, 2007.

Brenner, Susan. "RICO, CCE, and Other Complex Crimes: The Transformation of American Criminal Law." *William & Mary Bill of Rights Journal* 2, no. 2 (1993): 239–304.

Brown, Lawrence T. *The Black Butterfly: The Harmful Politics of Race and Space in America.* Baltimore: Johns Hopkins University Press, 2021.

Brownstein, Henry. H. *The Rise and Fall of a Violent Crime Wave: Crack Cocaine and the Social Construction of a Crime Problem.* Guilderland, NY: Harrow and Heston, 1996.

Burden-Stelly, Charisse. "Modern U.S. Racial Capitalism." *Monthly Review* 72, no. 3 (2020): 8–20. https://monthlyreview.org/2020/07/01/modern-u-s-racial-capitalism.

Cahill, Meagan. "Using the Weighted Displacement Quotient to Explore Crime Displacement from Public Housing Redevelopment Sites." *Cityscape* (2011): 103–134.

Caplan, Marvin Harold. *Farther Along: A Civil Rights Memoir.* Baton Rouge: Louisiana State University Press, 1999.

Caplan, Marvin, and Ralph Blessing. "Shepherd Park: Creating an Integrated Community." In *Washington at Home: An Illustrated History of Neighborhoods in the Nation's Capital,* 2nd ed., ed. K. Schneider Smith, 449–463. Baltimore: Johns Hopkins University Press, 2010.

Carlson, Tucker. "Smoking Them Out; How to Close Down a Crack House in Your Neighborhood." *Policy Review* (January 1, 1995). Retrieved March 11, 2022, from https://www.thefreelibrary.com/Smoking+them+out%3b+how+to+close+down+a+crack+house+in+your . . . -a016053747.

Chambliss, William J. *Power, Politics, and Crime.* Boulder, CO: Westview Press, 2001.

Collins, Charles R., Forrest Stuart, and Patrick Janulis. "Policing Gentrification or Policing Displacement? Testing the Relationship between Order Maintenance Policing and Neighbourhood Change in Los Angeles." *Urban Studies* 59, no. 2 (2022): 414–433.

Comrie, Donna. "Linking Public Housing to Education: A Comparative Case Study of HOPE VI." *Housing Policy Debate* 28, no. 4 (2018): 534–552. https://doi.org/10.1080/10511482.2017.1397725.

Contreras, Randol. *The Stickup Kids: Race, Drugs, Violence, and the American Dream.* Berkeley: University of California Press, 2013.

Cooke, Paul. "Present Status of Integration in the Public Schools of the District of Columbia." *Journal of Negro Education* 24, no. 3 (1955): 205–218.

Coppola, Lee, and Nicholas DeMarco. "Civil RICO: How Ambiguity Allowed the Racketeer Influenced and Corrupt Organizations Act to Expand beyond Its Intended Purpose." *New England Journal on Criminal and Civil Confinement* 38 (2012): 241–254.

Dantzler, Prentiss. "The Urban Process under Racial Capitalism: Race, Anti-Blackness, and Capital Accumulation." *Journal of Race, Ethnicity and the City* 2, no. 2 (2021): 113–134. https://doi.org/10.1080/26884674.2021.1934201.

Dembo, R., P. Hughes, L. Jackson, and T. Mieczkowski. "Crack Cocaine Dealing by Adolescents in Two Public Housing Projects: A Pilot Study." *Human*

Organization 52, no. 1 (1993): 89–96. Retrieved from http://www.jstor.org/stable/44126549.

De Vita, Carol J., Carlos A. Manjarrez, and Eric C. Twombly. "Poverty in the District of Columbia—Then and Now." Report prepared for the United Planning Organization, Urban Institute, Washington, DC, 2000. https://www.urban.org/sites/default/files/publication/62496/409454-Poverty-in-the-District-of-Columbia-Then-and-Now.PDF.

Diner, Steven J. "Crisis of Confidence: Public Confidence in the Schools of the Nation's Capital in the Twentieth Century." *Urban Education* 25, no. 2 (1990): 112–137.

District of Columbia. Office of Planning. *District of Columbia Strategic Neighborhood Action Plan: Neighborhood Cluster 17.* Washington, DC: Government of the District of Columbia, 2002.

Drew, Joseph. "Recurring Themes of Educational Finance in the History of Washington, D.C., 1804–1982." Studies in D.C. History and Public Policy Paper No. 3. University of the District of Columbia, 1982.

Duwe, Grant, and Valerie Clark. "Blessed Be the Social Tie That Binds: The Effects of Prison Visitation on Offender Recidivism." *Criminal Justice Policy Review* 24, no. 3 (2011): 271–296. https://doi.org/10.1177/0887403411429724.

Estes, Nick, Ruth Wilson Gilmore, and Christopher Loperena, "United in Struggle: As Racial Capitalism Rages, Movements for Indigenous Sovereignty and Abolition Offer Visions of Freedom on Stolen Land." *NACLA Report on the Americas* 53, no. 3 (2021): 255–267.

Farber, David. *Crack: Rock Cocaine, Street Capitalism, and the Decade of Greed.* New York: Cambridge University Press, 2019.

Fauntroy, Michael K. *Home Rule or House Rule: Congress and the Erosion of Local Governance in the District of Columbia.* Lanham, MD: University Press of America, 2003.

Forman, James, Jr. *Locking Up Our Own: Crime and Punishment in Black America.* New York: Farrar, Straus and Giroux, 2017.

Freeman, Lance. "Displacement or Succession? Residential Mobility in Gentrifying Neighborhoods." *Urban Affairs Review* 40, no. 4 (2005): 463–491.

———. *A Haven and a Hell: The Ghetto in Black America.* New York: Columbia University Press, 2019.

Gallagher, Carolyn. *The Politics of Staying Put: Condo Conversion and Tenant Right-to-Buy in Washington, DC.* Philadelphia: Temple University Press, 2016.

Gandhi, Natwar M., James Spaulding, and Gordon McDonald. "Budget Growth, Spending, and Inequality in DC, 2002–2013." In *Capital Dilemma: Growth and Inequality in Washington, DC,* ed. Derek S. Hyra and Sabiyha Prince, 177–197. New York: Routledge, 2016.

Gillette, Howard, Jr. *Between Justice and Beauty: Race, Planning, and the Failure of Urban Policy in Washington.* Philadelphia: University of Pennsylvania Press, 2011.

Gilmore, Ruth Wilson. *Change Everything: Racial Capitalism and the Case for Abolition.* New York: Haymarket, 2022.

———. *Golden Gulag.* Berkeley: University of California Press, 2007.

Gilmore, Ruth Wilson, and Craig Gilmore. "Beyond Bratton." In *Policing the Planet: Why the Policing Crisis Led to Black Lives Matter,* ed. Jordan T. Camp and Christina Heatherton, 173–199. London: Verso, 2016.

Glass, Ruth. *London, Aspects of Change.* London: Centre for Urban Studies, 1964.

Glotzer, Paige. *How the Suburbs Were Segregated: Developers and the Business of Exclusionary Housing, 1890–1960.* New York: Columbia University Press, 2020.

Goetz, Edward G. "Obsolescence and the Transformation of Public Housing Communities in the US." *International Journal of Housing Policy* 12, no. 3 (2012): 331–345. https://doi.org/10.1080/14616718.2012.709671.

Golash-Boza, Tanya. "A Critical and Comprehensive Sociological Theory of Race and Racism." *Sociology of Race and Ethnicity* 2, no. 2 (2016): 129–141.

Golash-Boza, Tanya, Hyunsu Oh, and Robert Kane. "Gentrification, White Encroachment, and the Policing of Black Residents in Washington, DC." *Critical Criminology* (2022). https://doi.org/10.1007/s10612-022-09670-9.

Golash-Boza, Tanya, Hyunsu Oh, and Carmen Salazar. "Broken Windows and Order-Maintenance Policing in Gentrifying Washington, DC." *Policing and Society* (2022). https://doi.org/10.1080/10439463.2022.2085268.

Gordon, Adam. "The Creation of Homeownership: How New Deal Changes in Banking Regulation Simultaneously Made Homeownership Accessible to Whites and Out of Reach for Blacks." *Yale Law Journal* 115 (2005): 186–226.

Gotham, Kevin Fox. "Racialization and the State: The Housing Act of 1934 and the Creation of the Federal Housing Administration." *Sociological Perspectives* 43, no. 2 (2000): 291–317.

Grandine, Katherine. "Brightwood: From Tollgate to Suburb." In *Washington at Home: An Illustrated History of Neighborhoods in the Nation's Capital,* 2nd ed., ed. K. Schneider Smith, 123–138. Baltimore: Johns Hopkins University Press, 2010.

Green, Constance McLaughlin. *Secret City: A History of Race Relations in the Nation's Capital.* Princeton, NJ: Princeton University Press, [1967] 2015.

Hanchett, Thomas W. "The Other 'Subsidized Housing': Federal Aid to Suburbanization, 1940s–1960s." In *From Tenements to the Taylor Homes: In Search of an Urban Housing Policy in Twentieth-Century America,* ed. John F. Bauman, Roger Biles, and Kristin M. Szylvian, 163–179. University Park: Pennsylvania State University Press, 2000.

Hansen, Carl F. *Danger in Washington: The Story of My Twenty Years in the Public Schools in the Nation's Capital.* West Nyack, NY: Parker, 1968.

Harrell, Rodney. "Understanding Modern Segregation: Suburbanization and the Black Middle Class." PhD dissertation, University of Maryland, College Park, 2008.

Hart, Christopher A. "Old Solutions for New Communities: The Failed Promise of DC's New Communities Initiative." Thesis, George Washington University, 2020. https://www.proquest.com/dissertations-theses/old-solutions-new-communities-failed-promise-dc-s/docview/2408524393/se-2.

Hartman, Sadiya. *Lose Your Mother: A Journey along the Atlantic Slave Route.* New York: Farrar, Straus and Giroux, 2007.

Harvey, David. *A Brief History of Neoliberalism.* Oxford: Oxford University Press, 2007.

———. *The Limits to Capital.* New York: Verso, [1982] 2018.

Heard, Sandra R. "Making Slums and Suburbia in Black Washington during the Great Depression." *American Studies* 57, no. 4 (2019): 5–22.

Heflin, Colleen M., and Mary Pattillo. "Kin Effects on Black-White Account and Home Ownership." *Sociological Inquiry* 72, no. 2 (2002): 220–239.

Helmuth, Allison Suppan. "'Chocolate City, Rest in Peace': White Space-Claiming and the Exclusion of Black People in Washington, DC." *City & Community* 18, no. 3 (2019): 746–769.

Henig, Jeffrey R. "Patterns of School-Level Racial Change in DC in the Wake of Brown: Perceptual Legacies of Desegregation." *PS: Political Science and Politics* 30, no. 3 (1997): 448–453.

Hinton, Elizabeth. *From the War on Poverty to the War on Crime.* Cambridge, MA: Harvard University Press, 2017.

Hobson, Julius. "The Employment and Utilization of Negro Manpower in the District of Columbia's Government and Private Enterprise." In *Civil Rights in the Nation's Capital: A Report on a Decade of Progress,* ed. Ben Segal, William Korey, and Charles Manson, 19–33. New York: National Association of Intergroup Relations, 1959.

Holt, Sidney L., Ana María del Río-González, Jenné S. Massie, and Lisa Bowleg. "'I Live in This Neighborhood Too, Though': The Psychosocial Effects of Gentrification on Low-Income Black Men Living in Washington, DC." *Journal of Racial and Ethnic Health Disparities* (2020): 1–14.

Hopkins, Daniel, and Katherine T. McCabe. "After It's Too Late: Estimating the Policy Impacts of Black Mayoralties in U.S. Cities." *American Politics Research* 40, no. 4 (July 2012): 665–700. https://doi.org/10.1177/1532673X11432469.

Hopkinson, Natalie. *Go-Go Live: The Musical Life and Death of a Chocolate City.* Durham, NC: Duke University Press, 2012.

Hostetter, Ellen. "The Emotions of Racialization: Examining the Intersection of Emotion, Race, and Landscape through Public Housing in the United States." *GeoJournal* 75, no. 3 (2010): 283–298.

Howell, Junia, and Elizabeth Korver-Glenn. "The Increasing Effect of Neighborhood Racial Composition on Housing Values, 1980–2015." *Social Problems* 68, no. 4 (November 2021): 1051–1071. https://doi.org/10.1093/socpro/spaa033.

Howell, Kathryn. *Affordable Housing Preservation in Washington, DC: A Framework for Local Funding, Collaborative Governance, and Community Organizing for Change.* New York: Routledge, 2021.

———. "'For the kids': Children, Safety, and the Depoliticization of Displacement in Washington, DC." *Journal of Urban Affairs* 40, no. 5 (2018): 721–739. https://doi.org/10.1080/07352166.2017.1360742.

———. "'It's complicated . . . ': Long-Term Residents and Their Relationships to Gentrification in Washington, DC." In *Capital Dilemma: Growth and Inequality in Washington, DC,* ed. Derek S. Hyra and Sabiyha Prince, 255–278. New York: Routledge, 2016.

Hwang, Jackelyn, and Robert J. Sampson. "Divergent Pathways of Gentrification: Racial Inequality and the Social Order of Renewal in Chicago Neighborhoods." *American Sociological Review* 79, no. 4 (2014): 726–751.

Hyra, Derek S. "Conceptualizing the New Urban Renewal: Comparing the Past to the Present." *Urban Affairs Review* 48, no. 4 (July 2012): 498–527. https://doi.org/10.1177/1078087411434905.

———. *Race, Class, and Politics in the Cappuccino City.* Chicago: University of Chicago Press, 2017.

Jackson, Kenneth. "Federal Subsidy and the Suburban Dream: The First Quarter-Century of Government Intervention in the Housing Market." *Records of the Columbia Historical Society, Washington, DC* 50 (1980): 421–451.

———. "Race, Ethnicity, and Real Estate Appraisal: The Home Owners Loan Corporation and the Federal Housing Administration." *Journal of Urban History* 6, no. 4 (1980): 419–452.

Jackson, Maurice. "An Analysis: African American Employment, Population, and Housing Trends in Washington, DC." Submitted to the Commission on African American Affairs, District of Columbia Government, 2017.

Jaffe, Harry S., and Tom Sherwood. *Dream City: Race, Power, and the Decline of the City.* 2nd ed. New York: Simon and Schuster, 2014.

Jones, Nikki. *The Chosen Ones: Black Men and the Politics of Redemption.* Berkeley: University of California Press, 2018.

———. "Working 'the Code': On Girls, Gender, and Inner-City Violence." *Australian & New Zealand Journal of Criminology* 41, no. 1 (2008): 63–83.

Jung, Moon-Kie, and João H. Costa Vargas, eds. *Antiblackness.* Durham, NC: Duke University Press, 2021.

Katznelson, Ira. *When Affirmative Action Was White: An Untold History of Racial Inequality in Twentieth-Century America.* New York: Norton, 2005.

Kelly, Clare Lise. *Montgomery Modern: Modern Architecture in Montgomery County, Maryland, 1930–1979.* Silver Spring: Maryland–National Capital Park and Planning Co., 2015.

Kerr, Audrey Elisa. *The Paper Bag Principle: Class, Colorism, and Rumor and the Case of Black Washington, DC.* Knoxville: University of Tennessee Press, 2006.

Kijakazi, Kilolo, Rachel Marie Brooks Atkins, Mark Paul, Anne E. Price, Darrick Hamilton, and William A. Darity Jr. "The Color of Wealth in the Nation's Capital." Urban Institute, 2016. https://www.urban.org/research/publication/color-wealth-nations-capital.

Kimble, John. "Insuring Inequality: The Role of the Federal Housing Administration in the Urban Ghettoization of African Americans." *Law & Social Inquiry* 32, no. 2 (2007): 399–434.

Kirk, Eileen M. "Obstructing the American Dream: Homeownership Denied and Neighborhood Crime." *Housing Policy Debate* (2020). https://doi.org/10.1080/10511482.2020.1793794.

Knoll, Erwin. "The Truth about Desegregation in the Washington, DC, Public Schools." *Journal of Negro Education* 28, no. 2 (1959): 92–113.

Kozol, Jonathan. *Savage Inequalities: Children in America's Schools*. New York: Crown, 2012.

Lacy, Karyn. *Blue-Chip Black*. Berkeley: University of California Press, 2007.

Laniyonu, Ayobami. "Coffee Shops and Street Stops: Policing Practices in Gentrifying Neighborhoods." *Urban Affairs Review* 54, no. 5 (2018): 898–930.

Lee, Logan M. "Far from Home and All Alone: The Impact of Prison Visitation on Recidivism." *American Law and Economics Review* 21, no. 2 (Fall 2019): 431–481. https://doi.org/10.1093/aler/ahz011.

Lees, Loretta. "Super-Gentrification: The Case of Brooklyn Heights, New York City." *Urban Studies* 40, no. 12 (2003): 2487–2509.

Leverentz, Andrea M. *Intersecting Lives: How Place Shapes Reentry*. Oakland: University of California Press, 2022.

Liebow, Elliot. *Tally's Corner: A Study of Negro Streetcorner Men*. New York: Little, Brown, 1967.

Littlejohn, Roy. "The Movement of Federal Facilities to the Suburbs." A Report of the Washington DC Advisory Committee to the United States Commission on Civil Rights, 1971. https://www2.law.umaryland.edu/marshall/usccr/documents/cr12f311971.pdf.

Lloyd, James. "Community Development, Research, and Reinvestment: The Struggle against Redlining in Washington, DC, 1970–1995." MA thesis, Ohio University, 2012.

Lotke, Eric. "Hobbling a Generation: Young African American Men in Washington, DC's Criminal Justice System—Five Years Later." *Crime & Delinquency* 44, no. 3 (1998): 355–366.

Lusane, Clarence, and Dennis Desmond. *Pipe Dream Blues: Racism and the War on Drugs*. Boston: South End Press, 1991.

MacKinnon, Timothy D. "Capitol Navy Yard: A 21st Century Transition." PhD dissertation, Rutgers University, 2017.

Malinowski, Shilpi. *Shaw, LeDroit Park and Bloomingdale in Washington, D.C.: An Oral History.* Charleston, NC: History Press, 2021.

Manning, Robert D. "Multicultural Washington, DC: The Changing Social and Economic Landscape of a Post-Industrial Metropolis." *Ethnic and Racial Studies* 21, no. 2 (1998): 328–355.

Manson, Steven, Jonathan Schroeder, David Van Riper, Tracy Kugler, and Steven Ruggles. IPUMS National Historical Geographic Information System: Version 17.0 [dataset]. Minneapolis, MN: IPUMS, 2022. http://doi.org/10.18128/D050.V17.0.

Marolda, Edward J. *The Washington Navy Yard: An Illustrated History.* Washington, DC: Naval Historical Center, 1999.

Martinez, R., Jr., R. Rosenfeld, and D. Mares. "Social Disorganization, Drug Market Activity, and Neighborhood Violent Crime." *Urban Affairs Review* 43, no. 6 (2008): 846–874.

Massey, Douglas, and Nancy A. Denton. *American Apartheid: Segregation and the Making of the Underclass.* Cambridge, MA: Harvard University Press, 1993.

Masur, Kate. *An Example for All the Land: Emancipation and the Struggle over Equality in Washington, DC.* Chapel Hill: University of North Carolina Press, 2010.

Matlon, Jordanna. "Racial Capitalism and the Crisis of Black Masculinity." *American Sociological Review* 81, no. 5 (2016): 1014–1038.

McKittrick, Katherine. "On Plantations, Prisons, and a Black Sense of Place." *Social & Cultural Geography* 12, no. 8 (2011): 947–963.

McNeeley, Susan, and Grant Duwe. "Keep Your Friends Close and Your Enemies Closer: Prison Visitation, Spatial Distance, and Concentrated Disadvantage of Visitor Neighborhoods, and Offender Recidivism." *Justice Quarterly* 37, no. 4 (2020): 571–589. https://doi.org/10.1080/07418825.2019.1568521.

Meyers, Travis J., Kevin A. Wright, Jacob T.N. Young, and Melinda Tasca. "Social Support from Outside the Walls: Examining the Role of Relationship Dynamics among Inmates and Visitors." *Journal of Criminal Justice* 52 (2017): 57–67. https://doi.org/10.1016/j.jcrimjus.2017.07.012.

Oliver, Melvin, and Thomas Shapiro. *Black Wealth, White Wealth: A New Perspective on Racial Inequality.* New York: Routledge, 2006.

Orfield, Gary, and Jongyeon Ee. *Our Segregated Capital: An Increasingly Diverse City with Racially Polarized Schools*. Los Angeles: Civil Rights Project, 2017. https://www.civilrightsproject.ucla.edu/research/k-12-education/integration-and-diversity/our-segregated-capital-an-increasingly-diverse-city-with-racially-polarized-schools.

Ostroff, Susan. "Maps on My Past: Race, Space, and Place in the Life Stories of Washington D.C. Area Teenagers." *Oral History Review* 22, no. 2 (1995): 33–53. http://www.jstor.org/stable/3675423.

Parenti, Christian. *Lockdown America: Police and Prisons in the Age of Crisis*. 2nd ed. New York: Verso, 2012.

Passow, A. Harry. *Toward Creating a Model Urban School System*. New York: Teachers College, Columbia University, 1967.

Pattillo, Mary. *Black on the Block*. Chicago: University of Chicago Press, 2010.

———. *Black Picket Fences: Privilege and Peril among the Black Middle Class*. Chicago: University of Chicago Press, 2013.

———. "Housing: Commodity versus Right." *Annual Review of Sociology* 39 (2013): 509–531.

Payan, Tony. *A War That Can't Be Won*. Tucson: University of Arizona Press, 2013.

Pérez, Gina. *The Near Northwest Side Story: Migration, Displacement, and Puerto Rican Families*. Berkeley: University of California Press, 2004.

Prince, Sabiyha. *African Americans and Gentrification in Washington, DC: Race, Class and Social Justice in the Nation's Capital*. New York: Routledge, 2014.

Provine, Doris. *Unequal under Law: Race in the War on Drugs*. Chicago: University of Chicago Press, 2007.

Reese, Ashanté M. *Black Food Geographies: Race, Self-Reliance, and Food Access in Washington, DC*. Chapel Hill: University of North Carolina Press, 2019.

Reuter, Peter, John Haaga, Patrick Murphy, and Amy Praskac. "Drug Use and Drug Programs in the Washington Metropolitan Area." Prepared for the Greater Washington Research Center, RAND Corporation, Santa Monica, CA, 1988.

Rosen, Eva. *The Voucher Promise*. Princeton, NJ: Princeton University Press, 2020.

Rothstein, Richard. *The Color of Law: A Forgotten History of How Our Government Segregated America*. New York: Liveright Publishing, 2017.

Rucks-Ahidiana, Zawadi. "Theorizing Gentrification as a Process of Racial Capitalism." *City & Community* 21, no. 3 (2021). https://doi.org/10.1177/15356841211054790.

Russello Ammon, Francesca. "Commemoration amid Criticism: The Mixed Legacy of Urban Renewal in Southwest Washington, DC." *Journal of Planning History* 8, no. 3 (2009): 175–220.

Ryder, Judith A., and Regina E. Brisgone. "Cracked Perspectives: Reflections of Women and Girls in the Aftermath of the Crack Cocaine Era." *Feminist Criminology* 8, no. 1 (2013): 40–62.

Satter, Beryl. *Family Properties.* New York: Picador, 2007.

Sharkey, Patrick. *Uneasy Peace: The Great Crime Decline, the Renewal of City Life, and the Next War on Violence.* New York: Norton, 2018.

Shinault, Carley M., and Richard Seltzer. "Whose Turf, Whose Town? Race, Status, and Attitudes of Washington DC Residents toward Gentrification." *Journal of African American Studies* 23, no. 1 (2019): 72–91.

Shoenfeld, Sarah. "Teachable Moment: 'Blockbusting' and Racial Turnover in Mid-century D.C." *Washington History* 30, no. 2 (Fall 2018): 50–54.

Shoenfeld, Sarah Jane, and Mara Cherkasky, "'A Strictly White Residential Section': The Rise and Demise of Racially Restrictive Covenants in Bloomingdale." *Washington History* 29, no. 1 (2017): 24–41. http://www.jstor.org/stable/90007372.

Smith, Neil. "Gentrification and the Rent Gap." *Annals of the Association of American Geographers* 77, no. 3 (September 1987): 462–465.

———. *The New Urban Frontier: Gentrification and the Revanchist City.* New York: Routledge, 1996.

———. "Toward a Theory of Gentrification: A Back to the City Movement by Capital, not People." *Journal of the American Planning Association* 45 (1979): 538–548.

Smith, Sam. *Captive Capital: Colonial Life in Modern Washington.* Bloomington: Indiana University Press, 1974.

Stoll, Michael A. "Spatial Mismatch, Discrimination, and Male Youth Employment in the Washington, DC, Area: Implications for Residential Mobility Policies." *Journal of Policy Analysis and Management* 18, no. 1 (1999): 77–98.

Summer, Rebecca. "Writing Out Black History in Washington, DC: How Historical Narratives Support a Performance of Progressiveness in Gentrifying

Urban Spaces." *Urban Geography* (March 22, 2021): 1–20. https://doi.org/10.10
80/02723638.2021.1902141.

Summers, Brandi Thompson. *Black in Place: The Spatial Aesthetics of Race in a Post-Chocolate City.* Chapel Hill: University of North Carolina Press, 2019.

Taylor, Keeanga-Yamahtta. *Race for Profit: How Banks and the Real Estate Industry Undermined Black Homeownership.* Chapel Hill: University of North Carolina Press, 2019.

Thompson, Heather Ann. "Rethinking the Politics of White Flight in the Postwar City: Detroit, 1945–1980." *Journal of Urban History* 25, no. 2 (1999): 163–198.

Tucker, Sterling. *Beyond the Burning: Life and Death of the Ghetto.* New York: Association Press, 1958.

Ture, Kalfani Nyerere, "Fighting the Farms: Structural Violence, Race and Resistance in Washington, D.C." PhD dissertation, American University, 2017. https://www.proquest.com/dissertations-theses/fighting-farms-structural-violence-race/docview/1881550137/.

Vale, Lawrence J., and Yonah Freemark. "From Public Housing to Public-Private Housing." *Journal of the American Planning Association* 78, no. 4 (2012): 379–402.

Vélez, María B., and Kelly Richardson. "The Political Economy of Neighbourhood Homicide in Chicago: The Role of Bank Investment." *British Journal of Criminology* 52, no. 3 (2012): 490–513.

Webb, Gary. *Dark Alliance: The CIA, the Contras, and the Cocaine Explosion.* New York: Seven Stories Press, 2011.

Werb, Dan, Greg Rowell, Gordon Guyatt, Thomas Kerr, Julio Montaner, and Evan Wood. "Effect of Drug Law Enforcement on Drug Market Violence: A Systematic Review." *International Journal of Drug Policy* 22, no. 2 (2011): 87–94.

Whitehead, Tony. "The Formation of the U.S. Racialized Urban Ghetto." CuSAG Special Problems Working Paper Series in Urban Anthropology. University of Maryland, College Park. September 15, 2000.

Wice, Paul. "Safe Haven: A Memoir of Playground Basketball and Segregation." *Washington History* (Fall–Winter 1997): 55–71.

Williams, Brett. "Beyond Gentrification: Investment and Abandonment on the Waterfront." In *Capital Dilemma: Growth and Inequality in Washington, DC,* ed. Derek S. Hyra and Sabiyha Prince, 227–238. New York: Routledge, 2016.

Wilson, Dreck Spurlock. *African American Architects: A Biographical Dictionary, 1865–1945.* New York: Routledge, 2004.

Wilson, William Julius. *The Truly Disadvantaged: The Inner City, the Underclass, and Public Policy.* Chicago: University of Chicago Press, 2012.

———. *When Work Disappears: The World of the New Urban Poor.* New York: Random House, 1997.

Index

Atwater, US Penitentiary at, 200, 208–10

Avalanche, Operation, 127, 150

Balderson, Mrs. Raymond, 62*fig.*

Ballard, Derrick, 136

Ballot Initiative 9, 101

banks, Black-owned, 56

Barr, William, 133

Barry, James, 40

Barry, Marion: arrest of, 109; Black middle class under, 105, 118; budget under, 103, 153; city workers under, 105, 118; police force under, 103, 105–6, 245n31; Summer Youth Employment Program of, 24; in War on Drugs, 103, 105–6, 119

Barry Farm: Black home ownership in, 40–41; city planning for redevelopment of, 195–99; displacement and dispossession in, 35, 40–41, 45, 195–97; eminent domain in, 41; FHA grading of, 41, 181–83; home values in, 198, 199*fig.*; household incomes in, 198, 199*fig.*; location of, 16*map*, 35, 36*map*, 181, 182*map*; official vs. local names for, 26, 40; origins of, 40–41; public schools in, 61; racial composition of, 183–84, 198, 199*fig.*; racialized reinvestment and gentrification in, 183–85, 195–99

Barry Farm Dwellings: beautification campaigns at, 41; construction of, 11, 35, 41, 183; demolition of, 184, 195–96; disinvestment from, 41, 72–73, 75–76, 196; drug trade in, 76; as landmark, 240n59; violence in, 76

Barry Farm Oral History Project, 196

Barry Farm Tenants and Allies Association, 195

Baum, Dan, 99–100

Belt, Detrice, 76

benign neglect, of public schools, 64

Bennett, William J., 103

Benson, Bonnie, 77

Benson, Ezra Taft, 77

Berman v. Parker, 40

BET. *See* Black Entertainment Television

Bias, Len, 102

Biden, Joe, 100

BIDs. *See* business improvement districts

biking, 205

Black boys and men: criminalization of, 4, 17, 159; in drug trade, 75, 89, 92, 109–15; as homicide victims, 20, 60, 69–70; unemployment among, 20, 75, 89, 94–95; violence and masculinity of, 70

Black boys and men, incarceration of, 2–4; displacement through, 210–12; in downward mobility, 3, 96; for drug trade, 109–15; gentrification and, 200–204, 210–12; rates of, 4, 12, 98, 109, 119; vs. White men, 119. *See also* drug prosecutions; returning citizens

Black Entertainment Television (BET), 105

Black in Place (Summers), 15, 156

Black-owned businesses, 56, 105

Black Picket Fences (Pattillo), 17

Black spaces, reshaped by gentrification, 156–57

Blandón, Daniel, 102

Bloomingdale: Black middle class in, 151; disinvestment in home values in, 151; downward mobility in, 96; gentrification in, 155, 156; household incomes in,

HOPE VI, 185–87; in Capitol View, 183, 186, 192–93; establishment of, 185–86; goals of, 186; in Navy Yard, 183, 186, 187, 192; vs. NCI, 186

Hopkins, Daniel, 245n31

Housing Act of 1937, 71–72

Housing and Urban Development, US Department of (HUD), 73, 139, 187

housing authority, DC: in demolition of public housing, 186, 187–88; in HOPE VI program, 186; location of public housing under, 56, 71; segregation of housing under, 35, 71; slum clearance by, 35; urban renewal policies of, 35; White public housing by, 38–39, 71. *See also specific public housing developments*

Housing Choice Vouchers, 186

housing projects. *See* public housing

housing segregation. *See* segregation

housing shortages, for Black residents, 35–37, 45

Howard, Oliver, 40

Howell, Beryl, 136

Howell, Junia, 214

Howell, Kathryn, 171

Howes, Paul, 137–38, 142

Hoyle, Mark, 131, 137

HUD. *See* Housing and Urban Development

Hughes, Langston, 157

Hughes, Ronald, 135–36

Hurd, James, 48, 49

Hutchinson, Dan, 135–36

Hwang, Jackelyn, 254n23

Hyra, Derek, 15, 156–57, 183

identification cards, to enter public housing, 74

incarceration: of Black youth, for drug trade, 109–15; displacement through, 210–12; downward mobility and, 3, 96, 98; educational opportunities during, 213–14; gentrification linked to, 200–204, 210–12; mandatory minimum sentences in, 100–103, 136; mass, 4. *See also* prisons; returning citizens

incarceration rates, DC: from 1970 to 2000, 104, 104*fig.*, 119; for Black men, 4, 12, 98, 119; for Black youth, 109; as highest in world, 10, 89, 119, 209; social class and, 11, 109; for White men, 119

Incarceration Reduction Amendment Act (IRAA), 112, 213

inclusion, predatory, 6, 227n14

inclusionary zoning program, 177, 202, 215

incomes: Black, increases between 1940 and 1970 in, 5; Black vs. White, downward mobility of, 96; household, 54, 96, 123; per capita, 54. *See also specific neighborhoods*

income taxes, 152

Independence Federal Saving & Loan, 56

Indigenous people, 34

Industrial Bank, 56

infrastructure investments, 44, 54

In Search of Respect (Bourgois), 110

interest rates, mortgage, 42, 55

intergenerational downward mobility, 92, 95–99, 98*fig.*, 113, 118

intergenerational poverty, 3–4, 113

intergenerational wealth, Black lack of, 172–78; disinvestment in, 4–5, 17, 56, 96–97, 118; downward mobility and, 96–97; home values in, 2, 56, 173, 175–76; inheritance of homes and, 99,

normalization, of violence, 70–71

North Capitol Citizens Association, 47–48

North Portal Estates, 46

Northwest quadrant of DC, 33, 35. *See also specific locations*

Norton, Eleanor Holmes, 190

Nugent, Antony, 131–32

OCCA. *See* Organized Crime Control Act

Odom, Nicole, 196–97

Office of Planning, DC, 155

Oliphant, Rose, 188

one-for-one replacement, 186, 187–88, 197

Operation Avalanche, 127, 150

Operation Clean Sweep, 105–7

Operation Violent Gang Safe Streets, 122–23, 130, 131, 141, 159. *See also* drug prosecutions

Opportunity Atlas, 95

oral histories, 18, 221–23

orange hats, 140

organized abandonment, 5

Organized Crime Control Act (OCCA) of 1970, 130–31

organized violence, 5

organizing. *See* community activism

overdoses, drug, 101–2

Parenti, Christian, 106

Parents United, 64

Park Morton, 186

Park View, 168–69

Parliament (band), 53

patriarchy, 70, 143

Pattillo, Mary, 8, 17

PCP, 101, 117

Peebles Real Estate Corporation, 105

Pell Grants, 213–14

pensions, 153

Pérez, Gina, 157

Perkins, Derrin A., 132–33

Perry, Diane Hinton, 49

Perry, Troy, 76

petition covenants, 48

Petworth: Black home ownership in, 6, 163*table*, 173–75; boundaries of, 26, 229n34; disinvestment from, 77–81; displacement and dispossession in, 35, 46–48; drug prosecutions targeting, 136, 139–40; FHA grading of, 47; home values in, 163*table*, 164–65, 173; household incomes in, 78, 79*table*, 162, 169; inclusionary zoning program in, 177; investors flipping homes in, 147, 164; location of, 16*map*, 35, 36*map*; official vs. local names for, 26; public schools in, 51, 77–81, 93–94; racially restrictive covenants in, 47; reinvestment in, 147; unemployment and poverty rates in, 78, 79*table*, 94, 162, 163*table*; violence in, 78–81; White flight from, 48–51, 54, 157; White home owners' role in segregation of, 47–48; White reclamation and gentrification in, 162–69, 163*table*; White subdivisions in, 46–48

Petworth Citizens Association, 47–48

police forces, DC: budget for, 101, 103; changes under Home Rule to, 104–5; in drug prosecutions, 127–32; gentrifiers calling police on Black people, 170–71; increases in size of, 89, 106; as majority Black, 101, 104–5, 245n31; misconduct by, 107; Operation

Avalanche by, 127, 150; Operation Clean Sweep by, 105–7; in Operation Violent Gang Safe Streets, 130; seizure of property by, 106–7; specialized units in, 107; statistics from, 18. *See also* carceral investment; Drugs, War on

political displacement, 156–57

population of DC, 154

population of DC, Black: change from 1930 to 1980 in, 35, 51, 52*table*, 53; geographic distribution of, 37

population of DC, White: change from 1930 to 1980 in, 51–54, 52*table*; after school desegregation, 62; in suburbs, 52, 53

Potomac Gardens, 112

poverty, in DC: under Barry, 105; Black rates of, 54; drug trade as escape from, 110–13; after end of antipoverty programs, 71–72, 94; geographic concentration of, 8, 41, 60; intergenerational, 3–4, 113. *See also specific neighborhoods*

poverty, US rates of, 101

Pratt, Sharon, 80

predatory inclusion, 6, 227n14

press coverage, of homicides, 66, 68–69. *See also specific publications*

pretrial detention, 100

Price, Donald, 137

Prince, Sabiyha, 15, 196

Prince George's County, 52, 120, 202–3

prisons, DC, 10, 153, 207–9, 260n5

prisons, federal: budget of, 104; challenges of family visits to, 208–10; DC residents in, 10, 153, 200, 207–10

private disinvestment: around public housing, 73, 75; in Black neighborhoods, 14, 44, 69

private housing: for Black families, FHA financing of, 42–44; segregation in, 37

private investment: around public housing, 38; in Black vs. White neighborhoods, 12–14; decline of, 59–60, 77; after demolition of public housing, 184; home values affected by, 215; in suburbs, 95

private reinvestment, 13–14, 151, 162. *See also* racialized reinvestment

Prologue DC, 46–47, 49, 230n14

property seizures. *See* forfeiture

property taxes, 152, 156

prosecutions. *See* drug prosecutions

pseudonyms, 225n1

P Street Crew, 126*map*, 133–35, 141

public disinvestment. *See* disinvestment

public housing: Black neighborhoods as sites of, 35, 56; construction of, 11, 35, 37, 71, 183; demand vs. supply of, 37; drug-related violence in, 11–12, 72–77; federal budget for, 72; legal segregation in, 35, 37, 71; in racialized reinvestment trajectory, 183, 183*fig.*; rents charged for, 72; repeated displacements from, 197; violence after disinvestment from, 11–12, 60, 71–77; for White residents, 38–39, 71. *See also specific developments*

public housing, demolition of, 180–206; through HOPE VI, 185–87, 192; through NCI, 186, 202; new-build gentrification after, 185–92; as new urban renewal, 157; number of units affected, 186; one-for-one replacement public housing, demolition of *(continued)* in, 186, 187–88, 197; in racialized reinvestment trajectory, 183, 183*fig.*, 184; returning citizens and, 200–204. *See also specific developments*

public investment: as anti-Black, 14, 179; in Black neighborhoods, 13; after demolition of public housing, 184; home values affected by, 215; in suburbs, 54; in White neighborhoods, 12. *See also* racialized reinvestment

public schools, in DC, 16*map*, 59–65; budget of, 60, 63; clothes in, 93; de facto segregation in, 63–64; desegregation of, 51, 61–63, 62*fig.*, 78, 211; disinvestment from, 59–65, 179, 211; dropout rates in, 64–65, 179, 237n21; number of students in, 63; racial composition of, 60, 63; Rhee's reforms to, 154; vs. suburbs, 61, 64, 237n21; violence in, 58–59, 65, 85–86, 160, 211. *See also specific neighborhoods and schools*

Rabaut Junior High School, 91

race, vs. class, in gentrification, 156

Race, Class, and Politics in the Cappuccino City (Hyra), 156–57

Race for Profit (Taylor), 6

racial capitalism: definition of, 13; displacement and dispossession in, 35; in drug prosecutions, 143; home and land values in, 13–14, 35, 179, 214; in intergenerational wealth gap, 12–13, 118, 215; racism in, 13, 183, 214; returning citizens and, 214

racialized reinvestment, 180–206; in Anacostia, 199–200; in Barry Farm, 183–85, 195–200; in Bloomingdale, 151;

in Capitol View, 183–85, 192–95; definition of, 3; forms of, 12; in Navy Yard, 181, 183–85, 187–92; racial composition of neighborhoods in, 183–85, 184*fig.*; returning citizens' experience with, 200–204; role in wealth gap, 3; trajectory of, 183, 183*fig.*

racial segregation. *See* segregation

racial wealth gap, size of: in DC, 3, 17; in US, 2

racism, anti-Black: definition of, 13; dismantling of, 215–16; in drug prosecutions, 143; in gentrification (*See* racialized reinvestment); of gentrifiers, 170–71; in home values, 3, 13, 118, 179, 215; in public investments, 14, 179; in racial capitalism, 13, 183, 214; returning citizens and, 214

Racketeer Influenced and Corrupt Organizations (RICO), 122, 130–36, 247n4

Rangel, Charles, 11

Rapid Deployment Unit, 107

Rare Essence, 168

Reagan, Ronald, 72, 101

real estate agents, 46, 49–52, 50*fig.*, 164

real estate investors and speculators, 147, 155, 164, 187, 198

reclamation. *See* White reclamation

redevelopment, city planning for, 155–56. *See also* gentrification; reinvestment; *specific neighborhoods*

Redevelopment Land Agency (RLA), 40

red hats, 140–41

redlining: in 1990s, 164–65; and disinvestment, 44; by FHA, 38, 55; and home equity, 164–65; scholarship on, 19

red zones, 108

drug trade, 75, 89, 93–95, 97–98; in Petworth, 78–80, 79*table*, 94, 162, 163*table*; youth, 20, 75, 89

Uniontown, 40

United States Attorney's Office (USAO), 131–32, 133

Universal Declaration of Human Rights, 209

Upshur Street, 162, 166

uptown neighborhoods: disinvestment from, 60, 77–84, 158–59; drug prosecutions targeting, 136–40. *See also* Eckington; Petworth

upward mobility, barriers to, 3, 4

urban renewal, 35–41, 157, 183

USAO. *See* United States Attorney's Office

vehicle searches, 108

Veterans Affairs, US Department of (VA), 18, 52, 55–56

Vietnam War, 97

Villabona-Alvarado, Mario Ernesto, 128

violence, 58–86; Black men as targets of, 60, 69–70; carceral investment as organized, 5; carceral investment as response to, 109, 211; impacts of living with, 66–71; in masculinity, 70; normalization of, 70–71; in public housing, 11–12, 60, 71–77; in public schools, 58–59, 65, 85–86, 160, 211; uptown, 60, 77–84. *See also* drug-related violence; homicides; *specific neighborhoods*

Violent Gang Safe Streets, Operation, 122–23, 130, 131, 141, 159. *See also* drug prosecutions

Volkov, Mike, 131–32

vouchers: housing, 186, 192–93, 196–97; witness, 137–38, 142

Wade, Benjamin, 40

walkouts, over desegregation, 61

Walmart, 193

Walton, Ellie, 188

War on Drugs. *See* Drugs, War on

warrior policing, 107

Washington, DC, creation of, 34

Washington, Walter, 104

Washington DC Economic Partnership, 199

Washingtonian (magazine), 131

Washington Navy Yard, 37–38. *See also* Navy Yard

Washington Post (newspaper): on Barry Farm Dwellings, 41, 75; on desegregation, 82; and drug prosecutions, 121, 130; on Eckington, 82, 83; on Hanover Place, 150; on homicides, 66, 68–69; on Petworth, 166; on police checkpoints, 108; on public architecture, 205; on public schools, 64, 82

wealth: barriers to building, 6–7; functions and importance of, 2; trickle-down economics on, 93. *See also* intergenerational wealth

wealth gap. *See* racial wealth gap

White, Antone, 131–32, 135–36

White citizens associations, 34, 45, 47–48

White flight, 48–54; end of racially restrictive covenants in, 48–49, 157; real estate agents in, 49–52, 50*fig.*; school desegregation in, 62–63; in White reclamation trajectory, 157–59, 158*fig.*; White resistance to, 51–52, 157. *See also specific neighborhoods*

White House, 34

White men: incarceration rates for, 119; masculinity of, 70

White public housing, 38–39, 71

White reclamation, 157–69; in Brightwood Park, 159–62, 161*fig.*; definition of, 12, 158, 158*fig.*; disinvestment as precursor to, 158–59; in Eckington, 159–62, 161*fig.*; in Petworth, 162–69, 163*table*

White subdivisions: in Brightwood, 34–35; in Eckington, 46–48; FHA financing of, 34–35, 46–48; FHA grading of, 47; forces behind creation of, 34, 45–48; in Petworth, 46–48; White flight from, 48–54

White supremacy, 209, 260n5

Wice, Paul, 51, 53

Wilkerson, Isabel, 80–81

William O. Lockridge Library, 205

Williams, Andre P., 132–33

Williams, Anthony, 153–54, 186

Williams, Donnell O., 133

Williams, John, 39

Williams, Michael D., 81

Williams, Nicolette, 70–71

Williams-Davis, Kevin, 132

Wilson, William Julius, 4, 8

Wilson High School, 85–86

wiretapping, 100

witness vouchers, 137–38, 142

women: drug trade and use by, 115–18, 143; home financing for, 6; as homicide victims, 70; violence and femininity of, 70

Women of the WIRE, 70–71, 115

Woodson High School, 44

Yards, The, 191

Yards Park, 190

youth. *See* Black boys

zoning: inclusionary, 177, 202, 215; mixed-use, 187; multifamily, 41

Zulu, Mustafa S. F., 112–13

Founded in 1893,
UNIVERSITY OF CALIFORNIA PRESS
publishes bold, progressive books and journals
on topics in the arts, humanities, social sciences,
and natural sciences—with a focus on social
justice issues—that inspire thought and action
among readers worldwide.

The UC PRESS FOUNDATION
raises funds to uphold the press's vital role
as an independent, nonprofit publisher, and
receives philanthropic support from a wide
range of individuals and institutions—and from
committed readers like you. To learn more, visit
ucpress.edu/supportus.